D0850796

DANGEROUS
Personalities

Also by Joe Navarro

Hunting Terrorists: A Look at the Psychopathology of Terror, 2nd ed.

Louder Than Words (with Toni Sciarra Poynter)

Advanced Interviewing Techniques, 2nd ed. (John Schafer, coauthor)

What Every Body Is Saying (with Marvin Karlins)

Phil Hellmuth Presents Read 'Em and Reap (with Marvin Karlins)

200 Poker Tells

Clues to Deceit: A Practical List

Narcissists Among Us

How to Spot a Psychopath

How to Spot a Histrionic Personality

How to Spot a Borderline Personality

Interviewing Terrorists

DANGEROUS
Personalities

An FBI Profiler
Shows You How to
Identify and Protect Yourself
from Harmful People

JOE NAVARRO, MA, FBI SPECIAL AGENT (RET.)
with Toni Sciarra Poynter

RODALE.

Copyright © 2014 by Joe Navarro

Rodale books may be purchased for business or promotional use or for special sales. For information, please write to: Special Markets Department, Rodale Inc., 733 Third Avenue, New York, NY 10017.

Printed in the United States of America

Rodale Inc. makes every effort to use acid-free ⊗, recycled paper ☺.

While the manuscript for this book was reviewed by the Federal Bureau of Investigation (FBI) prior to publication, the opinions and thoughts expressed herein are those of the author exclusively.

The Dangerous Personalities Checklists in this book have been adapted from the following books previously published by Joe Navarro and are used by permission:
Narcissists Among Us by Joe Navarro
How to Spot a Borderline Personality by Joe Navarro
How to Spot a Psychopath by Joe Navarro

Book design by Amy C. King

Library of Congress Cataloging-in-Publication Data

Navarro, Joe
    Dangerous personalities : an FBI profiler shows how to identify and protect yourself from harmful people / Joe Navarro, MA, FBI Special Agent (Ret.) with Toni Sciarra Poynter.
        pages   cm
    Includes bibliographical references and index.
    ISBN 978-1-62336-192-1 (trade hardcover)
    1. Crime prevention.   2. Criminals.   3. Crime.   4. Psychopaths.
    5. Antisocial personality disorders.   I. Poynter, Toni Sciarra.   II. Title.
    HV7431.N38   2014
    613.6'6—dc23   2014012528

Distributed to the trade by Macmillan

2   4   6   8   10   9   7   5   3   1   hardcover

We inspire and enable people to improve their lives and the world around them.
rodalebooks.com

FOR THE VICTIMS

There are two kinds of people in this world: those who fill your cup, and those who drain it. —Joe Navarro

CONTENTS

AUTHOR'S NOTE viii

ACKNOWLEDGMENTS.. ix

FOREWORD BY DR. LEONARD TERRITO.................................... xiii

INTRODUCTION: Why I Wrote This Book, and How to Use It.............1

CHAPTER 1: "It's All about Me": The Narcissistic Personality.......... 17

CHAPTER 2: "Fasten Your Seat Belts . . .":
The Emotionally Unstable Personality 57

CHAPTER 3: "Trust No One and You'll Never Get Hurt":
The Paranoid Personality 93

CHAPTER 4: "What's Mine Is Mine—And What's Yours Is Mine":
The Predator 127

CHAPTER 5: One Is Bad, Two Is Terrible, Three Is Lethal:
Combination Personalities 168

CHAPTER 6: Self-Defense against Dangerous Personalities.............188

SELECTED RESOURCES 212

NOTES 219

BIBLIOGRAPHY...223

INDEX 238

AUTHOR'S NOTE

THIS BOOK IS INTENDED TO inform the reader or to validate what the reader may have witnessed or experienced. It is not intended as a clinical guide and should not replace the services of a trained or licensed professional.

Whenever I talk to victims, I am keenly aware of what they have suffered and the need to protect their privacy and dignity, and so I have changed the names of all the victims I have interviewed. To further protect them, I altered slightly the details of events, dates, time, and location because some police reports and divorce filings are now searchable by specific words or groups of words. In the end, I have done my best to protect the victims without losing the character or manner of the offense and what they endured.

ACKNOWLEDGMENTS

ANYTIME YOU UNDERTAKE AN INTELLECTUAL journey, there are so many people to thank. The bibliography is full of such individuals who took the time to share what they know—they have my deepest appreciation.

The late Dr. Phil Quinn, who persuaded me to join the adjunct faculty at the University of Tampa's criminology department, served as a mentor for more than a decade as I studied and explored these individuals flawed of character and personality. To me, his perspective as a humanitarian, priest, psychologist, and criminologist was indeed unique and contributed significantly to my understanding of a complex subject.

Michel St-Yves of the Sûreté du Québec and fellow author has always honored me with his friendship and collaboration over the years on numerous projects here and in Canada, where he is a giant in his field. Once more, he did not let me down with his critiques of this book.

A special thanks goes to Kaja Perina, editor in chief at *Psychology Today,* who took time from her busy schedule to comment on early drafts of the manuscript. Dr. Leonard Territo receives my admiration as well as my thanks. While finishing his 12th book, he took the time from his cramped schedule to go through this manuscript meticulously with me line by line. His vast experience working with dangerous personalities, including Ted Bundy, was extremely helpful. His foreword is most kind.

This book would not be possible without Steve Ross, director of the Book Division at Abrams Artists Agency. Steve is the kind of literary agent who gets things done, and he is, without a doubt, one of the most interesting people with whom to share a meal.

I want to thank Alex Postman, Jennifer Levesque, and the rest of the team at Rodale Books who have an appreciation for the welfare of others both physically and mentally and who, upon seeing this manuscript, immediately understood its potential to save lives. To our editors Michael Zimmerman and Jeff Csatari, thank you for landing on this project on the run; you brought it all together—well done.

Early drafts of this work were carefully read and reread by Janice Hillary. I thank her for her insightful support and guidance. If only we could all have teachers like her—a teacher who cares about her students—even old ones like me.

My gratitude goes out to Elizabeth Lee Barron at the University of Tampa's Macdonald-Kelce Library, who generously assisted me with finding reference material and who, like my good friend Marc Reeser of the FBI, always makes me laugh.

To Toni Sciarra Poynter, I am indebted to you once again for shaping my words and thoughts, but more important, for being inquisitive, for sharing ideas and concepts that are transformative, and for being singularly meticulous. What a gift you have for writing and for making my task so much easier. Thank you, my friend.

Also, I must thank my family here and in Europe for tolerating my absences as I struggled with writing a manuscript that was three times larger than what the reader will see. To my wife, Thryth, for whom I have such a profound respect, I must thank you for who you are; for providing valued counsel and loving support; and for your patience as I struggled to work on this book for more than a year. You are a blessing in every sense of the word who all too often has to insulate me from distractions. And last, I thank my parents, who honor me by calling me their son and for having provided me a loving environment sans dangerous personalities.

Joe Navarro, MA, FBI Special Agent (Ret.)
Tampa
November 2013

I ECHO JOE'S THANKS TO Steve Ross of Abrams Artists Agency, to our editors Mike Zimmerman and Jeff Csatari, and to the team at Rodale Books for all their efforts on behalf of this book.

Thank you to Dona Munker for being the staunchest, most loving, caring friend and fellow writer anyone could have.

Love and gratitude to my husband, Donald, for being always in my army and in my corner, and for the way we can talk about the darkest of the dark and the brightest of the bright.

To Joe Navarro, thank you for our work together and for our many interviews and thoughtful conversations about the ways of dangerous personalities—a strange terrain you knew all too well. Thank you for your tireless work on every aspect of this book, for your dedication, for your humor, and for your ferocious joy in learning and work. When you e-mail me to say, "I'm on it," I know you are *on it*.

Finally, at the risk of sounding unserious, I am grateful that our cat Lucy was often curled soothingly within arm's reach on her fleece perch when it felt painful to write about these personalities.

Toni Sciarra Poynter
New York City
December 2013

FOREWORD

WHEN MY GOOD FRIEND AND colleague Joe Navarro completed the first draft of this book, he asked if I would review the manuscript and make some constructive comments where appropriate. Once I picked up the book and started to read it, I could not put it down. It is without question one of the most interesting, useful, and user-friendly books I have ever read on this subject. Although numerous academic studies have been conducted in the analysis of dangerous personalities, Joe has made a conscious decision not to load this book with social science jargon or with elaborate statistical analysis. He does, however, make it clear to the reader that his discussions and conclusions about these individuals are well founded and based upon his many years of experience as an FBI Special Agent and criminal profiler.

One of the main questions that came to mind as I read this book was: Who would find it both useful and interesting? I came to a one-word conclusion: *everyone*. This is because all of us at some time in our lives will most certainly encounter one or more of these dangerous personalities. In some cases, they may be family members, people we are dating or intending to marry, intimate or casual friends, or professional associates.

This book is valuable because it will help readers to understand that when they are dealing with one of these dangerous personalities, even casually, there is a good chance they will be victimized. These individuals are so flawed and callous that they can make us feel as though we are responsible for the suffering they cause, while they remain impervious to modifying or changing their toxic behavior.

If this book is carefully read, it will go a long way in accomplishing a number of objectives. First, it will assist readers in recognizing dangerous personalities and preventing them from entering their lives in the first place. Second, it will provide readers with specific suggestions on how to most effectively deal with such individuals if they must. Third, and most important, the admonitions set forth in this book, if adhered to, may save one's life or at the very least prevent someone from being seriously injured mentally, physically, or financially.

As a former homicide detective and still-active criminologist, I have personally witnessed the havoc these dangerous personalities inflict on innocent victims. They murder, rape, assault, steal, bully, and exploit anyone who falls within their sphere of influence and control. Based on my many years of law enforcement experience, as well as my own extensive research as a criminologist, I feel confident in saying that chances are, someone with a dangerous personality will come into your life or the life of someone you love. While vigilance is helpful, vigilance coupled with knowledge is optimal for keeping us safe. I can confidently say that Joe Navarro has written a remarkable book that fulfills that purpose.

Dr. Leonard Territo
Distinguished Professor of Criminal Justice, Saint Leo University,
Saint Leo, Florida, and Professor Emeritus, Department of Criminology,
University of South Florida, Tampa

WHY I WROTE THIS BOOK, AND HOW TO USE IT

ON JUNE 27, 1975, a young woman named Susan "Sue" Curtis went missing from an otherwise very safe college campus. She was 15 years old and attending a youth conference at Brigham Young University in Provo, Utah, where I was a rookie police officer.

I conducted the initial investigation into her disappearance. We interviewed friends and family for clues and learned that she'd gone back to her room to clean her new braces. But when I searched her room, her toothbrush was dry. She had never made it back.

We could account for some of her activity (her lunch ticket had been used), but we were limited in what we could reconstruct—this was before cameras were ubiquitous on campuses and cell phones kept us all connected.

We talked with her family. I still remember their fathomless pain and desperation. Their trauma was devastating and sad, so sad.

Sue was never found, and eventually all reasonable leads were exhausted. But the mystery of her disappearance always bothered me because I had been on duty that night, patrolling the campus, and somehow felt partially responsible. I kept a copy of the case file containing a large photograph of her, and for years afterward, I would scan crowds, looking for a face that even remotely resembled hers. I kept the file, too, to remind me of my failure to protect that innocent soul.

Years passed, and I went on to become an FBI agent. Then one day, I got a call from a Salt Lake City investigator. "There's something you should know," he told me. "We never found Sue Curtis. But we know who took her." He went on to say that a good-looking young man had been driving around campus in a Volkswagen that night, looking for a victim. That man had finally admitted to kidnapping and killing Sue Curtis. His name was Theodore "Ted" Bundy, a man who eventually would confess to the murder of 35 young women in four different states.

It's still hard to think about the almond-eyed girl with long hair whose photo I looked at day after day . . . whose diary I read . . . whose clothing I smelled for signs of where she might have been . . . whose shoes I felt for moisture or dirt as I desperately looked for any possible clue to her whereabouts. It's very possible that I had seen her killer that night driving about on campus. I would have looked twice at his car for not having a BYU student or faculty sticker—but many didn't that day, as there were so many visitors on campus. No illegal activity was seen or reported. It was like any other day, except that on this day there was a dangerous personality on campus: a predator and serial killer who would go on to kill many times more.

BYU is one of the safest campuses in the country, yet there had been an abduction and a life taken. How had this happened, and who would do such a thing? The realization that one person can do so much damage, not just to victims but also to their loved ones, was chilling. I was all of 22, a police officer in uniform, when I first truly understood that there are dangerous personalities on this planet, and that because of them, we can never be completely safe. I shudder to think what Sue Curtis, all of 15, was made to understand that night, alone with a predator, before she died.

I am convinced that this singular event drove me years later to serve as a criminal profiler in the Tampa Division of the FBI and later in the FBI's elite National Security Division Behavioral Analysis Program. I felt compelled to understand criminal and abnormal behavior, and this objective dominated much of my Bureau career. Sue Curtis disappeared on my watch. Those were my words and initials on that investigative report. That tragic event drove my passion to seek answers from those who knew best: the criminals themselves and their victims.

What I learned from them, over a period of 4 decades, is that there are certain personalities who hurt people the most. Over and over, they are responsible for crime, for torment, for misery, for financial losses as well as for loss of life. This book is about those dangerous personalities that cause us so much pain and suffering. What I learned about criminals, abnormal behavior, and dangerous personalities you should know also, because it may save your life.

THE REALITY OF DANGEROUS PERSONALITIES

By now, we're familiar with the grim headline: Lone killer walks into an office building, classroom, campground, or other area and, seemingly without provocation, opens up with an assault rifle or other weapons, killing or maiming scores of innocent victims. And after each of these events, after the mayhem is over and the victims are buried or patched up (the latter no doubt traumatized for life, as are their families), the question is asked: "Who could do something like this, and could it have been prevented?"

When these violent events happen, they dominate the news and preoccupy us for months (the massacres at Virginia Tech; at Columbine High School and Sandy Hook Elementary School; and in Oslo, Norway, to name just a few). Unfortunately, these horrible mass killings happen all too often. In America alone, they occur on average 18 to 20 times per year.[1] Coming at us with almost metronomic frequency—more than one per month—such events are almost numbing. "How many were killed this time?" we ask incredulously. Was it 8, 16, 26, or 77 (as in Utøya, Norway, on July 22, 2011, at the hands of Anders Behring Breivik)?

Yet as staggering as these violent events are, they don't represent the full picture of who victimizes most people. The sad truth is that for every mass killer, there are hundreds more who kill one child at a time, one date at a time, or one spouse at a time—and these events sometimes barely make it to page 6 in major newspapers. The mayhem that occurs under the radar, without making the national news, is the kind of crime, torment, and suffering many of us are more likely to experience.

The dangerous personalities among us harm us behind closed doors at home, at church, at school, and in the office, often preying in secrecy on the unsuspecting or the trusting—and for the most part, no one finds out until it's too late. When they do make the headlines, it's on those rare occasions when they get caught. They are responsible for many of the nearly 15,000 homicides, 4.8 million domestic assaults, 2.2 million burglaries, 354,000 robberies, and 230,000-plus sexual assaults that occur annually in the United States, many of which go unreported and unpunished.[2] Or, like Bernard Madoff, they may embezzle money from the elderly or even friends for years (on such a grand scale, in his case, that the economic well-being of thousands was compromised). They can go undisturbed for decades, destroying lives as convicted child rapist Jerry Sandusky did at Pennsylvania State University.

Think back to those times in your own life when someone stole something from you or took hurtful advantage of you. Perhaps your house was burglarized or your car was broken into. Perhaps you dated someone who turned out to be toxic, or you were bullied at school or at work. Perhaps you've been assaulted, mugged, or sexually abused and never reported it, or if you did, nothing came of it. Much goes on around us that is never reported, and when it is, it's rare that those responsible are incarcerated. For 60 years, criminologists have known that fewer than 1 percent of criminals are ever incarcerated for their crimes.

What this means for us is that most of the people who can hurt us—these dangerous personalities—will avoid official scrutiny, wreaking havoc in our lives without ever getting caught, or persisting for years before they're stopped. And that's just physical harm. Not all wounds are physical. Most of the people who cause us harm will also do it emotionally, psychologically, or financially. They, too, are dangerous personalities because they put us at risk in their own way.

HOW FOUR DANGEROUS PERSONALITIES CAME TOGETHER

While working for the FBI as a profiler, I began to see a pattern emerging as to the personality types who seemed to dominate our attention. These were people who were constantly making others miserable, breaking laws, engaging in risky behavior, taking advantage of or abusing others, and in general causing pain and suffering—not once, not twice, but repeatedly.

Through my own efforts and with the guidance of others, I learned that there are certain personalities who will always be nasty, who are deceitful and manipulative, who derive pleasure from taking advantage of others, and who don't respect people or laws. They are exhausting emotionally and can be cruel, callous, and exploitative. And they will repeat their behavior over and over without concern for the physical or psychological damage they inflict on others.

From investigating, arresting, and talking to rapists, murderers, kidnappers, bank robbers, white-collar criminals, pedophiles, and terrorists, I learned, sometimes the hard way, that dangerous personalities can be very deceptive. They may look and act quite normal on the surface. They may even be intelligent, interesting, charming, and attractive. But they are always dangerous.

In 1995, I met Kelly Therese Warren for the first time. Thirty years old, she lived in Warner Robins, Georgia, with her daughter and husband. Kelly had served in the military handling secretarial duties and had been discharged honorably after serving her tour in Germany. Her husband worked at a lumberyard, and she did various odd jobs, including babysitting and working at a convenience store.

Kelly always had a smile for me and would welcome me with a hug. What little food they had she willingly shared, and she always made sure to top off my glass of sweetened iced tea. She talked to me more than a dozen times over a summer, always with a smile.

Kelly told me what life had been like as a US Army soldier stationed in Germany and what it was like to grow up poor in the South. She was funny and cheerful and always quick to answer my questions and fill in the gaps. For nearly a year, she provided my FBI colleagues and me with information that we used to pursue a criminal—and not just a criminal, but a Soviet-bloc spy. For a year, we followed Kelly's every word. Every bit of information she enthusiastically volunteered, we pursued.

But something wasn't right. Nothing Kelly was telling us was panning out. It took a long time to figure out because most of the leads were in Europe, not in the United States. Finally, we were able to confront her with the facts. That's when we learned that not only had she lied, but that it was she who had placed her nation at risk. It was she who, in her mere twenties, at the height of the Cold War, had put all of Central Europe in danger by selling to the Soviet bloc highly classified war plans that she had typed.

Kelly, with her sweet smile and sweet tea, was yet one more example of how dangerous personalities can be charming, funny, and interesting, but they can also put a whole nation—or, in her case, a host of nations—at risk. Kelly is serving a 25-year sentence for committing espionage.

These individuals are flawed not only in personality but also in character—that is, in morality and ethics. In essence, they can't be trusted to tell you the truth, to care about and protect you, or to keep you safe. And because of their flaws, invariably their behavior leaves behind a debris field of human suffering.

Over time, I came to realize that there were four personality types responsible for most of the harm we were seeing. These four dangerous personalities daily put us at risk financially, emotionally, or physically, and they are the personalities we will focus on in this book:

- The narcissistic personality

- The emotionally unstable personality

- The paranoid personality

- The predator

MY INTENTION

Dangerous Personalities is my attempt to share with you what I know about those who will hurt you. Dangerous personalities are all around us. They may be your neighbors, friends, boss, date, spouse, relatives, or parent. They may be community leaders or professionals responsible for your education, money, health, or safety—and that is why we have to be particularly on guard.

A NOTE ABOUT TERMINOLOGY

Some readers may wonder why I chose to use nonclinical terms such as *predator* and *emotionally unstable* to describe two of the dangerous personalities in this book. This is a valid question.

I wanted to use terms that laypeople could understand immediately and that would transfer easily across cultures. It would have been very easy (and perhaps beneficial for book sales, as some friends suggested) to use the term *psychopath* to describe the predator. Unfortunately, the term *psychopath* has become so overused that even some professionals use the term carelessly, when the more discerning would tell you that *conduct disorder, sociopath, antisocial personality disorder,* or, as the World Health Organization prefers, *dissocial personality disorder* would be more accurate or precise.[3]

The medical and mental health literature clearly differentiates between a psychopath, a sociopath, an individual with antisocial personality disorder, and an individual with conduct disorder. To label someone using those particular terms, one must be very aware of the specific criteria established by the mental health community or by researchers such as Robert Hare.

Evil, crime, or suffering comes at us in many ways, and rarely does it wave a flag or blow a whistle to say, "Get ready, I'm coming!" In fact, from my own experience as an FBI Special Agent, I know that criminals are incredibly adept at getting close to us so they can take advantage. Dennis Rader, also known as the BTK killer, hid in plain sight for 30 years. Living in Park City, Kansas, near Wichita, Rader was a church council leader and dog catcher/compliance officer for the city. He was also a serial killer (at least 10 victims) who liked to bind, torture, and kill—thus the BTK appellation—something he kept secret from his wife and kids as well as from

As complex as this is for professionals, it is more so for the lay reader. That's why I decided to use the term *predator,* which encapsulates the fact that we are dealing with individuals who prey on others, take advantage of others, and have little regard for rules or for the rights and sanctity of others.

Similarly, terms such as *borderline personality, histrionic, conduct disorder,* or *bipolar disorder* are a mystery to most people not familiar with the full clinical meaning of these terms. So I use the appellation *emotionally unstable* to encapsulate the essence of this personality so that the average person, and that includes me, can understand.

I am also aware that some psychological terms, such as *borderline* or *histrionic,* have become so highly charged with negative meanings and connotations that they stigmatize or are used pejoratively while providing little clarity as to what is at issue. For these reasons, I avoided using those terms.

Narcissistic and paranoid personality were used, however, because these terms are widely understood, thanks to their long pedigree in mythology and in literature.

city officials and his church for 3 decades. David Russell Williams, a decorated Canadian Forces colonel, also hid a secret from his wife and his fellow officers: that he was a serial rapist and killer. Or how about the scores of Catholic priests who for decades hid their crimes of child abuse under the robes of the clergy?

It's cases like these that make us wonder, whom can we trust? How can we detect and avoid harm before it happens? In the end, we must rely on our own innate abilities to sense danger, our powers of observation, and the behaviors of others that alert us that something isn't right.

Sometimes, the only person making the key observations that may save you is you, sitting next to that odd or prickly person in a cubicle at work or behind that closed door at home. Consider the 2013 case of Ariel Castro, who held, tortured, and raped three girls in his house for more than a decade (more than 3,600 days—just think about that). Within hours of his arrest, neighbors spoke to news reporters of how bewildered they were, as Castro was "known as a sunny face, someone who was good with children."[4] One neighbor who lived two doors down and had known Castro for 22 years said, "I feel a little guilty, I should have spotted it."[5]

But what if those neighbors, family members, or his fellow musicians and band members (Castro played the guitar and sang) had been better observers? Most people, unfortunately, are simply not motivated to look closer. In fact, society frowns on meddling in other people's business, and frankly, most people simply don't know what to look for. Sadly, social blindness is the rule, not the exception.

I don't want you to be victimized. I don't want you to go through what I have witnessed and what so many have suffered. I want you to have a happy, fulfilling life. But I know there are dangerous personalities out there, ever ready to torment you or take what you value. If you have any doubt, just read the newspaper, and you'll know why we have to be prepared.

Invariably, a person who has been victimized later asks, "How could this happen to me? Why didn't I see the signs?" We've all experienced this, including me. While hindsight is 20/20, foresight is mostly blind. No one has taught us what to look for. We who work criminal cases know that there are almost always personality traits or behavioral cues that, to the informed, say, "There are issues here, pay attention, beware, or get away"— but either they weren't recognized or people chose to ignore them.

This is where *Dangerous Personalities* comes in. I want to help you anticipate when someone is going to try to take advantage of you or hurt you. Safety is our responsibility. It cannot be outsourced, and if we try to do so, we'll be disappointed. Police departments are notoriously overburdened, mental health clinics are swamped, the courts still let too many get away, and, as already mentioned, the majority of those who do wrong rarely get caught. Thus our safety is up to us.

How nice it would be if we could just block these individuals out of our lives as easily as we do spam or pop-up messages on the Internet—with one click. But we can't. That means we have to be on guard. I want to share this information with you because we don't have experts at our side 24/7 to turn to and ask, "What do you think, is he dangerous?" "Is he a good person?" "Can I trust her to care for my child?" "Should I invest with him?" "Should I let her be my roommate?" "Does this manager have the capacity to ruin my company?" "Should I bring him home and let him spend the night?" These decisions are our responsibility, yet few of us are prepared to assess others properly in order to answer these questions. When we fail to answer them today, we may find the sad answer on the front page of tomorrow's newspaper.

Now you can take an active role in ensuring your safety. *Dangerous Personalities* provides you with expert advice in a simple, practical way so that you can take control of your life. I want to help you learn how to assess others for flaws of character or personality to reduce the chance that you'll be taken advantage of emotionally, psychologically, financially, or physically. Benjamin Franklin said it best: "An investment in knowledge pays the best interest." I would only add that an investment in this kind of knowledge may save your life.

THE DANGEROUS PERSONALITY CHECKLISTS

In the world where I worked, we never had the luxury of days or weeks to assess an individual. Decisions about whom to investigate, focus on, follow, question, confront, engage, or arrest had to be made quickly. After all, when you're negotiating with a kidnapper, you can't say, "Hang on a minute; we have to ask a committee of experts what your personality is really like so we know how to deal with you." It doesn't work that way. Real life happens in real time, and decisions have to be made in an instant.

In crisis situations, our general knowledge of human behavior was critical, but so was the specific information we gradually collected as to how these dangerous personalities behaved. In time, as I studied and talked to these individuals, as well as to experts and to victims, their key features became formalized into checklists to help me assess these individuals in real time in the high-stakes situations we confronted daily in the FBI.

What only a select few FBI criminal profilers previously knew, and what I myself used repeatedly and refined over the years, I will now share with you.

Chapter by chapter, I'll describe the defining traits of each of the four personalities, how they behave, how they make us feel, and where and how we may encounter them, with examples from everyday life, my own crime files, and the headlines. I conclude each chapter with the Dangerous Personalities Checklist specific to that personality type, describing key warning signs in plain language. The checklists include a practical, easy-to-use scoring system to help you gauge where this person's behaviors fall on a spectrum from mild to moderate to severe—in other words, from irritating to toxic to dangerous.

The checklists will help you understand the following:

- The most common personality traits and behaviors that say, "Proceed with caution"

- The traits, behaviors, or events that appear normal but that, in fact, communicate danger

- What you can anticipate in the future from this individual

- The possible threat level to you and those who associate with this individual

Each checklist is very specific and highly detailed—far more detailed, in fact, than those used by mental health professionals when diagnosing personality disorders. As you look at the checklists, you may wonder why they are so long. The answer is simple. Assessing for dangerous personalities is often complex and subtle. The checklists are lengthy because they need to be. Details ensure accuracy and help avoid the risk of overlooking meaningful or nuanced behaviors that the layperson may have forgotten or may not have realized are significant but that are important in identifying a particular dangerous personality. When it comes to saving lives or keeping others safe, I have to consider what is useful to the widest readership, and also what is necessary. Just as an experienced pilot uses a lengthy preflight and landing checklist to ensure maximum safety for all on board, so we must use comprehensive checklists to be as careful and as precise as we can. When it comes to dangerous personalities, detail and accuracy trump brevity and ambiguity.

As you read this book and use the checklists, you will notice that unlike most books on the subject, there are very few statistics. There is, in my view, a valid reason for this. When we say that this or that personality type accounts for 1 or 6 or 2.8 percent of the population, I believe we're doing a disservice to readers by inviting them to focus on probabilities (statistics) rather than on behaviors. There's a risk that someone will say, "Well, I have a 96 percent chance of being safe, so I don't need to worry about dealing with that type of person." Many smokers delude themselves by focusing on the statistics relating to those who don't get lung cancer rather than on the behaviors and lifestyle that lead to lung cancer. This mind-set is precisely what we want to avoid. All it takes is *one* encounter with *one* dangerous personality—on the street, at work, in your car, in your house, in your bedroom—to completely ruin your life. Thus in this book, we focus on behaviors, not on statistics or probabilities.

I also know from the research (for more information, refer to the fifth edition of the *Diagnostic and Statistical Manual of Mental Disorders*, known

as the DSM-5) that certain disorders are more often diagnosed or associated with a specific gender: Antisocial personality disorder, for instance, is
more often diagnosed in males, while borderline personality disorder is
more often diagnosed in females.[6] These two disorders have many of the
behavioral traits of the predator and the emotionally unstable personality,
respectively, discussed in this book. For the same reason that it's inadvis-
able to focus too narrowly on statistics, it would be a mistake to associate
one disorder or personality type with a specific gender. We don't want to
be blinded by fixating on statistics or a gender bias. What we want to do is
focus on *behaviors*. Behaviors overwhelmingly will define the dangerous
personality type.

AN IMPORTANT CAUTION

As you read this book, keep in mind that I am not a mental health professional, and this is not a diagnostic book. Clinical diagnosis is reserved for
clinicians who have spent years training in the art and science of diagnosis
using specific criteria established by the American Psychiatric Association.
While professionals may find the material in this book helpful, this book is
not meant to be used for diagnostic purposes.

The checklists were designed as an assessment tool for those wanting
to identify dangerous personalities or behaviors associated with dangerous
personalities. Just as we prudently assess whom to allow into our homes or
whom to employ, this book and these checklists likewise help us to be more
thorough in our assessments of others. This is a descriptive book about
how to identify dangerous personalities through their behaviors. It's also a
book on how to protect yourself and your loved ones.

There are many excellent books and resources on mental illness, abnormal psychology, and personality disorders, as well as their possible causes

and treatment. This isn't one of them, and you should seek out those resources if that's the perspective you're looking for. This book is strictly from my perspective as a former FBI Special Agent who had to deal with these kinds of dangerous individuals on a frequent basis, either face-to-face, as the target of my investigations, or in consultations. My approach, therefore, is not from the healing arts—I leave that to mental health professionals.

The Selected Resources and the Bibliography offer a selection of valuable resources that draw from the healing arts, crisis centers, criminologists, law enforcement, and forensics, as well as insights from the victims themselves. I hope you'll explore these additional resources and continue to educate yourself long after you've finished this book. I truly believe you're best served when you consider what many authors have to say, rather than just one.

Many other books explore *why* these personalities are the way they are. You will not find that focus here, for this reason: When someone takes pleasure in humiliating you on a daily basis, has cleaned out your bank account, has molested your child, or is choking you with a belt, does it really matter *why* that person is this way? The only thing that matters, because you are not a clinician or a researcher, is your safety and the well-being of those you love.

During my decades in law enforcement, the more insight we had into a suspect's personality, the greater the probability we had of catching that individual or preventing further criminal acts. For example, in hostage situations, knowing whether we were dealing with someone who was primarily paranoid, a predator, a narcissist, or highly unstable could make a big difference in how we communicated with this person, how often, and by what means. It also helped us determine what actions might be taken to rescue the hostage. Knowing the individual's personality type gave us insight into the probable outcome of the situation, as personality traits often dictate the trajectory of how someone is likely to behave. Which is why we say in behavioral analysis, "The best predictor of future behavior is past behavior." Or to quote a legendary thinker on human nature:

We are what we repeatedly do.
—Aristotle

So if you seek to know the "why" of dangerous personalities, this is not the book for you. But if you want to know how they think and behave, if you want to protect yourself, your loved ones, or your business, then this is a good place to start.

ONE LAST THOUGHT BEFORE WE BEGIN

While my training and personal philosophy dictate that everyone deserves to be treated ethically and with respect, I also believe no one has a social obligation to be victimized. Let me repeat that: No one has a social obligation to be victimized. That's why I'm writing this book. I care about only one thing: your safety and well-being. I care about you, your children, your parents, or your grandparents not becoming victims.

My goal is not to scare you but to empower you. I want to sensitize you to these personalities so you can spot them before they can hurt you or those you love, and help you distance yourself if they're causing you harm. I want to help you develop your "safety radar" for detecting behaviors that signal *caution, be careful with this person, slow down, don't trust.*

The more we can do this as individuals, the better protected we'll be as a society. Then maybe the havoc wrought by the extremely dangerous personalities of the world can be contained long before they make headlines.

If this book helps you identify and protect yourself from someone who can hurt you physically, emotionally, psychologically, or financially—then I have accomplished my goal.

CHAPTER 1

"IT'S ALL ABOUT ME"

THE NARCISSISTIC PERSONALITY

OF ALL THE LABELS THAT are carelessly bandied about, *narcissist* is probably one of the most overused and least understood. It's a popular term with ancient origins (the Greek myth of Narcissus, who fell in love with his reflection), yet what it really means can be perplexing.

Many people think of a narcissist as someone who perhaps names hotels after himself or always wants to be in the spotlight—maybe a character on reality TV. Certainly plenty of people love the limelight. But the kind of narcissist we're talking about goes far beyond self-promotion by acting in ways that are toxic and dangerous. From this point forward, I will use the terms *narcissist* and *narcissistic personality* interchangeably.

Narcissistic personalities care only for themselves, their needs, and their priorities. While you and I appreciate attention, the narcissist craves it and manipulates people and situations to get it. While you and I work hard to be successful, the narcissistic personality connives to succeed and may cheat, lie, embellish the truth, or scheme to get ahead, uncaring of how others are affected.

These personalities can be found in every level of our society, right up to the top, where history's grim record shows that they've started wars and exterminated populations. But they're also found in the cubicle or on the bar stool next to you, at home, on the team, in the classroom, and even in your spiritual community.

"Cinderella," the classic tale of the cruel stepmother and stepsisters obsessed with themselves, epitomizes the exploitative nature of narcissism. These are people who live selfishly at others' expense. The most famous version of Cinderella is the Disney one, but historically there are more than 300 variants of this tale.[1] Apparently, many cultures have seen fit to warn us about this personality, and with good reason.

Like Cinderella's stepmother and stepsisters, these personalities see few faults in themselves and view anyone who doesn't value them as highly as they value themselves as nobodies to be denigrated or tormented. And while Disney's Cinderella enjoys a magical happy ending, in real life there's no fairy godmother or prince to save us from these bullies. When we're dealing with the narcissistic personality, our protection is up to us.

THE WAY OF THE NARCISSISTIC PERSONALITY

Narcissism isn't the same as confidence. True confidence reflects admirable strength of character. The narcissist's confidence is really arrogance—a character flaw leading to grandiose ideas and the relentless pursuit of the narcissist's desires, often at others' expense.

Some grandiose ideas can be good for society. Look at the advances that came from Edison's vision of a world powered by electricity and Kennedy's mission to land on the moon, to name just two. Walt Disney, too, had a grandiose idea: a "magical" place for children and adults to enjoy themselves—which would become Disneyland, Disney World, and Epcot.

The narcissist's grandiosity is entirely different. Consider Jim Jones, whose vision for Jonestown in Guyana was to create a place where people would pay tribute to him as a supreme individual. The price of admission? Your life savings and your free will. You also had to be willing to kill your own children and yourself by drinking cyanide-laced Kool-Aid along with more than 900 other followers.[2]

In the first instance, a grandiose idea leads to a place where we can fulfill our dreams. In the other, our worst dreams are fulfilled. The difference isn't one of ideas but of personality type and character flaws. One seeks happiness for all. The other seeks adoration and happiness only for himself. This is why I want to warn you about the defining traits of this dangerous personality.

Egocentric

As children, we all go through a phase where we feel we're the center of the world, with a high sense of entitlement. Narcissistic personalities essentially never outgrow this phase. Their childlike need to be constantly attended to leads them to do everything from the ridiculous to the unthinkable to be the center of attention or to get their way.[3]

They'll arrive late to meetings, parties, and family events, delaying activities, making others wait and even make sacrifices on their behalf. They may storm in or make dramatic entrances just to get everyone's attention. They have no hesitation about letting you know they're the smartest person in the room. Some are shameless name-droppers, habitually mentioning whom they know, whom they lunched with, and on and on, making sure you know that they associate with important people.

Looking good in every sense is vital to narcissists. You may see them preening in mirrors. They're highly aware of their physical appearance (which can lead to fitness or cosmetic surgery fanaticism) and use their presence to have an impact on others, whether it's making sure all heads turn at a party or ensuring everyone sees they've got the best, biggest, or most expensive everything.

Some narcissistic personalities present themselves as being very accomplished, but in fact they've accomplished little—which doesn't stop them from acting superior and seeing themselves as a great inventor, artist, musician, thinker, leader, or singer. When things don't go their way, they blame everyone but themselves. Maybe these individuals made mistakes, are incompetent, or just aren't well liked, but you'll never hear that from them. No, the system, society, the boss, the professor, the electorate, the world is against them. We simply fail to see how great they are.

When others don't treat narcissists as the special person they deem themselves to be, their reaction is infantile rage that ranges from sulking to whining to seething and, sometimes, to violence. They can berate and blame with impunity, hold grudges, and be vengeful—that is their nature.

Overvalues Self, Devalues Others

Because they see themselves as special and unique, narcissistic personalities tend to see everyone else as either marginal or inferior. They become masters at putting others down in order to elevate themselves—they are the bullies of the world. That's how businesswoman and hotelier Leona Helmsley got the moniker "the Queen of Mean."[4] But she wasn't just mean. She was by all accounts a bully toward anyone she deemed below her—no different from the kind of bullying we see today in schools.

If bullying seems to be on the rise and the consequences of bullying (absenteeism, depression, anxiety, suicide) are becoming ever more dramatic and extreme, it is no accident. Many clinicians are of the opinion that as narcissism has increased in the general population, so has bullying, which is a common characteristic of the narcissistic personality.[5] It seems persistent bullying and narcissism go hand in hand.

These days, the narcissistic personality doesn't even have to be with you to bring you down. On September 9, 2013, 12-year-old Rebecca Sedwick jumped to her death from an abandoned cement plant in Polk County, Florida, allegedly as a result of being tormented online (cyberbullied).[6] This is what can happen when people consistently overvalue themselves and devalue others—a common narcissistic trait.

Narcissistic personalities have an uncanny ability to identify weakness or insecurity in others and use it to put others down or make themselves look better. It may be something as subtle as noticing your new watch and then calling attention to their much more expensive one. At a cookout, they'll say things like "No steaks; only hamburgers?" loudly enough for all your guests to hear. They don't care how you feel; they thrive by belittling others.

They are the kind who, sensing someone's nervousness before giving a speech, would say, "It must be tough to follow a great speaker—I wouldn't want to be in your shoes." I know, because this happened to me right before speaking to a group in New Orleans.

Sometimes, these personalities betray their true nature by berating their spouses or children in public, at social occasions, or at kids' sporting events. If this is what they do in public, imagine what they do at home when outsiders aren't looking.

Or they'll make contemptuous comments with caustic indifference about how stupid or incompetent somebody is. They'll bark commands at a passing waiter for service and then turn to you with a smile as if nothing happened. At an event I attended years ago in Las Vegas, a speaker screamed at the hotel staff in front of about 150 attendees, "I didn't come all this way to look like a fool—fix it!" when the microphone stopped working. Everyone's jaw dropped. Such behaviors should serve as telltale clues to all who see or receive such treatment that they are in the presence of a narcissistic personality.

Instead of Empathy, You'll Find Arrogance and Entitlement

A person who feels superior to others will have limited ability to empathize. While most of us learn as children how to understand others' feelings and how our actions affect others, with these personalities, sympathy or understanding for your situation and feelings is limited or nonexistent. You could be in crisis and somehow you still won't be the center of attention, because nothing must detract from the needs, wants, and desires of narcissists. You may have a sick child you need to attend to, but they still want you to take them shopping at the mall. In fact, narcissistic personalities view revelations about needs, illness, or mistakes as weaknesses in others that confirm their superiority and justify their devaluing behaviors.

Some narcissists telegraph their arrogance and haughtiness; it's palpable in how they speak, react, and even carry themselves. Others recognize the need to at least appear to be empathetic. Their empathy, however, has an agenda—such as when a boss calls you at home when you're sick to ask how you're feeling but is only really concerned with when you're coming back to work. It may seem as if they care, until you discover how superficial and infrequent their interest in your life and well-being actually is—except when it affects them.

Still others betray their hypervaluation of themselves only when there is a crisis. Then their egocentric perspective on the world percolates to the surface.

On April 20, 2010, BP's Deepwater Horizon oil rig exploded in the Gulf of Mexico, killing 11 rig workers and causing the largest accidental marine oil spill in the history of the petroleum industry (or the world, for that matter). About the disaster and its effects on others, Anthony "Tony" Hayward, BP's CEO, remarked to a reporter on May 30, "We're sorry for the massive disruption it's caused to their lives. There's no one who wants this thing over more than I do. I'd like my life back."[7] The term *jaw-dropping* would apply here. We're talking about an environmental disaster of historic proportions coupled with the deaths of 11 humans, and he wants his "life back." Sometimes, it takes a crisis to reveal those narcissistic traits that say, "Nothing is more important to me than me."

The more you talk to narcissistic personalities, the more you get the sense that they don't care about you. They're not very inquisitive about you. What they really want is for you to pay attention to them and to their needs and desires, or to do their bidding. But because they're hyperaware of how they appear to others, they can, in many cases, modulate and moderate their behavior to control how they're perceived. They can do this for a while, but in the end, their true sentiments will come out.

Narcissists act nice to get their way, not to express true caring. In the movie *Goodfellas*, rising mobster Henry Hill (played by Ray Liotta) uses attentiveness to court Karen, his future wife, treating her to great restaurants, front-row seats, the best food, the best wine, no waiting in line. She is the focus of his total attention. Once they're married, boom, it's over. The narcissist worked for and got what he wanted, so what's the problem when he comes home drunk, smelling of other women? What his wife wants doesn't matter; the only thing that matters is what he feels he's entitled to. He has used attentiveness to ensnare, but he doesn't really care.

In real life, financier Bernard Madoff used connections and friendships to ensnare trusting people in his Ponzi scheme. The crushing difference between what they expected and what they got is the terrible truth of relationships with a narcissistic personality. You expect to be treated as an equal, as a friend, but a narcissist has no equal. For the narcissistic personality, friends are functional. They serve a purpose: to provide the narcissist with something wanted or needed.

The most dangerous narcissists are those whose utter lack of empathy and high levels of grandiosity verge on psychopathy: the ability to do harm without remorse. They have no conscience and will exploit others emotionally, financially, and sometimes physically. If you please them, you are convenient; if you displease them, you're more than an inconvenience—you're something they must debase or perhaps destroy. When we read about a parent who incarcerates, abandons, or murders his or her own baby so that the parent can have a good time and party, what we're dealing with, first and foremost, is a narcissistic personality: someone who overvalues himself or herself and devalues others with reptilian indifference.

That reptilian indifference is what we see in major cities and elsewhere in the phenomenon known as knockout assaults, in which the unsuspecting (including elderly women) are targeted for a blindingly fast punch without provocation, just to see if the person can be knocked out (usually causing a concussion) with a single hit. To behave with such callousness, one has to be able to devalue others—a trait the narcissistic personality has in abundance.

Takes Shortcuts, Bends Rules, Violates Boundaries

Because they feel entitled, narcissistic personalities may feel they don't have to work as hard as others, that they can take shortcuts to get what they want, or that the rules don't apply to them. This is how you end up with politicians who have affairs, father children, and attempt to deny their paternity (former US senator John Edwards); turn public funds into their own private piggy bank (former US representative Jesse Jackson Jr.); or are willing to sell political favors for a price (former governor of Illinois Rod Blagojevich).

One executive told me about hiring a manager who was fairly successful, but who then suddenly started flirting with his female co-workers. It was as if he just couldn't help himself with the sexual overtures. Every employee knew such behavior was not tolerated, but when he was confronted, he was enraged, maintaining that nothing in his behavior violated the terms of his contract and that he was merely being friendly. Remember, narcissists don't see that they're doing anything wrong; they feel entitled. They just get angry that someone's pointing out their inappropriate behavior.

Some create fictions about themselves to feed their need for recognition. For example, they'll say they're a decorated Navy SEAL, but they've never even served in the armed forces—and, of course, convincing proof is never available because their work is "secret." It's bad enough when someone pretends to be a military hero—an affront to all who served—but when someone pretends to be a doctor, pilot, or other professional, and people trust that person with their health, life, or savings, that is perhaps the ultimate betrayal of trust and ethics. Such violations undermine society and, in my experience, are most often committed by the narcissistic personality.

The narcissistic personality is quite gifted at bamboozling and conning others. This is exactly what Christian Karl Gerhartsreiter, a German immigrant, did, passing himself off as "Clark Rockefeller," a member of the iconic Rockefeller family. He ended up marrying Sandra Boss, a respected businesswoman, and having a baby with her.[8] When she discovered all his lies and sought a divorce, he kidnapped their child. Who could do such a thing? An unaccomplished narcissistic personality seeking to be recognized, that's who.

I remember when a woman named Sara, a widow, came to the FBI seeking our aid. I was assigned to interview her, as there might have been possible interstate issues involving fraud, which is a federal offense. Sara had just paid for her third and last child to finish college. With more free time, she turned her attention to a charismatic preacher who had recently established himself in town. She was captivated by his devoutness, his "knowledge of so many things," and how easily he made friends. His attentions led her to assist his "spiritual labors" to build up his church, committing almost $30,000 that she had saved. But after she handed over the money, the preacher vanished.

I talked to Sara 3 years after this happened, and she was still stinging from this financial calamity. She had lost most of her savings, and her children were upset that she'd fallen for this grifter, as other elderly women had done. But equally heartbreaking was her revelation to me that she had lost her "spirituality" and "trust in others."

With their boundless sense of self-importance, narcissistic personalities lack clear boundaries. They push the envelope with people, laws, rules, and social norms. As social puppeteers, they view others as extensions of themselves, commanding, directing, manipulating, and using people to meet their desires. For example, on a date, flirting, teasing, kissing, and caressing are inducements to sex for the narcissist. A woman may want to stop at some point and go no further, but the narcissistic personality feels entitled to do as he pleases, so for him the words *no* and *stop* have no meaning. Those words are speed bumps, not stop signs. This is what we mean when we say that the narcissist has no boundaries.

Every time you hear of yet another CEO who lies about the financial worth of the company and puts his or her employees at risk financially, you're witnessing a narcissistic personality in action. Jeffrey Keith "Jeff" Skilling and Kenneth Lay were responsible for the collapse of Enron in 2001—at the time the biggest corporate bankruptcy in US history. Both were convicted of conspiracy and fraud, but that was little consolation to stockholders who had been lied to and to the more than 20,000 Enron employees who were encouraged to invest in a company near collapse. They lost their jobs and their life savings. To allow something like this to happen requires a shocking degree of self-entitlement and grandiosity and a gross lack of empathy, qualities that the narcissistic personality has in abundance.[9]

When we read or hear about a priest, camp counselor, or coach who sexually violates a child, we're talking about a narcissistic personality who doesn't respect human rights. Ever notice that when these individuals get caught, they don't apologize? They don't because they felt entitled to violate children in the first place. When I look at Jerry Sandusky, retired Penn State coach and convicted serial child molester, I see a narcissistic personality and a deplorable human being who used children like a theme park. Not one apology came from his mouth. He deserves scorn as well as a lifetime in prison. He may have been a revered coach who did nice things, but he wasn't a good person—that is part of the narcissistic pathology.

Needs to Control

People sometimes joke that they're "control freaks," but if you've ever had a controlling boss or mate, you know it's no joke. A woman named Matilda fell for a handsome man who, like her, was from Latin America. She remained at home while he worked, and he was always on top of the family finances. That worked well in the beginning, but after a while, his control became suffocating. She grew tired of having to ask him for money for groceries, new clothes, and Christmas gifts. When she'd bring this up, he'd say, "Don't I take care of you? Haven't I given you everything? You shouldn't worry about such things."

He left her not long ago for another woman. This man who at first seemed so generous kept Matilda so much under his control that she had no idea how much money was in the bank or even where the money was. Now in her fifties, she's working several jobs. She has no money in the bank, no credit, no retirement savings, and he is unresponsive to her pleas. Her self-worth is as low as her financial worth. She tells me tearfully, "I have nothing, and I gave him everything." Here's a woman who placed her trust in someone who robbed her of her freedom and dignity. How did it get this way? As most things like this do: one step at a time into the abyss of life with a narcissist.

Narcissists often seek positions where they can control others. That's

Words That Describe
THE NARCISSIST

Over the years, I have collected the words of those who have lived with, worked with, or have been victimized by dangerous personalities. These are the words of those I've interviewed or who called the FBI or me personally, requesting assistance. When asked to describe these dangerous individuals, most people aren't politically correct and may not know clinical or medical terms, but they speak from the heart because of their trauma, hurt, or fear. These are their uncensored words, not mine. Perhaps some will sound familiar to you in describing someone you know. These words alone are instructive and sound a warning worth noting about these individuals:

Abusive, acting, actor, aggressive, amoral, arrogant, articulate, beguiling, bullshitter, bully, calculating, callous, chameleon, charismatic, charming, cheat, clever, cold, con man, conniving, contemptuous, controlling, criminal, cruel, cunning, dangerous, deceitful, deceptive, dehumanizing, deplorable, dishonest, disingenuous, disruptive, distracted, domineering, egocentric, evil, exploitative, fearless, forger, fraud, glib, grandiose, grandiosity, guiltless, hostile, imposter, inconsiderate, indifferent, infidelity, insensitive, insincerity, intense, interesting, intimidating, irksome, irresponsible, irritable, irritating, king, lawbreaker, liar, lord, loveless, Machiavellian, manipulative, mean, mesmerizing, narcissistic, Nazi, noxious, nuisance, parasitic, peacock, pedophile, player, predator, predatory, preoccupied, pretender, promiscuous, radiant, rattlesnake, risk-taker, ruler, sarcastic, seductive, self-centered, shallow, showman, slimy, smooth, snake, sneaky, superficial, swindler, tactless, temperamental, toxic, two-faced, tyrant, unapologetic, uncaring, uninterested, unreliable, unscrupulous, unsympathetic, vile, vindictive, witty.

why you tend to see more of them in jobs such as law, medicine, and politics or in high-level executive positions, where they can use their rank or status to take care of themselves. I recall an interviewee for an FBI position saying to me, "Once I get that badge, nobody will mess with me anymore." Needless to say, his application was rejected as soon as he left the room. It's not unusual for narcissistic individuals to seek jobs where they can exercise power and authority to control others rather than to help others.

In the end, it doesn't matter how high or low the position or the title; it will be used for the narcissistic personality's own gain. When you read that a member of a club, organization, or association is a self-centered tyrant or someone who has been embezzling money for years, think first and foremost of a narcissist—that is what they do.

THEIR EFFECT ON YOU

Narcissists can be hard to spot at first because they may be intelligent, engaging, and interesting, even exuding an aura of omnipotence. They can be charming to those who can help them, but eventually they show their true colors.

Sometimes, you'll see overt displays of arrogance, haughtiness, or grandiosity that give you insight and may also make you feel that something isn't right. At other times, they can be aloof, patronizing, and distant, which leaves you with an unsavory feeling. Sometimes, they withhold their affection, or they refuse to help or to honor their commitments. Whatever they do, the effect is always the same: They leave you feeling troubled, unfulfilled, or tormented.

Narcissists can also be subtly cruel. They will intentionally fail to validate something important that you've accomplished or any pain or suffering you may be feeling. By their deliberate indifference, they leave you to wither in lonely triumph or suffering—they are simply unwilling to take the slightest interest. To do so would be to make you feel good, and that is not what the narcissistic personality wants.

Because they are so limited in empathy, they are like "half people" looking for someone to complete them. Yet when they find someone, things go downhill because no one can really fulfill a narcissist. And they really aren't capable of fulfilling someone else. Thinking that you can make things work with a narcissist will take a terrible toll on you emotionally, psychologically, even physically.

And that's their chief effect: They wear on you. Narcissistic personalities see your needs, wants, or desires only as distractions or as obstacles to their own. If you're inconvenienced, unhappy, frustrated, or stressed out, it's of no concern to them. But if they don't get their way, then you see their reaction: eye rolls, contemptuous displays, pouting, impatience, petulance, huffiness, ranting, or they may just walk away. They're rather like children in adult bodies.

At times, we feel the pain of being with a narcissist instantly; at other times, it registers like a dagger stab a few seconds later ("Did I just see/hear that?"). We may be jolted awake at 2:00 a.m. as our subconscious kicks in and alerts us to something hurtful that they've done or lied about. Or their behavior triggers the sensation that something isn't quite right. Some people feel confused or physically queasy at these times. Some get sick or stressed out. I've had people tell me, "When I have to deal with this person, I don't eat breakfast because I feel like I'm going to throw up."

If you have these negative sensations, pay attention. Many of us have been taught to "forgive and forget," especially with family and friends. The narcissistic personality is counting on you to do that. Because when this person hurts you again and you're sitting there feeling startled, speechless, or defeated, the narcissist is feeling elevated, superior, and fulfilled. These emotional assaults will deplete you until you become putty in the narcissist's hands—or you have to take sick leave, as many do, just to cope.

Pathological narcissism can go to extremes where laws often fail us. One woman came to the FBI to seek our assistance in a domestic matter. Unfortunately, there was little that we could do other than refer her to social services. She reported that for years, her husband made her and her children sit on the floor whenever he called family meetings to castigate the family about this or that. Yes, he sat on a chair as if on a throne, and she and the kids had to sit on the floor as they were berated or made to reveal their failings.

Eventually, she was able to extricate herself and her children, but at great financial expense and not before she and her kids had suffered significant psychological damage. Here was a case of a narcissistic personality wanting to debase his family to feel superior. Police departments around the country and around the world see this every day—the details are different, but the intent is the same: the glorification of one at the expense of others.

When they aren't putting you down, narcissists are just being nasty. As Claire reported to me about her manager, "He'd pass my desk and literally dump work on it with a scowl. Files would scatter; coffee would spill. He didn't care what I was doing or that my desk wasn't his dumping ground. I can't tell you how many people he made cry. Cry. Who does that kind of thing?"

Every time I hear of a woman or child who is repeatedly berated in public, beaten, or subjected to some form of domestic abuse, the first thought that comes to my mind is there's a narcissist in that house who devalues his partner or children and overvalues himself so much that he can slap, strike, or beat a family member.

The case of Hedda Nussbaum and 6-year-old Elizabeth "Lisa" Steinberg, who lived with the Nussbaums, is a reminder of what it's like to live with a narcissist who gets away with abuse behind closed doors.[10] Nussbaum, a book editor at the time she met attorney Joel Steinberg in 1975, has been quoted as initially viewing Steinberg as "godlike," submitting to his direction on how to get ahead in business, but her life with Steinberg was anything but heavenly. He habitually criticized and denigrated her to the point of making her crawl on the floor like an animal. He would beat her almost daily, so much so that he disfigured her face. In 1987, in a fit of rage, he took it out on Lisa, killing her. It's a tragic example of how people involved with these narcissistic personalities over time are rendered pliant or inert. It was evident to prosecutors that Hedda had herself been so brutalized by Steinberg that she could not rise to defend an innocent child nor seek medical aid for Lisa. She personified what came to be called battered wife syndrome. More than 30 years later, it's still painful to think about what happened to Hedda and Lisa.

Not everyone who associates with a narcissistic personality will suffer as Hedda and Lisa did. But know this. Every person I've ever talked to who has associated with a narcissistic personality has said the same thing: One way or another, to one degree or another, they were forbidden to flourish. How did they feel? In their own words: "small," "insignificant," "inferior." Enough said.

THE NARCISSISTIC PERSONALITY IN RELATIONSHIPS

Narcissists cannot express love as we understand it. For them, it's conditional or comes with strings attached; in other words, "I will do this for you, but I expect certain things from you in return." For the narcissist, love is about quid pro quo: something for something. It is not altruistic.

People who've been romantically involved with a narcissist often tell me that in the beginning they were mesmerized by the person's charm, intelligence, attentiveness, and grand gestures—much as I described Henry Hill's early courtship with Karen in the movie *Goodfellas*. All of us are vulnerable to the narcissist's charisma and charm. But once an individual commits to the narcissistic personality, the charm quickly fades, leaving us at a loss to reconcile the alluring person we knew with the indifferent, manipulative partner we now face.

At home, these individuals may demand that everything stop when they walk through the door. If they're a stay-at-home spouse, then your whole existence is about catering to their needs. And whatever you do, it's never enough.

The narcissistic partner is never satisfied with your appearance, habits, tastes, activities, and abilities. Criticism can range from "that look" of disapproval to nagging to insults in private or in public. I asked one woman how often she was criticized by her spouse. Her answer was sobering: "Every day. Every single day of my life with him. I never did anything right in his eyes, and he taught the kids to criticize me and laugh at me as well."

A friend of mine (now divorced) tells of spending hours searching for the right gift for his former wife. When he finally presented it to her, she tossed it on the counter and said, "Thank you," as if being handed a glass of water. She didn't even take it out of the box, he said. This seems like a small thing, but she had done this to him so many times over the years that it bore witness to the fact that she didn't care about him but rather—as he discovered in other ways—cared only about getting ahead (she was using him to advance her career). This type of invalidation is consistent with the narcissistic personality. Want to make people feel worthless? Cheapen their efforts; don't recognize their goodwill; take no interest. That's how the narcissistic personality does it, and it hurts.

The narcissistic personality's craving to look good at all costs can have devastating consequences for the rest of us. That's what happened to Miriam, who sought the help of the FBI because her husband had moved overseas and left her with no money. She wanted the FBI to track him down to claim the money he took from their joint bank account. According to Miriam, her husband was obsessed with buying ever more expensive houses in better neighborhoods, nicer cars, and pricier jewelry, while insisting on membership in two country clubs. She began to sense something was wrong, she claimed, when he started telling her to cut back on outings, summer vacations, clothes for the children, and food expenses. The latter was the last straw. He was still spending nearly $3,000 a month in club fees while asking her to cut back. She finally confronted him, as she didn't work and wanted to know what was going on. He turned to her and said almost casually, "We are bankrupt." There was no money left in the bank.

Even though he owed millions, his narcissistic need to maintain his public image meant that he still had his hair and nails done every week and maintained his membership in two clubs while Miriam was cutting back on food expenses and having "anxiety and panic attacks." Eventually, he just walked away—fled the country and left her, clueless, penniless, and holding the bag, as she had cosigned on some loans. The depth of his callousness was breathtaking, as she discovered with each new phone call from a debt collector or attorney. When she eventually tracked him down overseas, his response was, "I owe you nothing. You had it pretty nice, thanks to me, for many years. You lived in a gated community. You should be thanking me."

The story of Kim is equally sad in a different way. She approached me at an event where I spoke and asked if she could talk to me about something personal. She had married a man older by 9 years: a man with big plans who'd pursued her with such vigor that eventually she and her parents relented, charmed by his "enthusiasm" and "persistence" and his grand vision for their life together.

But once married, she told me, nothing she did satisfied him. First, he insulted her privately, calling her "ignorant, dumb, foolish," but in a short time, he did it publicly, much to her embarrassment. He blamed her for his failures in politics, not realizing, as she and her parents later did, that he was just a lot of hot air, unable and unwilling to accomplish anything he set out to do.

Her friends disappeared, as he disapproved of people who didn't "measure up" and made their visits unpleasant. She told me she hadn't been visited by a friend in more than 10 years and rarely went out so as not to expose others to him or their troubled relationship.

When her kids were growing up, they were forever being chastised by him, and she was reluctant to step in except when "he spanked them really hard." Most of the time, she turned a blind eye to his "pelting with words" because, as she said, the pain of dealing with him wasn't "worth it." She had, as she put it, "nothing left to fight with, nothing left to defend."

Kim had been battered not with fists or a stick but with constant vitriol and humiliation. Pictures of her from 2 decades earlier show her vibrant, beautiful, happy, and radiant. But when I met her, she was in her late forties and had wilted emotionally and physically, her face reflecting the life she'd lived since turning 22. She looked defeated. Both Kim and Miriam, in their own ways, said the same thing to me: "If only I'd known what to look for."

As a parent, the narcissistic personality doesn't have the emotional bandwidth to be truly giving to children. Just as narcissists idealize themselves, so they may expect perfection from their children, pushing children to be the best, even at things the children don't like or aren't good at (but may try hard, attempting to win the parent's approval), and constantly raising the bar ("Why didn't you get an A?" "Too bad you didn't make varsity." "I know you can do better than that."). Picture the stage mother, the raging father at the kids' soccer game, the parent who sees the child's failure to get into his alma mater or join her sorority as a reflection on him or her.

Or these parents may use children as pawns to bring fame or fortune to themselves; for example, by pushing their children to win beauty contests or sports tournaments, make television appearances, or perform some other public or profitable endeavor. They'll swear that they're doing it for the child's benefit, never able to admit their narcissistic delight in fame by proxy. For narcissistic personalities, the light must in the end shine on them, even if it has to go through their children—but it must never fade.

A woman at one of my behavioral seminars talked about being so wounded by being relentlessly pushed as a competitive athlete by her narcissistic mother that in adulthood she cut off all communication with her. Her sense of "I am being used" left an emotional gulf between them.

If children fail to be perfectly athletic, studious, beautiful, or obedient, the narcissistic parent will begin to distance himself. Eventually, the child may be seen as more of a burden than a source of pleasure.

Some narcissistic parents view children as convenient labor. Carlina is one such mother. In her fifties, she started adopting children from what she herself called the "lower classes" and groomed them to work around the house. She'd say to them, even in the presence of outsiders, how they needed to take care of her in her old age because she had "rescued them" and it was their "debt." Sad, really, how easily some devalue others, especially the narcissistic personality. Eventually, according to the clinician who worked on this case for the state, these adopted kids were able to emancipate themselves from this very selfish woman. But they suffered. As one of them said to her court-appointed counselor, "Even in the orphanage life was better—I wasn't loved there, but at least I wasn't made to feel like a slave."

And you thought "Cinderella" was just a fairy tale.

It can be worse. There are untold cases of children going without food or medical assistance because their narcissistic parents just couldn't be bothered or didn't feel obligated. They may be tied to beds, locked in rooms, put up for adoption, or even killed.

It's heartbreaking to see how children desperately continue to seek the narcissistic parent's attention even as it's rationed out a few minutes here, a few hours there, not understanding that this parent can't love them as they long to be loved. As they grow older, they realize just how little they've been given, at what price, and with what strings attached. Any problems they have will be met with indifference or some version of "Get over it," "It's not so bad," or "Don't be a crybaby—that's nothing compared to what happened to me."

Amanda still carries the emotional scars of growing up with a narcissistic mother. She wrote to me seeking advice, having read some of my books. If you ask her, she'll immediately tell you she "never felt loved" as a child. Ever. How terrible that must be. It seemed to her that she could never please or do anything right. Her mother was always questioning, challenging, ordering; never asking, inquiring, or showing much interest in her needs, wants, or desires. She wonders aloud why she feels so empty. It all goes back to how she was treated—as if she were nothing.

Amanda reminded me that these childhood wounds then reopen repeatedly: What's the right Mother's Day gift for someone who criticizes everything? What do you write on the birthday card for a father who had no interest in you? If you move away, how often will you visit that person who didn't respect you or didn't show you love? Will you take on eldercare duties? What will you say and do at this parent's funeral? Will you even go?

Sometimes, parents who know no boundaries raise a child who also has none, overindulging their child as they do themselves. Thus the child internalizes the parent's narcissism, and narcissism moves from generation to generation. Yes, children can be taught indifference by their parents. They grow up having little sympathy or respect for others. You can socialize a child into being nasty, denigrating others while feeling entitled. It's no surprise, then, when these individuals become bullies, either in their youth or as adults. We shouldn't expect flowers when we have planted and watered weeds.

ENCOUNTERS WITH THE NARCISSISTIC PERSONALITY

Whether they're backstabbing you out of a promotion, belittling you in a meeting, or butting in line at the checkout, these personalities don't care if they inconvenience, intimidate, or infuriate you in their quest to take care of Number One—themselves.

Every time I hear of a boss, manager, coach, teacher, or co-worker who snaps, barks, yells, screams, throws things, or bullies, I know we're dealing with a narcissistic personality. There's no excuse for any of those behaviors, and shame on an organization that keeps such a person around. Adults who act like children do serious damage in the grown-up world, and the greater their authority, the wider and more devastating their wake.

Since narcissistic personalities have outsize egos, they also have an outsize sense of what belongs to them. In one FBI case I personally investigated, a government contractor who was working with highly sensitive and classified material contacted us for help after the computer systems administrator had taken over the company's computer. A review of his communications over the years with his superiors revealed him repeatedly bragging about how important he was and how "I did" this or "I did" that. He would often speak of or even insist that these were "my systems," "my network," "my codes," "my protocols." They weren't his, of course; he was an employee, but his narcissism was evident in his writings. In the end, outside experts had to come in after hours and reclaim the system. And that is the problem with narcissistic employees. It may be your company, your assets, or your job on the line, but they don't see it that way. They think it belongs to them and take risks at your expense. In the end, we pay the price for the narcissistic personality's excesses—often at great physical, psychological, or financial cost.

Narcissism isn't just about possessiveness; it can also escalate to violence that all too often goes unreported. A good example is the boss who throws things at you, grabs an arm, or (as in one case reported to me at a conference) blocks the doorway with his body and pushes a worker back into his office. What is unsettling is that the worker never reported this to his own organization. This wasn't the first time this had happened, nor the last—he had done it to others, but, as this employee related, "we had become accustomed to this bully."

Unfortunately, people often dismiss or ignore these and other outrageous behaviors, saying they "aren't so bad" or "won't happen again," or that it's easier to just tolerate the errant bully, especially if he's the boss.

So they let themselves be bullied and steamrolled, problems get swept under the rug, good ideas aren't brought up because no one wants to risk being belittled, and valued workers get fed up and quit. Sometimes, the narcissists' dysfunction becomes so entrenched that others cover for them, or they start to think that these out-of-bounds behaviors make sense, or excuse them because the person is "brilliant" or "okay most of the time." No, sorry, not okay, because you pay a heavy price for that kind of obnoxious nonsense.

These incidents need to be reported where possible. Certainly HR needs to be made aware immediately. If for whatever reason you can't or don't do so, then record it immediately on a calendar, in an e-mail to others or even to yourself, on a cell phone, anywhere—just make a record of exactly what happened, what was said, when, and where. Why? Because these individuals don't change. And if things get worse and the matter comes up for review or there's a civil action, whoever has the most accurate record of events wins. Narcissists aren't going to jot down, "I physically pushed so and so today" or "I called so and so a _____ today." They don't see anything wrong with what they did. But you need to write it down and share it with others. For more strategies on dealing with the narcissistic personality, see Chapter 6, Self-Defense against Dangerous Personalities.

At the end of a seminar I gave in Virginia on dangerous personalities, a high-level executive approached me and asked if I would mind calling his boss, who could not attend the conference. They had a "problem employee" who met the criteria of a dangerous personality, and he felt I should talk to the CEO. I was shocked by the phone conversation I had with this CEO on my way to the airport. This employee's behavior had gotten so out of hand that it threatened the company's solvency. This executive told me one gut-wrenching story after another of total abuse of trust on the part of this individual who had compromised the personal information of clients, credit card information of clients as well as fellow employees, vital strategic data about the company's plans, and more. As if that weren't enough, the employee was basically "gray-mailing" (i.e., stopping just short of black-mailing) the CEO and other executives by threatening to use that information if he didn't get his way.

The CEO had tried everything to placate this individual and work within HR department protocols, but they were getting nowhere. In fact, their efforts to reach out were actually empowering the narcissist. The CEO had been sickened to the point where he was seeing his family doctor and a psychologist to deal with the anxiety this employee was causing him. The narcissistic employee, of course, was just fine.

The CEO said this had been going on for about 18 months. I asked, "He is your employee, he makes everyone upset, he is unsettling you and making you sick, and he's being cavalier with private and proprietary information from the company, is that right?"

"Yes," the CEO replied.

"Then why is he being kept around?" I asked.

"Because I actually thought things would get better." That is a common answer from those who don't understand the narcissistic personality. They innocently, but ignorantly, think that things will get better. They won't.

Executives have told me that they've walked away from business deals because the other party was so toxic, so narcissistic, that they and their staff couldn't stand to be in the same room or even on the phone with them. Each time, they thought it would get better; it didn't. In fact, I've heard stories where it got so bad that some became physically sick from dealing with these individuals. As the owner of a shipping company said to me after one such event, "Joe, no deal is worth my best people getting sick over and me worrying the whole time whether I can trust this person. I walked away, and I'm happy I did."

Narcissists can reach high levels in high-powered or high-trust professions, where transgressions and abuses of authority can have devastating consequences. When you have a police officer who lies, cheats, and steals; a health professional who believes himself the arbiter of who lives or dies; a coach who sexually abuses trusting children, the potential to do damage increases exponentially.

Look at Rita Crundwell, comptroller and treasurer of Dixon, Illinois, who in 2012 pled guilty to embezzling $53 million over a 22-year period. This is an incredible amount of money, which she allegedly used, in part, to finance her interest in quarter horses.[11] Her position of trust as comptroller of the city gave her expansive access to city funds that she used as a personal checkbook.

We hear of corruption by government officials all the time, but the narcissistic personality can be found lurking anywhere. Anyone joining a religious sect that has a narcissistic personality as a leader can be assured of living a life that overvalues the leader at the followers' expense. As for cults, I've never studied one that didn't have a pathologically narcissistic individual as its leader. Jim Jones (Jonestown, Guyana), David Koresh (Branch Davidians), Charles Manson, Shoko Asahara (Aum Shinrikyo), Joseph Di Mambro (Order of the Solar Temple, also known as Ordre du Temple Solaire), Marshall Herff Applewhite Jr. (Heaven's Gate), Bhagwan Shree Rajneesh (Rajneesh movement), and Warren Steed Jeffs (polygamist leader and convicted child abuser) were or are all notoriously narcissistic, intolerant of criticism, preaching grandiose ideas, highly entitled, setting themselves above others and the law. These individuals will sell you dreams that come at a high price, and you will pay.

In November 1998, 1 year after the Heaven's Gate mass suicide in California and on the 20th anniversary of the Jonestown massacre in Guyana, a small group of FBI profilers gathered at the FBI Academy in Quantico, Virginia, to look at the events surrounding Jim Jones and his cult, the Peoples Temple. It was a sobering day for me because even though I had read about the event over the years, seeing the actual crime scene photographs of the bloated bodies of children and babies gave me a new perspective on the massacre, the Reverend Jim Jones, and his narcissistic personality. For those who are interested, you can go online to the FBI's virtual vault and retrieve the actual investigation of the massacre, which is code-named RYMUR (Murder of Congressman Leo Ryan) FBIHQ file number 89-4286, and examine some of the same documents that I viewed (http://vault.fbi.gov/jonestown/jonestown/).

If you read the thousands of pages from this online FBI report or from one of the many books written about Jim Jones and the Peoples Temple, some lessons prominently stand out:

❶ A striking number of people can be made to unconditionally put their lives in the hands of one individual.

❷ Under the cloak of religion, a dangerous personality can get away with a great deal for a long time with no outside scrutiny.

❸ Sect leaders can exert total control over the lives of their followers, ruling as if in a totalitarian regime.

❹ Repeated psychological and physical abuse may be used to hamper the efforts of those who want to leave the sect.

❺ Family and friends who fear for sect members will be persistently thwarted or frustrated in their efforts to help or rescue them.

❻ The narcissistic personality of a cult leader is palpable—as was evident in Jones's words and writings, which should have been warnings to prospective members.

❼ Only a handful of sect members may see the sect leader for what he is. Only a few saw Jim Jones as a toxic and dangerous narcissistic personality.

❽ Once vested and committed to the cult leader, followers are reluctant or unwilling to see the looming peril or to resist the urgings of the narcissistic personality, even when the lives of their children are also in peril.

For the profilers looking at the Jonestown massacre, our findings were sobering particularly because we had seen ample evidence of what we can expect from the narcissistic personality in past cult leaders (e.g., Charles Manson, David Koresh, Marshall Herff Applewhite Jr.) and the danger they present to the nonskeptical believer. Our limited analysis revealed the following:

❶ Cult leaders will continue to attract people who are unwilling or unable to discern when they are being manipulated or exploited.

❷ Cults that make leaving difficult (via psychological, social, or physical pressure) achieve compliance at a great psychological cost—even years later.

❸ Isolation of the sect is key to the narcissistic personality to avoid criticism, ridicule, or scrutiny and to control the sect.

❹ The narcissistic personality thrives in a leadership position within a cult and will do almost anything to remain the leader, including marginalizing or destroying those who oppose them.

❺ The narcissistic personality as leader of a sect acts with impunity in almost all cases, allowing the leader greater privileges (e.g., travel, clothes, luxury items, sex) than sect members.

❻ The narcissistic personality as sect leader purports to have all the answers and secrets to a better life and makes all the decisions.

❼ Because of constitutional protections around religion and voluntary associations, there is little that law enforcement can do to intervene in sects unless there is a clear violation of state or federal law. In most cases, because of secrecy, it is difficult to intervene, as we saw with the case of Warren Jeffs of the Fundamentalist Church of Latter-Day Saints in southern Utah in 2006 (sex with underage girls). Or, tragically, police come on the scene too late, as happened in Jonestown.

Those were our observations about cults, but if you think about it, many of these same characteristics (secrecy and isolation, psychological and/or physical abuse to weaken free will, absolute power concentrated in one person's hands) can be found in toxic work environments or organizations, in homes ruled by tyrants, or even in nation-states.

History bears witness to the fact that pathological narcissism is at the root of terrible suffering. Adolf Hitler, Joseph Stalin, and Pol Pot stand out as examples of leaders with narcissistic personalities who exterminated millions, all because of their extreme grandiosity—they believed that only they had the answers. These and more we'll discuss in later chapters.

But to give you a glimpse of how the narcissistic mind works, here's just one example that might be laughable if it weren't so lamentable. Joseph Stalin's unequaled capacity for cruelty was nearly equaled by his narcissistic craving for recognition, as reflected in the many official and honorary titles he subscribed to, including: Generalisimus of the Soviet

Union, Supreme Commander in Chief, Chairman of the State Committee for Defense, General Secretary of the Central Committee of the Bolshevik Communist Party, General Secretary of the Central Committee of the Communist Party, Chairman of the Council of People's Commissars of the USSR, the Coryphaeus (literally "the leader of the chorus") of Science, Father of Nations, and Brilliant Genius of Humanity. All these to mask his humble beginnings as Iosif Vissarionovich Dzhugashvili, a plebeian Georgian name that he later changed to Joseph Stalin to reflect his view of himself, literally, as the "Man of Steel" (Stalin means "steel" in Russian).[12] Such are the ways of narcissists, even when they are of humble origin.

YOUR DANGEROUS PERSONALITIES CHECKLIST

Warning Signs of the Narcissistic Personality

As I noted in the introduction, I developed various behavior-based check-lists during my career to help me assess individuals to see if they were dangerous personalities. This particular checklist will help you determine if someone has the features of the narcissistic personality and where that person falls on a continuum or spectrum (from arrogant and obnoxious to indifferent and callous to abusive and dangerous). This will help you decide more precisely how to deal with this person, determine his or her toxicity, and assess whether he or she may be a threat to you or others.

This checklist, as well as the others in this book, was designed to be used in everyday life by you and me—people who are not trained mental health professionals or researchers. It is not a clinical diagnostic tool. Its purpose is to educate, inform, or validate what you have witnessed or experienced.

Read each statement in the checklist carefully and check the statements that apply. Be honest; think about what you have heard an individual say or seen him or her do, or what others have expressed to you. Obviously, the best evidence is what you yourself have observed and how you feel when you are around or interact with this person.

Check only the statements that apply. Don't guess or include more than meet the criteria exactly. *If in doubt, leave it out.* Some items seem repetitive or appear to overlap—that is intentional, to capture nuances of behavior based on how people typically experience or describe these personalities.

It is very important that you complete the entire checklist, as designed, to increase its reliability. Each complete checklist covers very subtle yet significant issues that you may never have thought about. Some items may help you remember events you'd forgotten. Please read each statement, even if you feel you've seen enough or that the first few items don't seem to apply.

Gender pronouns (he, she, etc.) are used interchangeably in the statements. Any statement may be applicable to any gender.

We'll evaluate scores when you're done, but for now, check off each item below that applies.

- ☐ 1. Projects self-importance beyond position, experience, or what has been duly earned or deserves.
- ☐ 2. Has a grandiose idea of who he is and what he can achieve.
- ☐ 3. Often talks about his need to lead, to be in charge, to exercise power, or for achieving immediate success.
- ☐ 4. Believes she should only associate with other "special," "successful," or "high-status" people.
- ☐ 5. Requires excessive admiration from others.
- ☐ 6. Has a sense of entitlement, expecting to be treated as someone special or given priority at all times.
- ☐ 7. Is interpersonally exploitative of others and takes advantage of others for personal gain.

☐   8. Lacks empathy and is unable to recognize the needs or suffering of others.

☐   9. Is often envious of others or believes others are envious of him.

☐   10. Is arrogant and haughty in behavior or attitude.

☐   11. Has a tendency to see her problems as unique or more acute than anyone else's.

☐   12. Has an exaggerated sense of privilege that allows him to bend rules and break laws.

☐   13. Is excessively self-centered to the point of alienating others by being so "I" or "me" oriented.

☐   14. Is hypersensitive to how she is seen or perceived by others.

☐   15. Has regularly irritated or upset you, and others complain of the same.

☐   16. Routinely spends an inordinate amount of time on grooming, looking good, and being pampered.

☐   17. Tends to overvalue himself and his capabilities in almost all things.

☐   18. Has devalued others as being inferior, incapable, or not worthy.

☐   19. Has demonstrated little sympathy or empathy for others; nevertheless, she expects others to show her empathy.

☐   20. Has ignored the needs of others, including biological (food, water, etc.), physical (housing, clothing, etc.), emotional (love, touching, hugging, etc.), and financial needs, on multiple occasions.

☐   21. Is not happy when others succeed or receive recognition.

☐   22. Is considered to be or acts like a bully.

☐   23. Talks at you rather than with you.

☐   24. Needs to be the center of attention and does things to distract others to ensure being noticed (e.g., arriving late, wearing eye-catching clothing, using dramatic language, or making theatrical entrances).

☐ 25. When she communicates with you, it feels as if she is sending messages but is not receiving messages. Communication is only one-way.

☐ 26. Assumes others value him as much as he does himself and is shocked to learn that they don't.

☐ 27. Insists on having the best of everything (house, car, electronics, jewelry, clothes), even when she can't afford it.

☐ 28. Appears to have difficulty comprehending deep emotions. Seems emotionally detached at times when deeply felt emotions are most needed.

☐ 29. Has a need to control others and demands total loyalty at all times.

☐ 30. Behaves as though people are objects to be used, manipulated, or exploited.

☐ 31. Repeatedly has violated boundaries of rules, privacy, secrecy, or social decorum.

☐ 32. Only sees her own problems and repeatedly ignores the problems or struggles others may have.

☐ 33. Seems to lack altruistic qualities—everything is done for a selfish purpose; rarely does anything for the good of others.

☐ 34. Even without any kind of demonstrated achievement, acts self-important or accomplished.

☐ 35. Has a need to habitually inflate personal accomplishments, deeds, or experiences.

☐ 36. When others speak of accomplishments, he boasts of his own accomplishments or orients the conversation so that his accomplishments are also recognized.

☐ 37. Feels entitled to any one of these: success, fame, fortune, or sex, with no legal, moral, or ethical inhibitions.

☐ 38. At work, habitually competes with peers for attention or praise and devalues them to garner favor with those in authority.

☐ 39. When criticized, seems insecure and tends to lash out.

☐ 40. Has acted imperious at times, not wishing to know what others think, have planned, or are concerned about.

☐ 41. Has acted or believes self to be omnipotent, unwilling to realize her own weaknesses or frailties.

☐ 42. Is superficially charming or interesting.

☐ 43. Has presented himself as something he is not (impostor), such as a doctor, military officer, astronaut, or Navy SEAL, for example.

☐ 44. Is very interesting to be around at first, but after a while saps you of energy or interest.

☐ 45. Has made you feel that her cup must always be filled as yours runs empty.

☐ 46. Has devalued you or your work and made you feel worthless without any consideration for your feelings.

☐ 47. Has shown interest in and curiosity about how others achieved success, but is unwilling to dedicate or sacrifice himself to that effort.

☐ 48. Has grandiose fantasies of achievement (high political office) that are rarely fulfilled legitimately or at all.

☐ 49. Is preoccupied with achieving social acclaim or political office by any means.

☐ 50. Has repeatedly bought expensive or valuable things for herself, but refuses to do the same for family members.

☐ 51. Constantly underestimates others' ability and capacity to perform.

☐ 52. Sees himself as superior in intellect, capacity, or looks compared to others.

☐ 53. Enjoys putting others down so that she feels better about herself.

☐ 54. Has publicly belittled those who don't measure up to expectations, including his own children.

☐ 55. Is disinterested in knowing more about you and lacks normal curiosity in others.

☐ 56. At times, displays a certain coldness or aloofness that makes you worry about who she really is and/or whether or not you really know her.

☐ 57. When interacting with others, perceives benign actions such as seat adjusting, turning, checking of phone, or looking at watch as disinterest and becomes unnecessarily offended or irritated.

☐ 58. Treats those who are deemed to be below him with contempt and arrogance.

☐ 59. Only appreciates those who can do something for her.

☐ 60. Has interpersonal relationships that seem always impaired or in difficulty due to his ego and grandiosity.

☐ 61. Sees herself as having special knowledge or unique understanding and talks about herself that way.

☐ 62. Has a personality that wears on you, or you find him annoying.

☐ 63. Is inappropriately boastful of accomplishments.

☐ 64. The word "I" dominates conversations. She is oblivious to how often she references herself.

☐ 65. Comes across as self-righteous and above scrutiny.

☐ 66. Has achieved much success but at the price of others whom she rarely, if ever, properly credits.

☐ 67. Has commented that this person or that group is "inferior" or is "worthless."

☐ 68. Favors the use of cocaine (specifically) to potentiate his grandiosity, abilities, or self-worth.

☐ 69. Claims to be an exceptional lover or seducer. Boasts about repeated conquests.

☐ 70. Hates to be embarrassed or to fail publicly.

☐ 71. Doesn't ever seem to feel guilty for anything she has done wrong and never apologizes.

☐ 72. Believes he has the answer and solution to most problems, no matter how complex.

☐ 73. Believes herself to always be right and everyone else is wrong.

☐ 74. Sees those who disagree with him as "enemies."

☐ 75. Has resorted to cheating, conning, scheming, embezzling, or other white-collar crimes to achieve success.

☐ 76. Is often rigid, unbending, and insensitive.

☐ 77. Tries to control what others do or think.

☐ 78. Tends to be possessive of loved ones or family members and interferes with their freedom; doesn't like it when friends or outsiders visit.

☐ 79. Offers short-term, superficial, or self-serving demonstrations of empathy.

☐ 80. One senses he wants to destroy or spoil the fortunes of those he envies or is in competition with.

☐ 81. Has refused to look at or recognize a proud accomplishment of yours or fails to acknowledge pain and suffering of others.

☐ 82. Often reacts to criticism with retaliation, vilification, counterattack, rage, or callousness.

☐ 83. Can't be bothered to work, claiming it would interfere with "thinking," "planning," "networking," "studying," or "preparing."

☐ 84. Joined a club or purchased a golf membership or organization, just to be seen in the right places with the "right kind of people," but can ill afford to do so.

☐ 85. Sees flaws in others routinely, but none in herself.

☐ 86. Does not like to be critiqued, even when it is helpful.

☐ 87. Sees personal problems in others as signs of inferiority, weakness, or poor impulse control.

☐ 88. Consistently brags or boasts about expensive purchases (jewelry, toys, properties, cars, etc.).

☐ 89. At work, repeatedly overstates to management his value and contributions.

☐ 90. Very easily sees weaknesses in others and is quick to exploit those weaknesses.

☐ 91. Is in a parasitic or exploitative relationship, taking advantage of someone financially (refuses to work or contribute although healthy and capable).

☐ 92. Has at least once said that from an early age, felt "destined for greatness."

☐ 93. Seems to be highly dependent on tribute and adoration and will often fish for compliments.

☐ 94. Is not a very good listener or only listens when there is a compliment in it for her.

☐ 95. Demands that others make changes to suit his needs at their expense or inconvenience.

☐ 96. Is cunning and manipulative, seeking always to have the greatest advantage.

☐ 97. Doesn't seem to reciprocate in kind with attention, gratitude, or kindness to others.

☐ 98. Uses insults to establish superiority, dominance, or control.

☐ 99. Has made bogus claims about education or degrees (for example, claiming to have a PhD).

☐ 100. Maintains appearance of extravagant lifestyle despite being financially frail or having filed for bankruptcy.

☐ 101. Repeatedly fails to see or view things from others' perspective; lacks empathetic understanding of others and their needs or desires.

☐ 102. Likes to be around notable people to bask in their glory or likes to name-drop.

☐ 103. Thinks that not everyone is worthy to be around her.

☐ 104. Has a shallow emotional life and detests when others come to him with their "trivial" emotional problems.

☐ 105. Can be shy and solitary, but nevertheless is arrogant toward others and believes in her own superiority or uniqueness.

☐ 106. Has lied about the past, about accomplishments, or to conceal legal or ethical transgressions, including failure to act or notify.

☐ 107. Becomes indignant when others fail to show absolute loyalty.

☐ 108. Has intentionally kept you or others waiting or has extended meetings or conversations, inconveniencing others.

☐ 109. Is never appreciative or satisfied with compensation or perks at work, even though they are generous.

☐ 110. Doesn't hesitate to burden others with the trivial, even when others are occupied or attending to more important things.

☐ 111. Frantically tries to maintain a youthful body and appearance by overdoing workouts, physical exploits, cosmetics, or surgery.

☐ 112. Seems to be proving himself and affirming sexuality by having repeated extramarital affairs.

☐ 113. Most of her enjoyment seems to be from the tributes received from others.

☐ 114. Has taken pleasure in duping others, including parents, friends, and associates.

☐ 115. Rather than feeling happy for others' success, is jealous or petty and begrudges their success.

☐ 116. Has quit a relationship or a friendship once it no longer benefited him socially or financially.

☐ 117. Has actively looked for a trophy wife or partner to help with career or political ambitions.

☐ 118. Tactically plans day or events so as to garner attention and praise.

☐ 119. Is unable to identify the needs, wants, desires, and feelings of those closest to her.

☐ 120. Is impatient with others.

☐ 121. Incessantly talks about himself or his aspirations.

☐ 122. Tends to discuss personal issues or concerns in inappropriate or expansive detail, oblivious to time constraints or the sensitivities of others.

☐ 123. Often says things that are hurtful to others, yet shows no remorse.

☐ 124. One of these words usually applies to her: snobbish, disdainful, arrogant, patronizing.

☐ 125. Has criticized those who follow rules or who patiently wait in line.

☐ 126. Appears to be especially lacking in sadness and mournful longing.

☐ 127. Is only concerned with getting caught or being shamed in public, not with being ethical.

☐ 128. Even after many years, you feel like you really don't know this person.

☐ 129. Has used family or friends to lie on his behalf.

☐ 130. Is unwilling to acknowledge mistakes, wrongdoings, bad ideas, or perilous actions.

SCORING

☑ Count how many statements apply to this individual based on the criteria discussed at the beginning of this checklist.

☑ If you find that this individual has 15 to 25 of these features, this is a person who will occasionally take an emotional toll on others and may be difficult to live or work with.

☑ If the score is 26 to 65, this indicates that the individual has all the features of and behaves as a narcissistic personality. This person needs help and will cause turmoil in the life of anyone close to him or her.

☑ If the score is above 65, this person has a preponderance of the major features of a narcissistic personality and is an emotional, psychological, financial, or physical danger to you or others.

IMMEDIATE ACTIONS

Perhaps the checklist has confirmed for you that what you have long suspected is correct: You may be in a relationship or work with someone who meets the criteria of a narcissist. Perhaps you've been tormented and victimized, and completing the checklist now gives you validation and impetus to better deal with this individual, seek help, or change your situation. Congratulations—you have taken a giant step by educating yourself so that you can more effectively deal with these individuals.

What you do now will be based on many things, among them your situation and how this individual scored on the checklist. You may be able to ignore this individual at work. Or you may not have a choice: You may have to live with this person, and while this individual may be irritating, he or she may score low enough on the checklist to perhaps be tolerable. But maybe the person scored very high and presents you with the possibility of enduring torment, degradation, or even psychological damage. Only you can decide that, but now you have something concrete to work with as you come to terms with what's happening, whether you do that with friends, clergy, HR, your boss, a mental health professional, social services, or even the police.

But no matter what, your first responsibility is to yourself and your loved ones. Don't let anyone ever tell you that you have to stay in a relationship or in an organization where you will be bullied, tormented, or victimized. Do what you have to do to protect yourself.

Try to distance yourself from these individuals as much as possible. I know that sometimes this isn't easy to do for a variety of valid reasons, and I have heard them all. In those cases, try to set boundaries for what is permissible or acceptable, but don't be surprised when these boundaries are ignored and the offensive behaviors are repeated.

Here is the hard truth. You may need this individual, you may not be able to distance yourself from this individual, and this person may be a family member or a spouse, perhaps even your employer. I understand. But know this: The narcissistic personality will grind you down, and in the end, you will suffer emotionally, physically, psychologically, or financially. The higher a person scores on the checklist, the worse it will be. Distance, I have found, is often the best recourse with these individuals. That's the hard truth—and now you know it, too. For additional strategies in dealing with the narcissistic personality, see Chapter 6, Self-Defense against Dangerous Personalities.

"FASTEN YOUR SEAT BELTS . . ."

THE EMOTIONALLY UNSTABLE PERSONALITY

RESEARCHING EMOTIONALLY UNSTABLE PERSONALITIES AND talking to people whose lives they've turned upside down should concern all of us. While society and professionals more readily recognize the damage done by other dangerous personalities such as the predator (see Chapter 4), the havoc wrought by the emotionally unstable personality is rarely appropriately recognized. The damage this personality does tends to be more interpersonal, the kind the criminal system tends to overlook, yet often we live or work with people like this, and they can cause great harm.

This personality's key traits are pervasive emotional instability marked by behaviors that affect their well-being, relationships, and interactions with others. Changeable as the weather and far less predictable, they careen from one end of the emotional spectrum to the other, feeling on top of the world or like a princess one minute and a victim in the gutter the next.

They can be talented, charming, stimulating, and seductive, but they can also quickly turn hostile, impulsive, or even irrational. It is for this personality that the word *mercurial* was invented.

They have an overwhelming need to be loved and to feel secure but little ability to nourish or nurture healthy relationships. Get too close and they feel suffocated; give them space and they feel abandoned. Tragically, their inchoate quest for stability can lead to harm for themselves and others.

When I hear of yet another celebrity who's getting divorced for the fifth, sixth, seventh, or (in the case of Elizabeth Taylor) the eighth time, I have to wonder: Is this person emotionally unstable? Did the spouse have a clue? Did Richard Burton, who returned to Elizabeth Taylor a second time, think things would get better? They didn't—and they usually don't.[1]

People can be drawn to the intelligence, energy, seductiveness, or beauty of these personalities, viewing these characteristics as positive attributes for a successful relationship. But when they look below the veneer, beneath the managed public persona, they'll find the true emotionally unstable self. At home, at the office, or on the movie set, these bright but highly intense people disrupt, interfere, or become difficult to the point where nothing gets done or there is irreconcilable acrimony. Every biography you read about Marilyn Monroe attests to her emotionally unstable personality that adversely affected her and almost everyone she worked with.[2]

Similar to narcissistic personalities, emotionally unstable personalities must be catered to: They push boundaries, break rules, and have a need to be the center of attention. But while narcissists do these things because they feel they're perfect and entitled to special treatment, emotionally unstable personalities do them because they need constant support and affirmation, even from children, to feel good about themselves. Emotionally needy, they cling, tentacle-like, to those who will supply their needs and tolerate their behavior. But that kind of neediness is demanding of even the most giving person, and these individuals tend to be *very* demanding.

If you're involved with someone like this, be prepared for a life of extremes, exasperation, and exhaustion. The degree of turmoil depends on the person you're involved with and where his or her pathology lies on a spectrum, as each person is different. Some are less hostile and more tolerable, while others may be self-destructive or toxic to co-workers or even to their own children. At the very least, they'll be irritating and contentious; at worst, you'll experience profound emotional trauma and maybe even violence. As one psychologist described to me the excruciating stress of dealing with emotionally unstable personalities: "They don't always kill you. But they always seem to have a finger in your eye."

Many factors may contribute to making these personalities the way they are. There may be neurological or even biological reasons for their behavior, or it may be a result of past trauma, drug use, abuse, or parental indifference. No one knows for certain, though all of these must surely contribute, including hereditary factors.

What we do know, what has been reported to me, and what my experience has taught me is that these individuals eventually drain others of patience, understanding, compassion, and comprehension. Through their behavior and their emotional instability, they strain relationships with family, friends, co-workers, and managers to the breaking point.

Eventually, those around them just give up—they have nothing more to give. Some have reported being so emotionally taxed by an emotionally unstable personality that they're no longer capable of empathy or love. As one husband told me after many years of being married to a woman who was emotionally unstable, "I tried everything. I rolled over for her. But living with her was hell. She made me think of committing suicide—and that was the final straw. I was running on empty, thinking of hurting myself. Just because of her." I have heard this countless times over the past 35 years, both as an FBI Special Agent and later as a behavioral consultant.

These same sentiments have been echoed by others, including my late mentor Phil Quinn, PhD. From Dr. Quinn's perspective as both a Catholic priest and a psychologist, he was startled to learn early in his practice how people who had never thought about hurting anyone were driven to think about hurting themselves or wishing harm on someone else because of the other person's emotionally unstable personality.

Shocking? Yes. And a telling indicator of just how painful and damaging life with an emotionally unstable personality can be. After I posted an article on dangerous personalities on my *Psychology Today* blog, one reader wrote to me privately, saying, "I just want my mother to finally die. She stole my youth and all sense of security. I want the one person who has never defended me to at last die so that I can rest. So that I don't have to be on guard anymore." I was shocked to read this in her long, articulate letter—until I saw the things her mother had done and how this daughter had been tormented. Then I understood why she would feel that way.

Early in my law enforcement career, older police officers told me of the sad phenomenon of people being driven to hurt others because of how they were treated, and how it was common in many of the domestic calls they handled. That's the distressing reality when you deal with the more virulent form of the emotionally unstable personality. Their extreme behavior causes extreme reactions: The healthy are driven to unhealthy thoughts or actions. And while these thoughts can be understood, harming oneself or others can never be justified, nor is it excusable. These individuals need help every bit as much as those who are affected by them.

THE WAY OF THE EMOTIONALLY UNSTABLE PERSONALITY

There's such variety in how people with this personality behave that they're often difficult to detect or recognize. Some live in quiet pain and desperation. Others habitually look to argue or fight with everyone, especially with their spouse, whom they torment, sometimes violently. And there's the tempestuous seductress who's sexually alluring but so demanding that her clinginess becomes a turnoff. And much else in between.

Regardless of how the instability manifests, emotional highs and lows are the hallmark. While all of us feel moody, irritable, or anxious at times, these dangerous personalities feel this way far too often. They can have good days, weeks, or even months. But over time, their primary mode of reacting to the world is evidenced by emotional instability and mercurial outbursts.

That wouldn't matter if they lived alone in a cabin in the woods, but the effects are usually felt by someone close by: a parent, sibling, lover, spouse, child, or fellow employee. And there's the rub. The fundamental instability of this personality destabilizes others emotionally, psychologically, and even physically. While teenagers may be moody and experiment with risky behaviors, teenagers transition out of this stage. The emotionally unstable personality is persistently unstable over time, and this undermines relationships.

While many of these individuals are often aware of painful issues from their past that contribute to their erratic behavior, they seem powerless over their emotions and behavior. Even therapists find them difficult to deal with.[3] You try to reach out to them as best you can, but it's never good enough. Interacting with this type of personality has been described as being on an emotional roller coaster: You're their hero one minute and chewing gum on the sole of their shoe the next. Many on the receiving end of this volatility have told me of feeling both incredulity and despair as they wonder, "Where did that come from?" "Was that really necessary?" and "When will it happen again?"

The child of such a parent quickly learns to constantly assess the parent's mood. "How is she today?" becomes everyone's whispered watchword.

It saddens me to see how early these children begin to walk on eggshells because they know that out of that bedroom, on any given morning, can walk a saint or a monster bent on inflicting pain. When we read about children who want to divorce their parents (and many have), or who want early emancipation (before the age of 18), it's often because they've reached their limit for dealing with this kind of emotionally unstable personality. These radical steps are all they have left for their own mental well-being; enough is enough.

At work, we tiptoe around these unstable personalities, much like children: "Is the boss having a good day, or is he yelling or throwing things like yesterday?" People will literally hide in the bathroom or call in sick to avoid dealing with these volatile individuals. Their effect on an organization or a business can be demoralizing, which is why more and more businesses are becoming less tolerant of the emotionally unstable personality who acts out at work.[4] Some organizations have gone so far as to enact what has come to be known as Sutton's rule—establishing an "asshole-free" environment or zone at work. As Robert Sutton points out in his *New York Times* and *Wall Street Journal* bestseller *The No Asshole Rule: Building a Civilized Workplace and Surviving One That Isn't*, these individuals do more harm than good—it's better to just get rid of them than hurt your organization.

To emotionally unstable personalities, dating relationships are all about intensity. Things may escalate to raging arguments followed, at their insistence, by rabid "makeup sex." It's stunning how fast they can go from vicious arguing to hot sex. For the emotionally unstable personality, this isn't a problem. But for the rest of us, as many people have reported to me, the roller-coaster ride soon palls, and the more acrimony they experience, the less intimacy they want and the less contact they want; thus the die is cast for a failed relationship.

Hypersensitive

These personalities often don't take criticism well, are very sensitive to real or perceived slights, and can turn on you when they feel insulted. They're quick to feel victimized, so they immediately demonize others or accuse them of disloyalty based on unfounded suspicions. In one case reported to me by one of my university students, a mother ostracized her three grown daughters for months because they went to the movies without her. She accused them of "conspiring" to isolate her and of using the opportunity to "bad-mouth" her behind her back about how she reared them. These are typical roles these personalities play, reflecting the highs and lows of their emotional state—they're the queen or king (wanting to be worshipped by all) or the victim or outcast ("No one wants to play with me/everyone's against me").

These three sisters bent over backward to reach out to their mother to reassure her that they meant no harm by going to the movies without her, all to no avail. She sulked, acted injured for weeks, and wouldn't talk to them. This was par for the course: Mother's hypersensitivity to slights had been going on ever since her daughters could remember. And that's the problem. Hypersensitivity is this personality's default setting, and it's tiresome, manipulative, and emotionally draining.

But that's not the worst of it. Unstable personalities are perennial "wound collectors."[5] They stockpile and are constantly on the alert for social slights, mistreatment, incidences of inadvertent forgetfulness, or faux pas in order to later unleash reminders of them, like arrows, to hurt others. They're notorious for repeatedly bringing up examples from the distant past, sometimes decades old, of things that you've done, forgotten, or said that, justifiably or not, hurt them in some way. And because they're so fragile, their list of grievances can be quite long and petty, as they tend never to forgive human frailty in others. They are in some ways, as the renowned criminologist Dr. Leonard Territo put it so well, "victims in search of an oppressor."

Needy and Demanding, without Boundaries

To say they're "high maintenance" is an understatement. Unstable personalities have a childlike need to feel special. They crave the spotlight, whether it's having all eyes on them (think how actresses behave on the red carpet) or having your undivided attention when they're your client, patient, boss, friend, or lover. They'll even create divisiveness between others so they can sneak in and co-opt your attention. They divide to conquer with the skill of a surgeon.

They have such a need for others that they will fawn over or idolize you in an infantile sort of way as the "most wonderful lover," the "best doctor," the "most talented" professional, or "the most perfect friend ever." But should you fail them in some way, become disinterested or distracted, or if they tire of you, they'll turn on you and you'll instantly be demonized. It's remarkable how quickly they can shift to cold indifference, ignoring everything positive that has happened in the past and focusing only on their needs, your singular failure, or a perceived slight, no matter how trivial.

Often, they alienate the very people they seek by pushing the rules or boundaries, becoming too inquisitive, too demanding, too personal, too clingy, or too needy. At home or in business, if you give in to them, they'll walk all over you, always wanting more of your time, special treatment, attention, or rule bending. Refuse to accommodate and you're accused of being uncaring, bad, or disloyal. In a way, their reaction is similar to how young children react when they suddenly rant, "I don't love you anymore!" when they don't get their way.

For these personalities, there really are no boundaries or social conventions. Because they fear abandonment, when they feel needy, they need you *now*. Expect calls, e-mails, or text messages with no regard for your schedule, convenience, wishes, or business propriety. God help you if they get your cell phone number or the direct line to your office.

Physicians tell me that these personalities show up without scheduling an appointment, demanding to be treated immediately. When they're told this is not proper protocol, they become indignant and lash out at physician and staff. I was told of a case where one such patient slammed the door so hard that pictures fell off the wall in front of shocked patients. From adoration to fuming hatred in one instant—standard operating procedure for the emotionally unstable personality.

Some have been known to follow, surveil, read correspondence, eavesdrop on calls, and drop by unexpectedly to test loyalty and fidelity not only of lovers and spouses but also even of their own children. They've been known to travel great distances to follow a lover who has moved out, or they follow their beloved to and from work with eerie and persistent diligence. In essence, they become stalkers, but they can also become saboteurs.

Emotionally unstable personalities have been known to commit acts of vandalism to cars and homes that can run into the thousands of dollars. Sometimes, they barge into offices to confront ex-lovers, or they leave hurtful, acrimonious notes on dashboards or voicemail. Now with social media, they can be even more destructive and libelous. Nothing is off-limits when this personality is roused. Even laws don't matter.

In April 2000, a Gulf Coast Florida police department asked me to help with a peculiar case. A woman I will call Sheila was alleging that she had been raped three times in 5 years, each time by a total stranger, as she was getting into her car. The detective assigned to the case wanted me to profile the whole case, including the victim, as three rapes in 5 years happening to the same woman seemed improbable in a city that had statistically few rapes.

The first question that was asked of me was one I could not answer: "Was she lying?" As I told the detective, lying is very difficult to detect, but there are some things we can ask to assist us in determining the truth.

After reviewing the three cases, I noticed that the allegations always came either in late July or early August. Each time, the emergency room doctors were not able to find any semen for examination. She had been specific in her descriptive details of the perpetrator, and each time an all-points bulletin had been issued, resulting in the stopping of numerous individuals matching the description and the car he was supposed to have been driving. All without success.

When it was my turn to talk to her, there was little more I could ask, so I said, "Let's go to the police garage, where you can demonstrate the details of the encounter using your own vehicle." It was here where things began to fall apart. Her story sounded credible when told, but when asked to demonstrate where she was in relation to the suspect at all times, she seemed puzzled, she contradicted details she had been adamant about, or the story did not make logical sense. For example, she said that at one point the suspect, who had a knife, left her and went all the way around the car and opened the passenger door. All she would have had to do to evade him was press the lock button.

When these inconsistencies and issues were brought to her attention, she began to sob and eventually admitted that it was all a lie—there had been no rapes.

Why would she cause a city to spend tens of thousands of dollars in investigative time or cause numerous individuals to be pulled over, searched, and interviewed as potential suspects? Because she was an emotionally unstable personality—something that was later confirmed by talking to her workmates, friends, and family. At the height of summer, during school break (she was a teacher), she needed attention. Every time she called 911, the police would respond, as would the ever-attentive paramedics. The city's victim advocate would also be sent to her home, and friends and family would rally around her. In the emergency room, she received even more attention, and a detective would be assigned to work with her in case of an arrest or prosecution. A single phone call would bring attention that would last for weeks upon weeks.

It was recommended by a consulting clinician that the city not prosecute her if she would merely quit her job with the city school system and move; after all, she could have been prosecuted for her false allegations. Here again is an example of what happens when you are dealing with the emotionally unstable personality—a personality that is both needy and not married to the truth.

Manipulative

This personality will cry, rage, guilt-trip, feign illness, seduce, switch sides, flip-flop on issues, or engage in risky behaviors to get love, attention, or their own way. "No" to them is negotiable—especially if they know that with childlike persistence, "no" will become "maybe" and eventually "yes."

They may lie and connive for attention (such as telling a boyfriend that they're pregnant when they aren't in an attempt to hold on to a dying relationship, or claiming they had sex with someone else in the perverse hope of garnering greater fidelity). Their ability to deceive and manipulate is breathtaking in scope and capacity.

And when it comes to manipulating others, it can be argued, nothing works as dramatically as the threat of suicide. These personalities can be very dangerous to themselves, especially when they threaten self-harm or make actual attempts to harm themselves. These episodes may be more prevalent during times of distress, when they feel alone, or if they feel they're about to be abandoned.

It's always unsettling when threats of suicide are made, but the best way to handle such a threat is for you to stay calm. Your first reaction should be to tell the unstable person that you will call 911 (or the police, fire department, or ambulance) and then do so without hesitation. Whether the suicide intention is feigned or real, this is a matter for professionals, and this personality's behavior leaves you no choice. This is way beyond the average person's expertise to handle and should be left to professionals.

In my experience, once the police or 911 has been called, these personalities may change their demeanor. Or you may find that as you're about to dial, they back away from the threat. Make no mistake: Threats of suicide or self-harm should always be taken seriously. You are not a therapist, so it's best to leave this situation to a professional to handle, as these unstable individuals can hurt themselves and have done so. By calling for professional help, ethically you have done the right thing, and you also have not allowed yourself to be manipulated. You are not a puppet and do not deserve to be manipulated, no matter how sick or in pain someone may be.

One man I talked to at a conference said his wife threatened suicide or threatened to harm herself if she didn't get her way almost every time they had a "big argument." According to him, she had threatened suicide maybe "two dozen" times or more over the course of their painful marriage. Not once did he think to call emergency services, each time thinking this would be the last time or not wanting to call attention to himself and his family. Surprised? You shouldn't be. People will do what you will tolerate, and if you engage them or are benignly or naïvely permissive, as he was, emotionally unstable personalities will push those buttons to control you. Why? Because they can; because for them it is so easy; because they don't exercise self-restraint and only qualified professionals can help them—but only if they are willing to be helped.

If they can't get what they want and have exhausted manipulation, some will kill what they can't have. Remember, the behavior of these individuals exists on a continuum or spectrum. Some are just nasty to live with, but others can be brutal and, under certain circumstances, murderous if they don't get their way. Just read the newspaper of any major city and look for news stories in which perennial but escalating turmoil in a domestic setting leads predictably to greater instability, greater turmoil, violence, and, all too often, death.

The tragic death in 1998 of comedian Phil Hartman serves as a reminder of the danger of living with an emotionally unstable personality. His wife, Brynn, shot him and then herself. For years, friends had been aware of her emotional instability and the turmoil it was causing in the marriage—something their two surviving children will forever contend with.[6] Sadly, there are many examples like this.

Irrational, All-or-Nothing Thinking

Don't expect emotionally unstable personalities to respond to logic when they're upset or acting out. They tend to react emotionally rather than logically when stressed or critiqued. Their thinking is binary: all or nothing, good or bad, black or white; there are no shades of gray. You're either with them or against them; friend or foe—and, sadly, that includes children.

They will publicly test your loyalty in front of others by asking questions such as, "Are you with me or with her? Whose side are you on?" These obvious manipulative acts are annoying and embarrassing, orchestrated to test your allegiance as if you were back in grade school. Yes, that's how needy they can be.

Their behavior is as unpredictable as their thinking. You can never guess what they'll do. One father told me of packing the family in the car for a 3-day vacation and driving more than 100 miles when his wife, a very emotionally unstable personality, kept escalating a small incident. Sensing that the children were siding with the father, she began to lash out at the kids verbally. What came next shocked even he who was used to these

Words That Describe
THE EMOTIONALLY UNSTABLE PERSONALITY

Here are the uncensored words that victims use to describe the emotionally unstable personality:

Abnormal, alluring, aloof, angry, ass, asshole, atomic, beguiling, bewildering, bitch, bitter, borderline, calamitous, catastrophic, chameleon, chaotic, clingy, cold, complainer, complex, conflict, confusing, conniving, consternation, controlling, coquettish, crazy, creepy, critical, criticizes, cruel, cunning, dangerous, deceptive, dehumanizing, dejected, delusional, demanding, demeaning, denigrating, depressed, depressive, desperate, despondent, destructive, disconnected, disillusioned, disorganized, disquieting, distant, diva, draining, dramatic, dysfunctional, emotional, empty, envious, erratic, exasperating, exciting, exhausting, explosive, fearful, flirt, flirtatious, freaky, frightening, frustrated, frustrating, histrionic, horrendous, horrible, hysterical, imbalanced, impossible, impulsive, inappropriate, incomplete, inconsistent, incredible, instability, intense, intricate, irrational, irresponsible, irritable, irritating, lascivious, lecherous, lethal, liar, lies, lively, *loca*, loco, lustful, malevolent, malignant, masochistic, mean, mercurial, miserable, moody, morbid, nasty, negativistic, neglectful, neurotic, nuts, nutty, nymphomaniac, odd, painful, perplexing, pitiful, prick, problematic, psycho, queen, rage, relentless, resentful, risky, sadistic, salacious, sarcastic, scary, schemer, seductive, seductress, seesaw, seething, sexual, sexy, short-fused, sick, sickening, special, stalker, storm, suffocating, suicidal, tantrums, temperamental, tempestuous, tense, threatening, tiresome, tormented, tormentor, torn, tornado, train wreck, tumultuous, turbulent, unappreciative, unbridled, uncaring, undependable, unforgiving, ungrateful, unhappy, unhinged, unpredictable, unreasonable, unreliable, unstable, untrusting, unyielding, vengeful, victim, vindictive, violent, vixen, volatile, weird, whirlwind, wicked.

outbursts. With anger and rage on her face, she barked, "Turn this fucking car around or I will throw myself out!" As she said this, she opened the car door and leaned out. The kids were screaming and scared, as they were on I-95 heading toward Orlando, driving in excess of 65 miles per hour. Another vacation ruined, kids shaking and in tears, hotel deposits lost—all because he had forgotten to "pack her favorite suntan lotion." There's no excuse for this kind of behavior. That traumatizing event stayed with those kids and with him for years. Humans don't have Erase buttons, and when children witness events like this, they pay a price for living with an emotionally unstable personality.

Some unstable personalities can be gullible and susceptible to fads. Many seek out gurus or cult leaders who can provide a rigid belief system. Cults are attractive to unstable personalities because of the attention they're given by the cult members, the unconditional acceptance they receive, the group bonding that is common, and the structure that's provided that they can't seem to get in normal society. This susceptibility to cults and charlatans, however, makes them vulnerable to exploitation and often leads to arguments with family or loved ones who challenge their adopted lifestyle, seeing that they're wasting their time, money, or opportunities. Think for a minute about the kind of people commune leader, habitual criminal, and convicted killer Charles Manson attracted and you get the picture: emotionally unstable individuals who think Charles Manson is okay.[7] "Gullible and susceptible" does not even begin to cover it.

Impetuous, Impulsive, Sensation Seeking

Whether to feel more alive or to escape feeling bad, these personalities can be reckless and impulsive, deciding on a whim to engage in behavior that puts them or others at risk, saying and doing things that are improper, offensive, or seductive at the most inappropriate times. They may be perceived as "troublemakers," "problematic," "a bastard," "a prick," "a drama queen," or "out of control." Often they crave attention through sexual exploits.

When reality TV personality and *Playboy* model Anna Nicole Smith died, multiple men stepped up to claim paternity of her child, and it appeared they all had been intimate with her. These personalities may find sex a formidable elixir, and so they engage in sexual behavior that can have dangerous consequences. They may have scores upon scores of lovers with all the attendant pathologies, including venereal diseases, jealousies, unwanted pregnancies, and violence; but little warmth or love. The movie *Looking for Mr. Goodbar* was about such a person. Theresa Dunn, played by Diane Keaton, is chronically empty, using sex to garner intimacy, but never feeling fulfilled.

They might hook up with "bad boys" or run with the wrong crowd. That is the emotionally unstable personality at its saddest. For a parent, the emotional drain of witnessing a young adult child's life misspent or on the edge of danger is horrendous. The unstable woman may gravitate to the law-breaking predator: Remember Bonnie Parker, who ran away with Clyde Barrow, who together formed the notorious duo Bonnie and Clyde? By all accounts, she was an emotionally unstable personality, and it showed in her behavior, which led directly to her tragic death.

If alcohol or drug abuse becomes their method of dealing with the stresses of the world, their decision making will be further skewed by chemical dependence, and their health may be compromised in other ways as well.

Some turn to impulsive, pathological, or destructive behaviors that on the surface may not seem so terrible, yet serial shoplifting, running away, gambling, binge eating, reckless driving, and bulimia, to name some, have terrible collateral effects on these individuals, their families, and society.

These personalities can veer into compulsive pleasure- or pain-seeking behaviors—for them, sadly, these might be one and the same. It's not unusual for some to engage in self-abuse such as cutting themselves, pressing lit cigarettes to their skin, picking at scabs, pulling out their hair, even banging their head on the wall to feel something or to blot out a feeling.

They sometimes speak of being bored and of feeling a pervasive emptiness. Marilyn Monroe often spoke to her various therapists and friends of this chronic emptiness that no one could fill, despite having many admirers, lovers, and husbands.[8] Then there are those who habitually seek to aggravate others or want to argue or pick fights. One senses that they actually derive pleasure from antagonizing or fighting with others. Some clinicians have described it as a very pathologically sadistic need to injure, coupled with a masochistic need to partake in a cycle of acrimony and discord so that they feel something. I asked one such personality, "Why do you treat him like that?" Her answer was so revealing: "Because," she said, "that is the only way I get a rise out of him. That is the only time I see him come alive." And she said it with a smile.

THEIR EFFECT ON YOU

It's easy to be engulfed by this personality's compelling blend of hero worship and neediness. But in the end, you'll feel mentally and emotionally drained by these individuals' ups and downs, manipulations, and outbursts. When they feel down, you'll be reassuring them. When their risky behavior gets them in trouble, you'll be rescuing them. When you disappoint them by not providing what they need, you'll be the target of their rage. The closer you are, the more likely you'll be in their crosshairs, as they tend to attack the very people they claim to love.

They can run through money breathtakingly quickly buying clothes, drugs, or sex or by gambling. If they get picked up for driving under the influence, fighting, drug possession, or sexual solicitation, there will be legal fees and bail. They're apt to cajole you for loans till they can "get back on their feet." Or they may steal your money to get high or seek other thrills. If they're wealthy, you'll read about how they went through millions of dollars living it up. If they're not, then you and I will be the ones to bail them out.

People involved with these personalities feel constantly hyperalert, unable to relax and enjoy the good times and dreading the bad spells. They're not living their own life so much as living in fear of these personalities' moods. What will set them off? Will they blow up? Will they hit the child who comes home with a bad grade? Will they steal what isn't theirs? Will they flirt shamelessly with people they shouldn't? Many have told me that from the moment they got involved with an emotionally unstable personality, they had to be on guard or constantly prepared to defend themselves, their actions, and eventually their sense of self-worth.

When you live with someone like this, as relatives often report, you may have physical symptoms of anxiety and chronic stress. After a while, you mirror the unstable person's roller-coaster emotions as your limits are breached repeatedly and all you're doing is just trying to keep up. Resisting the manipulations and maintaining proper boundaries are exhausting. Many report sleep problems, depression, behaving in ways they never behaved before, and arguing as never before.

This personality's rage can escalate from verbal to physical: throwing or destroying things, hitting or slapping others, or harshly punishing children. A woman once reported to me how her mother used to beat her with a spatula almost daily as a child. Then there's the executive who arrived home to find his wife had slashed all of his business suits with a box cutter over an argument the night before. Or how about not just a plate of spaghetti but a whole pot of sauce thrown at the wall? Others report treasured mementos, gifts, or even knives going flying. It's hard to imagine things like this happening, but they do. And then there are the incidents where guns are fired in anger. As any police officer will tell you, "domestic" calls are dangerous precisely because often the people involved are emotionally unstable, and they may become further disturbed by drugs or alcohol.

By now the cruelty of movie star Joan Crawford toward her adopted daughter Christina Crawford is well known. If you haven't read Crawford's book *Mommie Dearest*, I recommend you take a look—but not before bedtime, or you may have a restless night. That is what life with an emotionally unstable personality is like.

This personality's instability can infect entire groups, as no one in the family, on the team, or at work wants to be on the receiving end of the vitriol. Everyone walks on eggshells, afraid to say no or be the bearer of bad news.

Add testosterone to the mix and you have a higher potential for danger and violence. All too frequently, these are the men who beat up their spouses on the weekend or when they walk through the front door. Police officers are familiar with these domestic calls. These are usually repeat scenarios featuring the same cast of characters: unstable personalities who pick fights, punch, tackle, choke, smother, bind, or burn spouses as a matter of routine. It makes them somehow feel good—that is the sadistic side of this personality.

Can associating with this personality be life threatening? Not always, but yes. Remember, they dread abandonment. If they can't have you, they may decide no one else can, either. Just take a look at the case of Jodi Arias, who made headlines during her trial in 2013 for brutally killing her ex-lover Travis Alexander in 2008, making Glenn Close's character Alex Forrest in the 1987 movie *Fatal Attraction* seem harmless.[9] There is no way her victim, Travis Alexander, would have been brutally killed (she stabbed him multiple times, slit his throat, and for good measure shot him in the head) but for his association with this emotionally unstable personality who could not deal with abandonment.[10] This is one case that became notorious because of the television coverage, but yearly in the United States, there are thousands of cases where the emotionally unstable personality violently goes after a lover or former lover—all too often ending in injury or death.

THE EMOTIONALLY UNSTABLE PERSONALITY IN RELATIONSHIPS

Like narcissists, unstable personalities move in fast when dating—but while narcissists do it for dominance, these personalities do it for stability and the emotional high of feeling adored. They want that feeling to go on forever and may push hard for commitment, but even when they get what they want, an emptiness persists that no one and nothing seem to ease.

They can go over the top in their desperate efforts to bond, flirting outrageously or making implausible or outrageous statements. One man I spoke to reported to me how within minutes of meeting an individual who, as it turned out, was an emotionally unstable personality, she just blurted out, out of the blue, "You have no idea how much you mean to me." He elaborated further: "She actually lingered there holding my hand almost too long, leaning in too close, embarrassing me in front of others, telling me how 'special' I was in her eyes and that she would be 'dreaming of me later.'" This was at a business meeting—needless to say, he was aghast.

It's not surprising, given these individuals' neediness, how much such statements sound like those of a smitten seventh grader. What's surprising is how often people fall for it—something this personality knows and exploits. Sadly, what no one realizes is that the object of this outsize affection will in time feel suffocated and struggle desperately to get extricated from this clingy person.

At first, there may be hot sex and idealizing, but with the inevitable fall from the high precipice, things devolve into irritability and endless acrimony. Try to leave, however, and the unstable personality becomes frantic, fighting to keep you even while lashing out and devaluing you. The fact that you're at work won't stop this personality from barging into your office and causing a scene; nor from calling dozens of times per hour; nor from scratching your car door at work; nor from calling your boss to tell her that you are "a slut" or "a pig." Anyone who's lived this will tell you it's surreal: The person screams, yells, and calls you names—but doesn't want you to leave.

Even if you manage to end the relationship, unstable personalities still want you to remain loyal. They may stalk you, read your mail, threaten you, beat you up, enter your home, go through your things, or confront your current date. Nicole Brown Simpson reported some of these experiences to the police for years, but little was done until she was killed.[11] O. J. Simpson, according to Nicole, simply could not let go of her; even after their divorce, he would come over, threaten her, and beat her up. The police photos showing her facial trauma attest to the violent side of this dangerous emotionally unstable personality.[12]

They may harass you through your parents, friends, or social media. If they ever took or somehow obtain pictures of you naked or doing anything that compromises you, these images will be used against you. If you can imagine it (or even if you can't), they will do it. One woman reported to me that new boyfriends would find notes on their car windows from her ex-boyfriend, telling them what a "whore and a slut" she was.

Women involved with such men may think, "He'll get better," or "This will be the last time," or "I can fix him."[13] They can't, and most likely these individuals won't change. A female police officer I know told me it took her 3 years to break up with someone like this who would occasionally beat her up. Even this trained law enforcement professional found herself emotionally trapped, embarrassed to seek help, vested in someone she thought she could fix. She couldn't. It can happen to anyone, and I repeat, it never gets better unless the unstable personality makes heroic efforts to change—and that rarely happens.

If you have children and are dating this kind of personality, you may be putting not just yourself but your children at risk of psychological and possibly physical danger. I am speaking from my law enforcement experience when I say that the very nature of the emotionally unstable personalities puts children, especially those not their own, at greater risk of psychological or physical harm.

Earlier I mentioned a woman whose mother used to beat her with a spatula. After these beatings, her mother would say things like, "See what you made me do? Now come here and hug me." This, unfortunately, isn't the first time I've heard of this kind of pathology. In response to my books and articles, grown children from all over the world have written to tell me how their mothers used a kitchen utensil, a broom, or an old belt on them for the slightest transgressions and then expected the child to comfort their abuser. You don't have to be a clinician to realize how damaging this is.

If children express feeling hurt or upset, the parent may dismiss them: "Oh, stop it, it wasn't that bad" or "Toughen up; you'll get over it." If children ask for hugs or attention, this self-absorbed parent may say, "Not until you stop being this way" or "Can't you see I'm busy?" This response leaves the child with a Grand Canyon–size void that the child never seems to overcome. This is how such a parent's emotional instability reverberates into the next generations.

Children of these personalities grow up psychologically damaged. The life lessons they pick up make me sad just writing about them: Stifle your emotions, ignore your needs, expect to be hurt, never say no, don't make waves, you don't matter, but above all comfort me. They learn to be secretive, to hide their feelings; or they act out to get a reaction; or they learn to lie, experiment with drugs, or mindlessly seek out anyone who will pay them attention. They may become bullies, adopting the preemptive "hurt them before they hurt you" mind-set they absorbed so well from their unstable parent. And they are forever on guard, like sentinels, having been taught from an early age to be both fearful and hypervigilant, never knowing what mood their parent will be in or how the parent will react. This is no way to grow up.

Imagine how it feels to discover that children in other families are loved, while you are merely tolerated or tormented. It comes as no surprise, then, when the adult children of the emotionally unstable personality write to me saying they're torn between wishing their parent was dead and dreading it happening, since then they'd have to decide whether or not to attend the funeral and pretend they care when they don't. As one woman recently told me, "All I wanted was to be loved. How hard is that? You don't know what it is like not to be loved by a mother. It will be a relief when she dies."

If you have children with a parent like this, you have a responsibility to try to provide safety and respite for them. Sadly, in my experience, most parents fail to act because they don't want to deal with the volcanic reaction of the emotionally unstable parent. This is a terrible disservice to an innocent, powerless child. If ending the relationship and gaining custody of the children isn't an option, everything possible should be done to set boundaries to protect the child and provide opportunities for relief (for example, facilitating anything the child loves to do—school activities, hobbies, extracurricular sports, reading, music, art) to keep the youngster away from the toxic parent. But I have to be honest here, perhaps more honest than a therapist may be with you. The long-term prospects are dismal. Protect your child and get away, please, for their sake and yours.

ENCOUNTERS WITH THE EMOTIONALLY
UNSTABLE PERSONALITY

Often these personalities have a veneer that allows them to function in society, but not always. A lot of euphemisms are used to describe them: "My neighbor's very irritable," "My cubicle mate is crazy," "Her highness is having a fit," "He's prone to outbursts," "There's too much drama here." I believe we should never sugarcoat what can hurt us. Through their behavior, these individuals confirm that they're emotionally unstable and toxic. Through their behavior, they cause others to react negatively and create needless interpersonal conflict.

A telltale clue is how people in business will do almost anything to limit their communications and interactions with the emotionally unstable personality. Word soon gets out. People will say things like, "Is he on the team/project/committee/attending the event? Because if he is, I'm out." They'll avoid having to call, talk to, socialize with, work with, or even sit next to this toxic person and will exclude him or her from meetings, events, and the information loop.

In the film *The Devil Wears Prada*, a staffer describes Miranda Priestly, the terrifying editor of a top fashion magazine, played with chilling precision by Meryl Streep: "Miranda Priestly is impossible. Always has been, always will be. Your job is not about pleasing her. It's about surviving her."[14] It's a perfect description of life with an unstable boss, coach, manager, or leader. You work your fingers to the bone, but there's no appreciation. No one wants to break bad news or tell this person something can't be done.

Sometimes, these personalities have the capability to get the job done and things look good to the outside world—for example, to senior management, to a commanding officer, or to voters. But talk to those who work for or with them, and you'll hear stories of people being chewed out, of cruel things being said, of intentional divisiveness sown in the ranks. Maybe they get the job done, but at what cost? The losses in turnover, sick days, illnesses, insurance, and lawsuits are considerable.

If you read the newspapers or biographies, you'll find accounts of many who stand out as having characteristics of the emotionally unstable personality. While it would be easy to make snap judgments about people based on media accounts of their behavior, this is something we should resist doing. First, we don't know the full story of how this person behaves nor any extenuating circumstances of the situation. For example, Amy Winehouse, the singer-songwriter who tragically died of alcohol poisoning in 2011, appeared to have a number of the characteristics of the emotionally unstable personality. Maybe she was, maybe she wasn't; the complete details are not available to most of us. So while we may read or see accounts that give us pause or put us on alert, generally we need more information to fully understand if someone is an emotionally unstable or dangerous personality.

Second, the principal methodology we discuss in this book is based on your direct observations, not on what you may read in the headlines. So while what we glean from news reports may give us pause, we need to be careful in our assessments. Personal turmoil, whether in politics, entertainment, or just next door, certainly gets our attention, but we can never know for sure if this is an emotionally unstable personality until we experience that personality directly.

As with most of the dangerous personalities in this book, the public hardly notices the emotionally unstable personality until or unless the person does something outrageous, grotesque, or criminal. For the most part, emotionally unstable personalities do most of their damage privately, one-on-one behind closed doors. Even if those doors are at 1600 Pennsylvania Avenue, otherwise known as the White House. Most people are not aware that Mary Todd Lincoln, wife of president Abraham Lincoln, brought much turmoil into their relationship, the executive government, and the

White House with her notable emotional instability.[15]

There are, of course, those the media seem to track with frequency because they're in the entertainment industry, but for the most part, we endure the emotionally unstable personality in private. What I most often hear from those involved with an emotionally unstable personality is "I suffered alone."

Nevertheless, when I see, hear about, or meet someone who repeatedly violates social boundaries, someone who has a short fuse or is "temperamental," someone who causes me or others to feel inferior or troubled, or someone who likes to argue and fight, my "safety radar" goes on alert, and I look for other clues that this individual might be an emotionally unstable personality so I can take steps to protect myself and those I love. So should you.

YOUR DANGEROUS PERSONALITIES CHECKLIST

Warning Signs of the Emotionally Unstable Personality

As I noted in the Introduction, I developed various behavior-based checklists during my career to help me assess individuals to see if they were dangerous personalities. This particular checklist will help you determine if someone has the features of the emotionally unstable personality and where that person falls on a continuum or spectrum (irritating and dramatic to caustic and mercurial to threatening or dangerous). This will help you decide more precisely how to deal with this person, determine his or her toxicity, and assess whether he or she may be a threat to you or others.

This checklist, as well as the others in this book, was designed to be used in everyday life by you and me—people who are not trained mental health professionals or researchers. It is not a clinical diagnostic tool. Its purpose is to educate, inform, or validate what you have witnessed or experienced.

Read each statement in the checklist carefully and check the statements that apply. Be honest; think about what you have heard an individual say or seen him or her do, or what others have expressed to you. Obviously, the best evidence is what you yourself have observed and how you feel when you are around or interact with this person.

Check only the statements that apply. Don't guess or include more than meet the criteria exactly. *If in doubt, leave it out.* Some items seem repetitive or appear to overlap—that is intentional, to capture nuances of behavior based on how people typically experience or describe these personalities.

It is very important that you complete the entire checklist, as designed, to increase its reliability. Each complete checklist covers very subtle yet significant issues that you may never have thought about. Some items may help you remember events you'd forgotten. Please read each statement, even if you feel you've seen enough or that the first few items don't seem to apply.

Gender pronouns (he, she, etc.) are used interchangeably in the statements. Any statement may be applicable to any gender.

We'll evaluate scores when you're done, but for now, check off each item below that applies.

- ☐ 1. You are constantly on the defensive around this person.

- ☐ 2. Displays of intense anger and outbursts are disproportionate to the circumstances or the event.

- ☐ 3. Since knowing or entering into a relationship with this person, you have become less happy, less confident, or less sure of yourself.

- ☐ 4. Relationships are a roller coaster of highs and lows.

- ☐ 5. The person is unable to appreciate the consequences of his statements or behavior and how it may affect others, including family members or society.

☐   6. Behaves in ways that at times are inappropriate or outrageous.

☐   7. Seems to fall apart under stress with some frequency.

☐   8. Arguments that should last a few minutes may go on for hours or days with no effort to ameliorate or end them.

☐   9. Seems to play role of victim or princess with regularity.

☐ 10. Hates being alone and constantly seeks companionship.

☐ 11. Has threatened suicide.

☐ 12. Frequently displays or expresses feelings of panic, anxiety, irritability, sadness, or anger.

☐ 13. Often feels or has expressed feeling emptiness; gets bored very easily, needs excitement.

☐ 14. Intense anger has been observed toward family members.

☐ 15. There are recurrent instances of fighting, arguing, or physical confrontations with others.

☐ 16. Verbal altercations seem to be a way of life for her.

☐ 17. You can't seem to relax, chill out, or "stand down" around this person.

☐ 18. This person has mentioned multiple times that someone or some group has it in for him and is conspiring against him.

☐ 19. Fellow workers describe her as "trouble," "difficult to work with," "irritating," or "impossible."

☐ 20. When you are around him, you feel emotionally and even physically drained.

☐ 21. After spending a few hours with her, you feel as if your world has been turned upside down. You may ask yourself: "What just happened?"

☐ 22. Those who are closest (e.g., you, family, children, spouses) routinely have to "check" to see what is the current "mood."

☐ 23. Frantically works at avoiding real or imagined abandonment by lovers or friends.

☐ 24. At times, this person's behavior seems theatrical or overdramatic for the circumstances.

☐ 25. Arguments are bitter and ugly—full of invective and cursing.

☐ 26. Is excessively demanding of others as it relates to favors, time, attention, or money.

☐ 27. Has thrown, torn, or broken objects out of anger or disapproval.

☐ 28. Has threatened suicide in order to avoid abandonment.

☐ 29. Rather than make amends or bring to closure, likes to wallow in argument and prolonged acrimonious discourse.

☐ 30. Is described by others as "unpredictable," "unreliable," or "unstable."

☐ 31. Attachments are often made too quickly and too intensely with someone new.

☐ 32. Likes to get tattoos in order to "feel something."

☐ 33. Is known to seek or harbor grievances for a very long time.

☐ 34. Easily denigrates or criticizes others, causing humiliation or embarrassment.

☐ 35. Claims to forgive but never does: Wrongs or injustices are remembered specifically for use in future arguments.

☐ 36. Has a short fuse, and frustration level is very low.

☐ 37. Seems incapable of consistent empathy, caring, or love.

☐ 38. It's not uncommon to hear people say, "Don't get upset, but . . ." when starting a conversation with this person.

☐ 39. There are indications that relationships are always stormy.

☐ 40. Marriage has been bitter and full of acrimony.

☐ 41. Seems to always be attracted to the wrong kind of person (criminals, drug users, thrill-seekers, or irresponsible individuals).

☐ 42. Doesn't seem to care if others are offended by his behavior.

☐ 43. Not happy being herself—wants to be someone else.

☐ 44. Takes part in risky behavior or thrill-seeking behavior that is criminal or puts others at risk.

☐ 45. Is very sensitive to what others say and think about him—tends to lash out when criticized.

☐ 46. Changes in plans are very upsetting and cause anxiety or irritability.

☐ 47. Known to have self-inflicted injury by cutting, scratching, biting, piercing, burning, or pulling out her own hair.

☐ 48. If ignored or not treated as special, gets upset or indignant.

☐ 49. Acts as though she wants to be the center of attention—doesn't want to feel left out.

☐ 50. Does not hesitate to lie or fabricate if it favors him.

☐ 51. You have felt reluctant to speak or take action out of fear of this person's reactions toward you or that they may hurt themselves.

☐ 52. Known to orchestrate sympathy to get attention (e.g., feigns illness or malady).

☐ 53. Her suffering, illness, or injuries are always worse than everyone else's.

☐ 54. Places difficult demands on the time and attention of others.

☐ 55. Uses nurturing of others as a tool to garner attention and devotion from them.

☐ 56. Has adopted children for the specific purpose of ensuring being "taken care of when old."

☐ 57. Does not understand or practice altruistic love.

☐ 58. You feel trapped by this person in some way.

☐ 59. It seems that this person's emotions are always so intense.

☐ 60. Is known to have unstable and intense interpersonal relationships.

☐ 61. Has complained of feeling inferior repeatedly.

☐ 62. Everything that this person does for others seems to come at a price or with strings attached.

☐ 63. Has been depressed or anxious for a long time or episodically.

☐ 64. Changes loyalties quickly, leaving you or friends frustrated and bewildered.

☐ 65. Seems to be very insecure and vigorously attempts to overcompensate.

☐ 66. Has admitted experimenting with or using "all kinds of drugs"—both in quantity and variety.

☐ 67. Has reported being emotionally out of control but can't explain why.

☐ 68. Has threatened to hurt himself or commit suicide merely to manipulate others.

☐ 69. Associating with this person lowers your self-esteem.

☐ 70. Fears anyone getting too close or keeps people from getting too close.

☐ 71. Has complained of a persistent vague illness or condition that affects her moods or energy levels.

☐ 72. Has relationships that are intense but short-lived.

☐ 73. Self-image is seemingly unstable (doesn't like who she is, how she looks, or where life is taking her).

☐ 74. Has an overwhelming need to be loved, adored, and cared for exclusively.

☐ 75. Claims to suffer from migraines, fibromyalgia, ulcers, colitis, irritable bowel syndrome, or frequent headaches.

☐ 76. Grown children refuse to have anything to do with this person.

☐ 77. Is very resourceful at blaming others when things go wrong.

☐ 78. Turns any criticism into countercriticism, even if it is illogical or false.

☐ 79. This person is in a constant power struggle with you or others.

☐ 80. Is stubborn and argumentative—seems to always want the last word.

☐ 81. Often exhibits poor planning (fails, for example, to bring food or water or even money for taking care of children), as if priorities are a last thought.

☐ 82. Fluctuates between extremes of idealization (loving) and devaluation (hating) of others.

☐ 83. Seems to live for the moment: There is little planning for the future (financially or with regard to work).

☐ 84. Doesn't seem to learn from previous relationships or from life experiences.

☐ 85. Desires relationship with an "ideal person" who will be all caring, all giving, and omnipresent—at their total disposal: i.e., an idealized person who doesn't exist.

☐ 86. When not fulfilled, becomes severely disappointed and devalues others.

☐ 87. Is impulsive as it relates to one or more areas such as promiscuous sex, unrestrained spending, substance abuse, reckless driving, binge eating, gambling, excessive drinking, or risk taking.

☐ 88. Even after a short meeting, this person causes you or others to feel anxious, troubled, angry, or infuriated.

☐ 89. Is constantly looking for excuses or cabals within organizations that are out to get her or keep her from being promoted or recognized.

☐ 90. Intentionally seeks a relationship with someone who is married or already in a relationship.

☐ 91. Dates have complained about feeling odd or that something is wrong or weird, even after a short date.

☐ 92. "Psycho" or "nuts" is a term you or others have used to describe this individual.

☐ 93. Seems capricious and temperamental without cause.

☐ 94. Has turned against loved ones dramatically without reasonable cause.

☐ 95. If in therapy, has turned against the therapist, despite having previously praised the therapist.

☐ 96. Likes the "fast" unencumbered life or engages in irresponsible behavior.

☐ 97. Has failed to comply with obligations such as getting heating oil, paying bills, or paying taxes—despite having money.

☐ 98. Her own children seem to be an inconvenience to her rather than a joy.

☐ 99. Uses humiliation as a form of punishment.

☐ 100. Has neglected children to hang out with friends, party, or go drinking.

☐ 101. Has a history of attracting too many men, and often the wrong kind of men.

☐ 102. Children complain about being ignored, ridiculed, or even abused by her at home.

☐ 103. Seems emotionally distant, even when trying to be close.

☐ 104. Has repeatedly accused you of being the cause of his problems or unhappiness.

☐ 105. Feels secure and happy with an entourage or a group—doesn't like to be alone.

☐ 106. There seems to always be tension (almost everything is taken negatively) in her life.

☐ 107. Seems temperamentally sensitive.

☐ 108. Has placed demands on you to take sides against someone else.

☐ 109. Seems impervious to acts of kindness or generosity even from people who care or have tried to help.

☐ 110. Seems hyperalert to signs of abandonment or of losing someone.

☐ 111. Has reported anxiety or depression at various times in the past.

☐ 112. Has repeatedly stalked someone or has repeatedly harassed someone from his or her past.

☐ 113. Refuses to let scabs on the skin heal (picks at them even in public); pricks skin with sharp objects when stressed.

☐ 114. Is seemingly unable to control outbursts of anger or animosity.

☐ 115. Has been diagnosed as anorexic or suffering from bulimia nervosa.

☐ 116. Two or more nonclinical terms such as "horrible," "bitchy," "psycho," "impossible," "nut job," "crazy," or "wacko" have been used to describe this person.

☐ 117. Has joined a cult or claims to have a guru, master, or coach, which she follows without question.

☐ 118. You feel you have to walk on eggshells around this person.

☐ 119. Is known to be afflicted with a personality disorder such as but not limited to histrionic personality disorder, borderline personality disorder, or paranoid personality disorder.

☐ 120. Has physically hit a spouse or lover on more than one occasion when angry.

☐ 121. Has been diagnosed as being bipolar, manic/depressive, or as having severe mood swings.

☐ 122. Has talked about or has actually physically retaliated against someone (let air out of tires, scratched a car door with a key, sent hate mail, etc.).

☐ 123. Has gone to great effort or expense or traveled great distances to follow, observe, or harass someone.

☐ 124. At work, has displayed intense anger toward fellow workers.

☐ 125. Has vandalized or destroyed property of a former co-worker, friend, roommate, lover, or family member.

SCORING

☑ Count how many statements apply to this individual based on the criteria discussed at the beginning of this checklist.

☑ If you find that this individual has 15 to 35 of these features, this is a person who will occasionally take an emotional toll on others and may be difficult to live or work with.

☑ If the score is 36 to 65, this indicates that the individual has all the features of and behaves as an emotionally unstable personality. This person needs help and will cause turmoil in the life of anyone close to him or her.

☑ If the score is above 65, this person has a preponderance of the major features of an emotionally unstable personality and is an emotional, psychological, financial, or physical danger to himself or herself or to others.

IMMEDIATE ACTIONS

If you're involved with an emotionally unstable personality, realize that these individuals need help from professionals who know how to deal with this kind of complex and conflicted personality. The process can be lengthy, but they can be helped by very intense therapy—if they're willing to be helped and with great effort on their part.

You can try to reach out to them, but you may find yourself being attacked for your efforts. If being with this kind of person has caused you to be irritable, upset, angry, or depressed, or if they've victimized you through their behavior, you may need professional assistance yourself.

These individuals can be so toxic that they can traumatize without being physical.

Set strict boundaries about what you will permit. While this may trigger resistance at first, it may establish some stability, if only for a while. If they insist on violating boundaries or if they further traumatize you, then you have confirmation that they are seriously troubled and that you need to distance yourself. No one expects you to be mistreated or victimized, even by the emotionally unstable. Having said that, if you decide to continue to associate with this person, don't be surprised if the behaviors continue, creating turmoil in your life.

If the person in question is considering, talking about, or threatening to harm himself, call 911 (or police, fire department, or ambulance) without hesitation, as these are issues best handled by professionals. If you have children, remember that they are helpless against this personality and need your protection. Take steps to protect yourself and any loved ones. You have a moral obligation to spare children the wrath of these individuals. For additional strategies, see Chapter 6, Self-Defense against Dangerous Personalities.

CHAPTER 3

"TRUST NO ONE AND YOU'LL NEVER GET HURT"

THE PARANOID PERSONALITY

IN THE 1999 MOVIE *American Beauty*, actor Chris Cooper brilliantly plays the part of the reclusive neighbor Colonel Frank Fitts, a retired US Marine. Just from the nonverbals, we can tell something's wrong in that family. Fitts's wife is almost robotlike—afraid to speak. When the doorbell rings, everyone freezes. Fitts reacts as he has always done: Rather than go to the door, he interrogates his wife and son about who's there.

Fitts fears strangers and inquisitive neighbors, locking everything up in the house. To him, the world is falling apart, and he's one of the few who recognizes that. Fortunately, he has all the answers for what to do about it. He bashes gays, foreigners, blacks—even his own imperfect son. He mistrusts his family, constantly questioning their loyalty. There's no laughter or romance in the Fitts household. It's been years since friends came over. Everything must be done his way. Everyone moves slowly, methodically, avoiding anything that could rouse his suspicions or incite his ire.

Inflexible, irritable, and highly moralistic, Fitts has made life miserable for anyone who comes in contact with him, especially his family. Fitts is a paranoid personality.

No one's really like that, you say? You'd be wrong. There are millions of people like this to one degree or another. One of them was my neighbor.

Mr. "P," my neighbor where I grew up in the suburbs of Miami, rarely came out of the house. When he did, it was to shout at the kids who were playing in the neighborhood. He was retired, and he sat by the window keeping an eye on anyone who passed by. His wife had no friends and rarely went out. We said hi to her once, and he yelled at her for waving at us. He poisoned several animals that had strayed onto his property and bragged about it to us as a warning.

I never saw Mr. P smile or laugh—there was no joy in him. Once, when a salesman came to our house with two suitcases full of fabric samples for curtains, Mr. P called the police. I'm not sure what he thought, but I do know my mother had to leave work to deal with that inconvenience and many more over the years.

The kids in the neighborhood just thought he was weird. We thought it odd that his wife wasn't allowed to talk to the neighbor moms. Some might say he was eccentric. What society doesn't teach us is that this individual is a paranoid personality. Had we known, we might have given him the space he craved and avoided the repeated humiliation my parents endured trying to befriend him, only to be snarled at.

Paranoid personalities are consumed by irrational mistrust and fear. Their suspicions know no bounds. Their rigid thinking is impervious to reason and makes them judgmental, biased, and uptight. They see only the cloud around the silver lining. Do something nice for them, and they'll suspect ulterior motives. Altruists, to them, are opportunists with hidden agendas.

All of us have an inner warning system that alerts us to danger. But with the paranoid personality, it's as if this system is stuck in overdrive, sounding alarms about you, me, neighbors, co-workers, ethnic groups, foreigners, the government, and on and on. Their skewed perspective dominates their life and can dominate anyone involved with them.

When I lecture, I often ask for a show of hands from those who know someone like this. At first, just a few hands go up. But as I list the key traits—easily insulted; argumentative; jealous; holds grudges; questions motives; challenges the rules; fears, dislikes, or hates those who are different—I see the proverbial lightbulbs going on as more and more hands rise. Sometimes, people chuckle or roll their eyes as they recognize someone at work everyone has learned to avoid. Or they close their eyes with the heavy look of one who has been badly hurt.

Countless times during my years in law enforcement, we dealt with the damage these individuals inflict. Yet even we tended not to describe or understand them properly. That kind of failure can have deadly consequences.

Jerry Kane and his son Joseph Kane of Little Rock, Arkansas, were paranoid personalities, deeply suspicious of government officials and the police, believing that the law didn't apply to them. So when Officer Bill Evans and Sergeant Brandon Paudert pulled them over for a minor traffic violation, there was no talking. The Kanes opened up with automatic weapons, killing both officers. This event was captured on the police dashboard camera and can still be seen on YouTube. If those officers had known that they weren't dealing with people who were just odd or eccentric but rather with paranoid personalities who were virulently antigovernment and anti-law enforcement, perhaps they'd be alive today.

Look around and you will see these personalities:

- The driver who thinks you cut him off intentionally, so he tailgates you with horn honking, headlights flashing, rude gestures, and cursing. He may even follow you all the way home.

- The man who thinks everyone's hitting on his wife or girl-friend, so at parties he sticks his nose into every conversation she has, especially with men, and makes sure those men don't loiter very long.

- The date from hell who considers you merely an audience for his Mr. Know-It-All act, argues with everything you say, or puts your ideas down (not surprisingly, you discover he has no friends).

- The relative who's habitually trying to convince you of some pseudoscience remedy or has found yet another guru who sees the world just as he does.

- The fellow employee who frequently files grievances and then questions why others got promotions or bonuses and he didn't.

- The complainer who shows up at government offices almost weekly to rant about issues or threaten to file a lawsuit.

- The anonymous author of an acrid online attack, accusing you of having a hidden agenda and knowing what you "really meant."

- The reclusive neighbor who insists on telling you about the new world order or conspiracies or secret organizations that control the federal government.

- The former employee or ex-boyfriend who, angry about how he's been treated, shows up at the office unannounced and armed.

- The brilliant scientist no one listens to, so he moves to a smelly cabin in Montana where he can warn us of the threat of technology by sending bombs (16 in all) through the mail that killed 3 and injured 23 ("Unabomber" Theodore John "Ted" Kaczynski, PhD).

These are more than cranky people. They're driven by irrational fear and distrust. They're thin-skinned and hyperreactive. And when crossed, rejected, or embarrassed, they may lash out and can be extremely dangerous.

When coupled with narcissism, the paranoid personality drives violence on every level: from criminals to cult leaders to dictators who live by their own rules, vilify others, and annihilate anything that gets in their way. All that's needed is some unpredictable triggering event and you end up with a Christopher Dorner (a former Los Angeles police officer), who was hypersensitive, feeling slighted, and incapable of reconciling his fears, so in 2013 he went after his former employers, killing two and leading officers into a standoff that ended with a shoot-out.

Despite the danger they pose, these individuals are some of the least studied and understood. They're difficult to treat in part because they don't think there's anything wrong with them, and they question the intentions of anyone trying to help. Too often they're at the mercy of their pathology—and so are we.

THE WAY OF THE PARANOID PERSONALITY

Every FBI Special Agent who works complaint duty, as I did, will tell you that FBI reception rooms and phone lines are full of these personalities. They come in or call to carp about threats, enemies, conspiracies, cabals, or failures of the government to respond to their requests.

I remember how sometimes their spouses sat quietly, faces furrowed from the agony of living with this person, as the diatribe went on. Others wanted us to mediate because their mate (usually the husband) had spent a fortune on weapons, emergency shelters, 2-year supplies of food, and water purification systems. The FBI complaint desk was their last resort after family members had given up—and, of course, there was no money to visit a psychologist.

Because I hadn't been clued in to this pathology during training, I wasted precious hours attempting to use logic to persuade or convince these individuals of their errors—hours I could have spent solving crimes. In time, I learned to simply listen, not to set the record straight or try to present contrary evidence. All the paranoid personality wants is validation of his or her beliefs, and that requires one thing: a pliant audience.

Movies and television often portray the paranoid personality as a wild-eyed, crazed individual similar to the Jack Torrance character played by Jack Nicholson in the 1980 psychological horror film *The Shining*. But that's Hollywood. The reality is much different, much more nuanced.

Some paranoid individuals are quiet and reserved, almost shy, yet they view the world with unyielding suspicion. Others are dramatic, vociferous, even combative. They often turn up the heat in conversations because they enjoy arguing. These individuals may show up at demonstrations and make it a point to not just argue but to be vitriolic, even physical, pushing others, blocking cars, damaging property. They skate very close to being unstable—all it takes is a trigger.

Some are mental lightweights, while others have high IQs and achievements to their name. Ted Kaczynski had a very high IQ and a real knack for making bombs and hiding their origin. Howard Hughes was smart and rich but very paranoid—so much so that he cocooned himself in hotel rooms during the last 10 years of his life, allowing no outsiders to see him. He died isolated from the world in a Las Vegas hotel room in 1976. Jimmy Lee Dykes won medals for his US Navy service but over the years repeatedly frightened his neighbors in Midland City, Alabama, with his "eccentric" and menacing behaviors (e.g., threatening to shoot trespassers, making nocturnal armed tours of his property). Neighbors reluctantly tolerated this paranoid personality, but it all unraveled on January 29, 2013. On that day, shortly before he was slated to appear in court on a charge that he had menaced his neighbors yet again, Dykes boarded a school bus, killed the bus driver, and took a 5-year-old child hostage. The child was held captive in an underground bunker for 6 days before an FBI SWAT team rescued the boy, killing Dykes in the process.[1] What drove the behavior of Kaczynski and Dykes? Simply this: irrational fear—the essence of the paranoid personality.

At home or at work, there's always something for this personality to be suspicious about. Perhaps it's a neighbor, the neighbor's children, the planes that fly overhead, or the electric lines that sit close to the house. They seek space, isolation, and distance to calm their fears. Sadly, that can't be done because the paranoia comes from within them.

Some isolate themselves at a school, at work, in a city, or even within a family—they become the loners. Some take it a step further and live in the wilderness (the desert Southwest, Idaho, Montana, and Alaska are favorite choices) to get away, avoid others, or "prep" for some apocalyptic event. They may find refuge in organizations that believe as they do, joining a group or a cult where they don't have to convince others of their fears or eccentric beliefs.

Then there are those who are truly eccentric. They may dress oddly (military camouflage fatigues), carry a large knife, or dress to intimidate or to offend, such as when they wear the Nazi swastika. Naturally, others notice and talk about their strangeness. This, of course, fuels their paranoia that they're being talked about.

The paranoia of some drives them into the camps of those who hate. They listen to it on the radio; attend rallies; and wear the emblems, signs, clothes, and tattoos of hatred. These are the dangerous ones who seek like-minded "true believers," as Eric Hoffer warned us in his landmark book on mass movements and totalitarian governments.[2] They join the KKK, the skinheads, Aryan Nations, and any other extremist group that seeks to hate and do away with others because passionate hatred and fear give purpose and meaning to an otherwise unfulfilled life.[3]

Or they hook up with just one other like-minded paranoid personality for support in doing harm. This is what happened with the 2013 Boston Marathon bombers—the Tsarnaev brothers. Similarly, Timothy McVeigh joined forces with Terry Nichols, a fellow like-minded personality, to blow up the Alfred P. Murrah Federal Building in Oklahoma.

And when they cannot find anyone with whom to commiserate, they act alone, like Anders Behring Breivik, the right-wing extremist who feared the influx of minorities in Norway, so he went out and massacred 77 souls, mostly children, in Norway in 2011.[4]

The paranoid personality spectrum, as you can see, is broad and ranges from irritating and obnoxious to extremely flammable and dangerous, but to one degree or another, these people share defining characteristics.

Hypersuspicious, Fearful, Secretive

These personalities' irrational suspicion drives them to constantly monitor the words and actions of others to gauge evil or malicious intent. Even inadvertent social slights may be viewed as suspect. They tend to be secretive and not reveal much about themselves. They may lie to protect their beliefs, whereabouts, or true intentions. Even at home, they may lock things away from their spouses or fellow family members. It's not unusual for them to have a locker or sometimes a room no one else can enter. As you can see, this is where normal maintenance of privacy and security crosses over into the paranoid realm—the realm where even family members can't be trusted.

It's impossible to catalog all the things the paranoid personality may fear. It could be blacks, Catholics, Jews, Mormons, Baptists, Mexicans, Muslims, Africans, non-English speakers; electrical grids, cell phone towers, the food supply, fluoridation of water, the neighbors, planes flying overhead, foreign accents, abortion clinics, animal research, pharmaceutical companies, the new world order, anyone wearing a blue beret, Europeans, microphones, the government, the IRS, nonwhites, technology, and on and on and on. Oh, and let's not forget the cubicle mate, the boss, the manager, the HR department, the computer system, the insurance company, the e-mail system at work—or, perhaps, you. Each one of these individuals has his or her own particular fear, gripe, or insecurity. Eventually, if you associate or interact with the person long enough, these will be revealed to you—if not in words, then through the person's paranoid, eccentric, or dangerous behavior.

Some are so mistrusting that they keep lists of the comings and goings of co-workers, neighbors, family members, strangers, or anyone who passes by. Ted Kaczynski did just that from his remote cabin in Montana. President Richard Nixon, who had many of the features of the paranoid personality, kept an enemies list and repeatedly stated to others that he just could not "confide in anyone."[5]

Opinionated, Argumentative, Prone to Hate

Adaptability is a hallmark of a healthy human being. We can embrace new ideas and change in response to circumstances. While we hold steadfast to certain beliefs (for example, religious or political views), we recognize that others feel differently. Not so for paranoid personalities. They think their hypersensitivity is a form of superior insight, so there's no room for debate with them. Logical or even empirical proof, to them, is meaningless. Try to reason with them and you may be seen as a conspirator working against them, or worse, as an enemy.

Paranoid personalities select and distort facts and history, stringing together disparate events and ideas to fit their views and justify their actions—for example, exterminating doctors who perform abortions.[6] When Paul Jennings Hill assassinated John Britton, MD, and his friend James Barrett in 1994 as Britton walked into a women's abortion clinic in Pensacola, Florida, in Hill's paranoid mind, his killing of the doctor and his friend (who was acting as his bodyguard) was justified to save unborn babies. Such is the mind of the paranoid personality—skewed, rigid, moralistic, or unyielding—where murder is justified to save the unborn.

This personality tends to know a lot about very little, fixating on a narrow idea—a passage of the Bible, or a legal, social, or political issue that may be of little or no consequence to most of us. Timothy McVeigh focused on the militarization of police SWAT teams in the 1990s. He didn't like their military-style tactics targeting reclusive Randy Weaver and his family at Ruby Ridge in northern Idaho in 1992. For his beliefs and for his hatred of the federal government in general, he blew up the Alfred P. Murrah Federal Building in Oklahoma, killing 168 innocents, including children.[7] Paranoid personalities are not sticklers for logic or empirical evidence. They will cite dubious or obscure examples from history, esoteric works, unknown authors, or even law dictionaries to support their arguments.

Combine rigid thinking, a fixed ideology, and selective memory with irrational fear and you have the toxic broth of hate—not the dislike you or I might feel, but an uncompromising, dehumanizing hate.[8] Add pathological narcissism to the mix and you have people willing and able to act on their hatred with horrific cruelty: walking into classrooms and calmly gunning down students as they scream and cower. This is exactly what happened at Columbine High School (1999), thanks to two paranoid teenagers, Eric Harris and Dylan Klebold, who narcissistically saw themselves as special and entitled to take the lives of others.

For many of these paranoid personalities, violence becomes the solution because nothing else will achieve their out-of-bounds aims or do so fast enough for them. So you get "magical thinking" that goes something like this:

If I kill enough scientists, I'll stop the advance of technology.

—"Unabomber" Ted Kaczynski, who mailed 16 bombs, killing 3 and wounding 23

If I blow up a building, I'll stop the FBI and do away with SWAT teams.

—Timothy McVeigh, bomber of the Alfred P. Murrah Federal Building in Oklahoma City, killing 168 women and children and injuring hundreds

If I set off a bomb at the Atlanta Olympics, then abortions in America will cease to be performed.

—Eric Rudolph, Olympic Park bomber, 1996, Atlanta

If I kill enough Americans, the United States will leave the Middle East.

—Usama bin Laden, mastermind of the 9/11 attack on the United States that killed nearly 3,000

If I kill enough Norwegian children, then surely the government will recognize my warnings about the threat of Muslims and foreigners migrating to Norway.

—Anders Behring Breivik, killed 77 (mostly children) in Norway

It's clear to everyone but them that their actions will not have the effect they desire and that, in fact, their thinking is not just magical but pathological. Violence doesn't fix what they crave to change, but such is the thought process of the paranoid personality at the more volatile end of the spectrum.

Wound Collector, Grudge Holder

The paranoid personality, much like the emotionally unstable personality, is a perennial "wound collector"—only more so. Any innocent mistake or perceived wrong, no matter how unintentional, becomes a black mark on your character and an indicator of your disloyalty. No transgression—including those you didn't do—will be forgotten or forgiven. Once you're the enemy, the paranoid person will feel justified in holding grudges or taking action against you, be it avoiding you, backstabbing you, plotting against you, sabotaging or destroying things that belong to you, or, in some cases, killing you.

History is full of paranoid wound collectors. Usama bin Laden used events from the Crusades in the 11th century to justify the killing of Americans in 2001. Ted Kaczynski collected wounds and grievances from the time of the industrial revolution in the 18th century, while Timothy

Words That Describe
THE PARANOID PERSONALITY

Here are the uncensored words victims use to describe the paranoid personality:

Adversarial, alarmist, alone, aloof, angry, apocalyptical, apprehensive, armed, aroused, assertive, barricaded, biased, bigoted, bluffer, boastful, cagey, calculating, callous, cantankerous, careful, cautious, circumspect, cold, combative, complainer, confused, confusing, contemptuous, contentious, contrarian, control freak, controlling, cracked, crackpot, crank, crazy, creepy, critical, cruel, crusty, daft, defensive, delusional, demanding, demented, deranged, difficult, disbeliever, distrustful, disturbed, doubtful, draining, dry, eccentric, envious, erratic, evasive, extremist, fanatic, fearful, fixated, flake, fruitcake, fussy, grandiose, guarded, gullible, hardheaded, hater, hates, haughty, hidden, hiding, high strung, hostile, hubris, hypercritical, hypersensitive, impossible, impressionable, incredulous, inflexible, inhospitable, injured, insular, intolerant, irascible, irrational, irritable, isolated, jealous, know-it-all, kook, lame brain, leery, liar, litigious, loco, loner, loon, loony, lunatic, mad, maniac, mean, menacing, mental, millennialist, mistrustful, mobilized, narrow-minded, nasty, neurotic, nonconformist, nut, nuts, nutty, obdurate, obscene, obsessed, obsessive, odd, offensive, opinionated, out, overcritical, overly sensitive, peculiar, perplexing, persecuted, pessimistic, picky, prejudiced, prickly, provocative, psycho, quarrelsome, querulous, questioning, radical, rebel, recluse, remorseless, repulsive, rigid, scary, self-important, skeptical, squirrely, startled, stiff, strict, stubborn, survivalist, suspicious, tense, terse, testy, threatening, touched, touchy, treacherous, trigger-happy, truculent, "truther," unbalanced, unbelieving, unbending, uncompromising, uncultured, unforgiving, ungenerous, unromantic, unstable, unwavering, unwelcoming, unwell, unyielding, uptight, victim, victimized, vindictive, wary, watchful, weird, whiner, withdrawn, worried, zealot.

McVeigh's dissatisfaction with the federal government and wound collecting began just a few years prior to his bombing of an Oklahoma City federal building, during the events at Ruby Ridge (1992) and the siege of the Branch Davidians in Waco, Texas (1993). For paranoid personalities, wound collecting is a necessity. They use it to justify their actions, and there's no statute of limitations on how far back they'll reach to collect those wounds nor how wide a net they will cast.

This personality has fantastic recall of adversarial situations, historical wrongs, and social slights. These collected wounds feed their paranoia and justify their hatred and behavior. Hitler's *Mein Kampf,* if you can bear to read it, is one long, rambling collection of historical wounds focusing on the Jews going back 2,000 years to the time of Christ.

THEIR EFFECT ON YOU

Working the complaint desk in the FBI taught me how paranoid personalities gradually alienate everyone around them, slowly exhausting the goodwill, patience, and charity of others.

I remember one visit in particular from a paranoid personality and his wife because I was struck by how sad she looked as she patiently sat with her husband while he ranted about this or that while pulling newspaper clippings from a worn shoe box, making endless allegations against the government and the United Nations. There was nothing the FBI or I could do for him and his outrageous allegations, so after an hour or so they left. Later that day, his wife called from a pay phone to apologize and to thank me for lending an ear. She explained that he had become this way after the Vietnam War and was getting worse each year. Their kids no longer came around, and his fixation on government wrongs was all consuming and frankly was overwhelming her.

I told her that there was no need to apologize but wondered if she was okay. Her answer surprised me. "No, I'm not okay," she answered, holding back tears. "He makes my life a hell, but what can I do? I'm stuck." And then she hung up. Police training doesn't prepare you for this. I can still picture her pathetically sitting there, patiently listening to yet another rant.

This is one of the reasons why I decided to include the paranoid personality in this book: because much of the damage this person does is psychological. Family members often expressed to me that they were "emotionally broken down" as a result of living with a paranoid personality. Those are strong words with huge implications.

Let's be clear: Paranoid personalities will suck the joy out of your life. They will make you tense, worried, irritable, and edgy. You see, you must view and fear their enemies as they do; otherwise, in their opinion, there is something wrong with you. You can't relax around them, and if they perceive you as disloyal, they'll take out their contempt or anger on you. Your wishes and desires are of no concern as you quickly learn they have a one-track mind or a single fixation.

You won't be alone in your inability to break through or establish trust when they are at the more virulent end of the paranoid personality spectrum. No one can—not family, not therapists, and not the police. They'll air their grievances at work, on vacation, in line, at the lunch counter, anytime they see an opportunity. Conversations devolve into diatribes. Even compliments can rouse their suspicions—such as the time my father told Mr. P, our neighbor, that he liked the used car Mr. P had just purchased. That just made Mr. P even more suspicious of my father.

They can force you to change the way you live, making you constantly adapt to that foreboding world they fear. When they bicker at work and get laid off, it is you who has to step in and work extra hours to make up the difference in income. When they become obnoxious with the neighbors, you will have to do the fence mending. You'll have to change your routine to accommodate paranoid people because they tend to become insular and withdrawn, and they expect you to be as well. Conversely, at the other end of the spectrum, they can become difficult and argumentative. No matter what, they expect you to believe as they do and see the world through their paranoid prism, whether you like it or not. Their enemies must become your enemies.

In extreme cases, they may take their whole family to live in the middle of nowhere, as happened when former Green Beret Randy Weaver and his wife took their family to live in a cabin they constructed in Ruby Ridge, Idaho, in 1992. These personalities can seek extreme isolation, believing that some apocalyptic event is imminent, joining the ranks of the "preppers" who are prepared for some horrendous catastrophic event, often exposing their family to deprivation as well as ridicule.

They can expose you to danger for reasons you may never fathom. To me, the saddest situations occur when the paranoid personalities decide to isolate themselves with their children within the confines of a cult, as we saw with those who followed Jim Jones to his compound in Guyana. Exposing their children to the squalor of a dengue-infested jungle and the paranoid rantings of a narcissistic megalomaniac wasn't enough. The final act was to kill their own children and themselves with cyanide-laced Kool-Aid (November 18, 1978). Nine hundred eighteen died that day because they—or, in the case of innocent children, their parents— believed.

Like Jim Jones's followers in Guyana, everyone who associated with David Koresh, head of the Branch Davidian sect in Waco, Texas, in the 1980s and early 1990s was in danger also, as he truly believed he was divine, that only he had all the answers, and that an apocalyptic end was coming. Both he and Jim Jones demanded blind and unconditional obedience; anyone who was against them was in peril. Remember, if you're not with them, you're against them.

THE PARANOID PERSONALITY IN RELATIONSHIPS

With so much perceived danger all around, don't expect effusive intimacy from paranoid personalities. They may care for you in their own way, but they're too preoccupied to think much about what others feel and too guarded to share themselves fully with partners or friends. Conversations tend to be one track, circling back to their favored issue(s). They have no real interests other than the agenda on which they're currently fixated. The result is limited, one-dimensional relationships.

Because they view any conflict as an attack, they can't handle the normal ups and downs of relationships. So unless you feel like arguing with them constantly, you end up becoming compliant. In fact, spouses of the acutely paranoid personality become like Colonel Fitts's wife in *American Beauty*: automatons, lacking emotions, perennially fearful of a backlash.

Most people aren't aware when they first start dating a paranoid personality that they're being assessed for their pliability and willingness to go along with this person's ideas. This personality will quickly move on rather than spend time trying to convince someone with a skeptical mind and will most likely select mates who are receptive and nonjudgmental, and who don't question. The problem is, many of us don't recognize this up front because no one has warned us about the paranoid personality, and once we're committed, it may be too late.

The wife or girlfriend of the paranoid personality often complains that her mate is always jealous with absolutely no cause, calling frequently or dropping by work or home unannounced—not out of caring, but to test her. This personality may scour your calendar, address book, phone records, or e-mails for signs of disloyalty or activities not approved of. At a seminar I led on paranoid personalities in relationships, one woman told me she'd found evidence that her husband had paid a surveillance team to tail her—and she was just going to visit a friend in another city.

Paranoid personalities will insist on isolating you socially, so eventually you lose contact with family and friends. Why? Because no one is to be trusted. Even their own relatives will pull away, tired of the suspicion and vitriol. Chances are, none of their friends will be people you'll want to spend a lot of time with, as they tend to attract other odd, eccentric personalities who dress, behave, and believe as they do—again, other *true believers.*

The whole family's life becomes limited by the circumscribed world of the paranoid personality, who may monitor or control communication—for example, not letting family members have cell phones or other devices, or tracking keystrokes on computers with special software to see what you really think or have been up to or to keep you from being "corrupted" by the outside world. Dating may be forbidden, and staying out late, dancing, or even wearing makeup may rouse the ire of the moralistic paranoid personality.

One woman came to the FBI to ask what she could do about the fact that her husband didn't want the kids to go to public school anymore. He would even put chalk marks on the car tires to make sure the car wasn't moved while he was away on business. What do you say to that? That is life with a paranoid personality.

Paranoia can be inculcated in children as well as in adults. JoAnn McGuckin and her husband moved with their seven children to rural Idaho to isolate themselves from the world. After JoAnn's husband died, their eldest daughter, 19-year-old Erina, recognized things just weren't right in their home—which had little food, no running water, and no heat—so she went to the authorities. Consequently, JoAnn was arrested in June 2001 on a variety of charges based on neglect and deprivation of the children.[9]

When the police later returned to take the remaining children into protective custody, the children, rather than being grateful to be released from deprivation and squalor, went to battle stations consistent with the paranoid personality. They set 20-plus dogs loose on the sheriff's deputies, screaming, "Get the guns!" Those children then barricaded themselves against the police with weapons for a week.[10] JoAnn and her husband had taught their children to be paranoid—to trust no one. Events like this cause relatives and loved ones terrible stress and grief, not to mention the cost to the city and county for mobilizing police, emergency, fire, ambulance, and social welfare resources for days on end.

This is precisely what happened in Waco at the Branch Davidian compound when law enforcement officers tried to arrest David Koresh. That attempt transformed itself into a threat against those who believed in the divinity of Koresh. When government agents tried to rescue the children from within the compound, the Davidians themselves set fire to the buildings, immolating themselves rather than allowing the breakup of the group. The siege lasted 51 days and 76 people died, including many innocent children.[11] Once again, paranoia overrode parental sensibilities, just as in Jonestown.[12]

ENCOUNTERS WITH THE PARANOID PERSONALITY

As several clinicians have said to me, you see these personalities in every organization and most are functional, but they make life difficult for those around them.

In school, they may have the intelligence to do well but don't seem to succeed or thrive, lacking the interpersonal skills to be a contributing member of the community. They alienate students and teachers, who don't want to give them recommendations—which, of course, just proves their suspicions that others want them to fail.

Sometimes, these personalities look unkempt or dress like recluses or "mountain men"—inappropriate for most work settings. Or they wear paramilitary clothing and carry weapons to appear threatening. Or they cultivate a hostile, sinister, rebellious look with prominent tattoos, Mohawk-style haircuts, or shaved heads.

Most will find work, but they're always suspicious of management, of how decisions are made, of why they don't get promoted. They're the office malcontents, whether openly irritating and obnoxious or quietly plotting in their cubicles, often spreading discontent.

Then there are the office saboteurs. They make sure that little things don't get done properly, reports are delayed, deliveries are late, cars get scratched, calls aren't returned, or bills are lost—especially if things don't go their way. So the paranoid personality can use passive and not-so-passive aggression to sabotage those around them, especially those they deem enemies.

Even if they're functional at work, they may be hypercompetitive, irritating, and contrarian, grumbling and complaining endlessly. If they see a group talking quietly, they'll think they're being talked about. At times, they can be seen muttering to themselves, which, of course, makes them an oddity. If they hear other workers speaking a foreign language—a valued skill set for any organization—they're the first to complain that they're being secretly talked about.

With grandiosity in the mix, they'll think they're smarter than everyone, including the boss, and are being overlooked for advancement. Negotiating anything with them can be very difficult as they're so mistrustful, and they're notorious for arguing with the boss, harboring suspicions of management's motives, spreading rumors, questioning procedures, suspecting favoritism, or bringing frivolous lawsuits. They may embark on endless letter-writing campaigns to air their grievances with superiors or may go outside the organization to bring scrutiny from public officials.

It should be noted that there are very successful businesspeople that meet the criteria of a paranoid personality. But they come with their own quirks and odd behaviors consistent with this personality type. Billionaire

Howard Hughes suffered from OCPD (obsessive-compulsive personality disorder), but he was also paranoid. He lived in isolation, thought his phones were bugged, and grew to detest meeting people and insisted on dealing only with a few people he absolutely trusted (they were called his Mormon Mafia because he mostly hired members of the Church of Jesus Christ of Latter-Day Saints to be around him).[13]

Companies may transfer a "problem" employee from department to department thinking that this is the best way to deal with the paranoid personality. It isn't, because these individuals will be a problem wherever they work, and one has to keep in mind that the paranoid personality can be volatile—we just never know what that trigger will be or when. Even police officers can be surprised by this personality's volatility when making traffic stops, serving warrants, or responding to domestic disputes. If the person has been drinking or is on drugs such as cocaine, amphetamine, or methamphetamine, the potential for violence is even greater.

Although by now the terms "school shooting," "disgruntled employee," "road rage," and "going postal" are almost clichés, they're hardly ever associated with the paranoid personality, yet they should be, since paranoia is what most of these individuals who unleash massively violent rage tend to have in common. Teachers, students, and fellow workers may see behaviors they think are odd or moody but don't recognize the warning signs of the paranoid personality on the brink of explosion.

And when paranoid individuals rise to leadership positions or governance, the damage they can do boggles the mind. Some of history's worst atrocities have been driven by the paranoid personality's uncompromising hypersuspicion, fear, and hatred. Joseph Stalin, Adolf Hitler, and Cambodian dictator Pol Pot were all acutely paranoid. They irrationally feared nonexistent enemies and required that their followers do the same. The cost in lives is so staggering that words cannot do justice to their crimes. One life lost is a tragedy. How, then, do we characterize the loss of more than 30 million (Stalin), more than 5 million (Hitler), or more than 1.2 million (Pol Pot)?—and these are conservative estimates. It's unfathomable. We cannot comprehend such large numbers. But if we look away, if we don't act, if we don't call things what they are, we passively abet ignorance of a fundamental truth: When the paranoid personality rises to the top, mayhem ensues.[14]

In the end, paranoia's most enduring damage is the instability it sows between people. It tears at trust, harmony, and cohesion in relationships, in families, in organizations, in communities, and between nations. That is the toxic, tragic legacy of the pathologically paranoid personality.

YOUR DANGEROUS PERSONALITIES CHECKLIST

Warning Signs of the Paranoid Personality

As I noted in the Introduction, I developed various behavior-based checklists during my career to help me assess individuals to see if they were dangerous personalities. This particular checklist will help you determine if someone has the features of the paranoid personality and where that person falls on a continuum or spectrum (from narrow-minded, argumentative, and rigid to annoyingly suspicious and questioning all the way to highly unstable, volatile, or even dangerous). This will help you decide more precisely how to deal with this person, determine his or her toxicity, and assess whether he or she may be a threat to you or others.

This checklist, as well as the others in this book, was designed to be used in everyday life by you and me—people who are not trained mental health professionals or researchers. It is not a clinical diagnostic tool. Its purpose is to educate, inform, or validate what you have witnessed or experienced.

Read each statement in the checklist carefully and check the statements that apply. Be honest; think about what you have heard an individual say or seen him or her do, or what others have expressed to you. Obviously, the best evidence is what you yourself have observed and how you feel when you are around or interact with this person.

Check only the statements that apply. Don't guess or include more than meet the criteria exactly. *If in doubt, leave it out.* Some items seem repetitive or appear to overlap—that is intentional, to capture nuances of behavior based on how people typically experience or describe these personalities.

It is very important that you complete the entire checklist, as designed, to increase its reliability. Each complete checklist covers very subtle yet significant issues that you may never have thought about. Some items may help you remember events you'd forgotten. Please read each statement, even if you feel you've seen enough or that the first few items don't seem to apply.

Gender pronouns (he, she, etc.) are used interchangeably in the statements. Any statement may be applicable to any gender.

We'll evaluate scores when you're done, but for now, check off each item below that applies.

☐ 1. Believes that others seek to exploit or harm him in some way.

☐ 2. Is preoccupied with unjustified doubts about the loyalty of others.

☐ 3. Is reluctant to trust others—perceives them as deceitful.

☐ 4. Has unwarranted fears that others will use information maliciously against her.

☐ 5. Perceives others as demeaning or threatening, no matter how benign their intentions.

☐ 6. Holds grudges for a long time and is not forgiving of slights, even after many years.

☐   7. Is very sensitive to how others view him.

☐   8. Has angry reactions to minor slights—seems to always have an ax to grind.

☐   9. Frequently questions fidelity of spouse or lovers without cause.

☐   10. Has a pessimistic view of life or believes she is being persecuted.

☐   11. Habitually questions the intentions of others, including his spouse, intimate relations, family, or workmates.

☐   12. Is suspicious (without need) of people, events, objects, or anything foreign.

☐   13. Is quick to anger or has been described as having a very short fuse.

☐   14. Is jealous with little or no justification.

☐   15. Is distrustful of others, particularly foreigners or minorities.

☐   16. Seems to have a high degree of anxiety in her life.

☐   17. Feels a need to be guarded, secretive, devious, and scheming, or thinks others around him are that way.

☐   18. Is reluctant or unwilling to entertain alternative views; readily dismisses them.

☐   19. Thinks jokes have hidden meanings that are aimed against her.

☐   20. Is unbending in thoughts and ideas—stubbornly holds on to beliefs.

☐   21. Seems to know a lot about very little, arguing arcane information of little interest to anyone else.

☐   22. Thinks he is very logical but in fact his logic is at times faulty or skewed.

☐   23. Argues frequently or provokes arguments with regularity.

☐   24. Exaggerates and personalizes difficulties.

☐ 25. Sees herself as a victim of one or more of these things: life, society, government, family, workers, conspiracies, cabals, etc.

☐ 26. Intentionally collects and hangs on to social slights, incidents of forgetfulness, or wrongs.

☐ 27. Has a reputation for making a mountain out of a molehill, always thinking the worst, or blowing things way out of proportion.

☐ 28. Has an inability to relax and seems constantly guarded, almost always serious, lacking in humor.

☐ 29. Lacks tender passion or softness; everything is tension producing and threatening.

☐ 30. Is constantly hostile, stubborn, or defensive.

☐ 31. Is envious of power and seeks to achieve it through shortcuts, cheating, or illegal schemes.

☐ 32. Is incapable of having anything nice to say about others.

☐ 33. Is reluctant to confide in others or reveal things about herself.

☐ 34. Space is a big issue—doesn't like it if you get or stand too close.

☐ 35. Doesn't like it when people look at his house or his car and tends to lash out at them.

☐ 36. Communications all too often are full of anger or hatred toward authority figures.

☐ 37. Even at a great distance, has the same reaction as you might if someone stood too close to you.

☐ 38. Wears or displays ornaments, tattoos, signs, or other emblems (e.g., bumper stickers) that indicate hatred or fear of others.

☐ 39. Seems to be always guarded as to what she is doing or contemplating.

☐ 40. Has very few friends or none at all.

☐ 41. Constantly looks for signs that others are conspiring or planning something against him.

☐ 42. Acts, behaves, or is referred to as being eccentric or odd.

☐ 43. Feels that institutions (government, IRS, work, church, school, employer) are seeking to do him ill or keep him down.

☐ 44. Claims that past failings at work or in relationships have been the fault of others.

☐ 45. Claims to have perfect recall of events and uses them to argue—yet those recollections are often faulty or biased.

☐ 46. Thoughts, beliefs, and prejudices are rigid and inflexible—becomes truculent when challenged.

☐ 47. Has belonged or currently belongs to a hate group or to an organization that is intolerant of others.

☐ 48. Criticizes the promotion of others at work as being the work of a cabal or a conspiracy or done to perpetually punish or keep him down.

☐ 49. Has a pervasive suspiciousness of others—even of those she knows.

☐ 50. Is excessively self-important or believes he is infallible.

☐ 51. Has found ways to isolate from others, be it at school, at work, or even in a big city—is considered a loner.

☐ 52. Strongly believes that others will eventually disappoint or take advantage of him, and so he is always guarded.

☐ 53. Even when others are kind, suspects that in time their "true face" or feelings will show.

☐ 54. Refuses to let children attend school—fears they will be adversely influenced or "polluted."

☐ 55. Seems to have an unrelenting level of anxiety or apprehension in her life.

☐ 56. Tries to control what others think.

☐ 57. Has a generalized anxious feeling of pending doom, or destruction, or that some sort of harm will come.

☐ 58. Seems to view the world in general as being untrust-worthy—full of deceit.

☐ 59. Avoids going to the doctor because of distrust of physicians, medical equipment, or the medical profession in general.

☐ 60. Is intolerant of others' opinions.

☐ 61. Spouse or family is concerned when he goes out because they never know if he will argue or cause a scene.

☐ 62. Has repeatedly gotten into arguments with superiors.

☐ 63. Feels that the school, school system, or teacher(s) has it in for him or his children.

☐ 64. Seems to have little respect for superiors and thinks of herself as better than they are.

☐ 65. Brings up different events from history to point out how things are conspiring against her or others.

☐ 66. Prefers that others stand at a greater than normal distance when they talk to him, and if they violate that space, gets very anxious, irritable, or angry.

☐ 67. Has purchased a weapon or keeps a weapon nearby because he fears someone or a group is coming after him.

☐ 68. Has had multiple run-ins with the law.

☐ 69. Is distrustful of strangers even when seeking them out.

☐ 70. Literally rates people by how trustworthy they are.

☐ 71. Has a fear of institutions, technology, scientists, food, or some other unspecified entity or organization.

☐ 72. Collects articles, clippings, pictures, or license plate numbers of or about individuals or institutions that are conspiring against her or that she distrusts.

☐ 73. Is a known user of cocaine, amphetamine, "speed," or methamphetamine.

☐ 74. Thinks telephone calls are intercepted or the room is bugged with microphones.

☐ 75. Feels that doctors do more harm than good or distrusts modern medicine or pharmaceutical companies.

☐ 76. Believes himself to be above the law or a "sovereign citizen" and that he doesn't have to pay taxes or even have a driver's license or license plate to drive.

☐ 77. Has a need to control family members very strictly.

☐ 78. Goes into a fit of rage when people accidentally trespass on his property.

☐ 79. Routinely sticks nose into other people's business, especially of family members.

☐ 80. Seeks to control the opinions of others, insisting they see things her way.

☐ 81. Often has an unrelenting one-track mind about this or that issue.

☐ 82. Has threatened a spouse or significant other for revealing personal information about him.

☐ 83. Conducts what he calls "emergency," "immediate reaction," or "bug out" drills as preparation for dealing with threats, the "end days," or some other apocalyptic event.

☐ 84. Forbids family members to talk to outsiders, even the mail carrier.

☐ 85. Gets upset when family members spend too much time talking to friends on the phone.

☐ 86. Has obtained a weapon or made an explosive device to punish or get back at others.

☐ 87. Is highly moralistic and judgmental.

☐ 88. When spouse or kids come home, they are questioned as to where they've been and about their activities and are required to provide a full accounting of their activities.

☐ 89. Cell phones of family members are routinely examined to see telephone activity.

☐ 90. Has stalked or placed a tracking device on the spouse's vehicle.

☐ 91. Has called (redialed) numbers or made queries to determine who has called and the purpose of the calls.

☐ 92. Refuses to give family members access to cell phones, computers, or other electronic devices so that they cannot communicate with outsiders or to avoid "evil" influences.

☐ 93. Becomes very upset when you challenge or ridicule her ideas, thinking, logic, or examples.

☐ 94. Has called others fools and naïve for not seeing the threats that he sees.

☐ 95. Has curbed or restricted the activities of family members (spouse, children) so as not to be influenced by outsiders, disbelievers, or those who think differently.

☐ 96. Only she has a clear understanding of the threats that are out there.

☐ 97. Tends to be demanding and arrogant.

☐ 98. Has been fired for arguing with workmates or boss.

☐ 99. Is highly moralistic and sees the world as white or black— there is no gray area, no flexibility in thinking.

☐ 100. Tends to be unromantic, lacking tenderness or empathy in his interpersonal relations.

☐ 101. Has been taken advantage of by someone who purportedly believes similarly.

☐ 102. Is inconsiderate of others or is considered rude.

☐ 103. Fears that physicians will use his body for experiments or implant his body with some sort of device.

☐ 104. Continually pursues reinforcement of beliefs or fears through reading, radio, Internet, or other means.

☐ 105. Spouse or loved ones often have to act as buffers with others or have to apologize for his actions or behaviors.

☐ 106. Has talked in ways to frighten others repeatedly or to make others fear for their safety.

☐ 107. Has killed or tried to poison dogs or cats that have accidentally crossed onto his property.

☐ 108. Frequently complains to city officials about minor grievances.

☐ 109. Perceives people in social and personal relationships to be either with him or against him.

☐ 110. Has alienated at least one family member because of her beliefs or because of unrelenting need to argue, accuse, or challenge.

☐ 111. Writes letters, e-mails, or other forms of communication that are always attacking something.

☐ 112. Thinks helicopters or airplanes are following her.

☐ 113. Seeks to find other individuals who are also suspicious and distrustful.

☐ 114. Has expressed that he "trusts no one" but himself.

☐ 115. Doesn't like people standing behind her—this causes her to become irritable, nervous, or visibly uncomfortable.

☐ 116. Prefers only the company of those who agree with his odd, peculiar, extremist, or eccentric ideas.

☐ 117. Never seems to be happy—all too often is on edge or irritated.

☐ 118. Has the appearance of someone who is always troubled by something.

☐ 119. Keeps a secret place in the house or at work where no one is allowed.

☐ 120. Has talked about or actually moved out into the country, away from others, expressing mistrust about having people close by.

☐ 121. Has joined or looked into a group, organization, or cult that believes as he does.

☐ 122. Lacks any interest in art or music except in what supports her thinking.

☐ 123. Routinely drills with weapons to make sure he is ready to deal with any threat.

☐ 124. When he hears or sees vehicles, he hurries to examine them or even keeps a list of cars he routinely sees that he claims are conducting surveillance.

☐ 125. Actually keeps a list of enemies or those she deems suspicious.

☐ 126. Has gone out at night or at odd times to conduct reconnaissance to check on neighbors or someone he deems suspicious or a threat.

☐ 127. Seems to be unsettled, always on the move; can't hold a job for very long.

☐ 128. Has a constant looming fear of a major catastrophic or apocalyptic event.

☐ 129. Is known to others as a complainer, instigator, or malcontent.

☐ 130. Has been rejected by others for being odd, eccentric, or stubborn.

SCORING

☑ Count how many statements apply to this individual based on the criteria discussed at the beginning of this checklist.

☑ If you find that this individual has 20 to 25 of these features, this is a person who will occasionally take an emotional toll on others and may be difficult to live or work with.

☑ If the score is 26 to 60, this indicates that the individual has all the features of and behaves as a paranoid personality. This person needs help and will cause turmoil in the life of anyone close to him or her.

☑   If the score is above 60, this person has a preponderance of the major features of a paranoid personality and is an emotional, psychological, financial, or physical danger to you or others, even to him- or herself.

IMMEDIATE ACTIONS

If you're involved with an individual like this who meets the preponderance of the criteria for a paranoid personality, you have a tough road ahead. When the features of such individuals are mild, they will wear on you because they question everything and are suspicious and untrusting of others, including you. Over time, they can become even more suspicious, more stubborn, more single-minded, and more rigid in their thinking. That is a challenge for any long-term relationship or for a family.

If they're at the more extreme or toxic end of the spectrum, they can be very difficult, argumentative, hypersuspicious, or just plain dangerous. The problem is, no one can predict their reactions nor what will trigger rage or violence on their part. What we do know is that the more features of paranoia they have, the greater their instability and danger. And, of course, they can become radicalized extremists, bringing danger to others and themselves, much as "Unabomber" Ted Kaczynski did.

Trying to convince, persuade, or argue with them is usually nonproductive and, in fact, may backfire, as you may be seen as the enemy for disagreeing with them or not seeing things with their unique or special clarity.

Trying to get them professional help may not be easy, either. No matter where they are on the spectrum, low or high, they don't think anything is wrong with them, which is why these individuals rarely seek help. That alone is a tough or an impossible hurdle to overcome.

You can try to get them some professional help, if they'll go, but please be very careful. Because these personalities are suspicious of others and are perennial wound collectors, your efforts may turn them against you, making them more suspicious of you or propelling them to violence.

At work, these individuals may be aggravating because they question everything. They can create problems among colleagues and drive wedges in an otherwise collegial work environment. Frankly, most bosses get tired of having to explain or justify decisions or hear their complaints, so they marginalize them.

There's no doubt that having a paranoid personality in the workplace is a liability, not just from the divisiveness they sow but also because of how they may lash out at perceived slights. Individuals who score high on the paranoid personality checklist need to be monitored for signs of aggression, especially if they're reprimanded, cautioned, or demoted, but particularly if they're fired.

In situations where the spouse of an employee has all the features of the paranoid personality, there's also the danger that a domestic dispute, jealousy, or paranoid ideation may expose people at work to danger that had origins at home. When I read about an ex-husband coming to his ex-wife's workplace to shoot her and everyone else in sight, I have to wonder, yet again, if this was the work of an acutely troubled paranoid personality.

If you are in an industry against which activists have made threats or that has been targeted by extremists (abortion clinic, medical research, chemical industry, animal research, timber industry, construction, atomic energy, coal production, electrical grid, plastics, to name a few), you may become the focus of a paranoid personality; thus the potential for danger or violence is much higher.

Care needs to be taken when dealing with the paranoid personality at home or at work, especially if there are indications that the individual has a history of violence or weapons use. Since we can't predict what will trigger someone's violent behavior, all we can do is look at past behaviors, where they reside on the Dangerous Personalities Checklist, if there have been recent stressors (divorce, relationship breakup, demotions, job loss, increased drug or alcohol use, etc.), and the presence of weapons in the person's life. If these things are all present, it makes for a very dangerous mixture. Just remember the story of Jimmy Lee Dykes mentioned earlier—his neighbors' experiences, the killing of a bus driver, the abduction of a child from a school bus, barricading himself with the child in his bunker—all because this paranoid personality received a summons.

While history is replete with examples of those who fit the criteria of the paranoid personality who did great harm, most of the harm these individuals do is on an interpersonal level at home or at work. Nevertheless, we have a responsibility to warn others if we have confirmed that this person has a majority of the features of a paranoid personality—we may just spare them a lot of pain and agony.

If you encounter these individuals, recognize what they are first and foremost. Don't try to argue with or convince them. If they appear dangerous in any way, or if they ask you to assist in committing dangerous or criminal acts, the best action is to get away and warn others if possible.

If their behavior becomes too much for you to bear—if it's too taxing or too dehumanizing (this happens a lot in cults) or if they drain the happiness out of your life—then distance yourself. You don't have to suffer needlessly. If you decide to stay, you now have been forewarned of what you can expect, so don't be surprised if things don't get better. Don't end up like the wife of Colonel Frank Fitts in the movie *American Beauty* or, for that matter, like my neighbor's wife in Miami: empty, resigned, joyless.

But be careful, because if these individuals self-isolate, isolate you, become convinced that there are no alternatives left, or become radicalized, they can become extremely violent. For additional strategies, see Chapter 6, Self-Defense against Dangerous Personalities.

CHAPTER 4

"WHAT'S MINE IS MINE—AND WHAT'S YOURS IS MINE"

THE PREDATOR

THE EYES FIXED ON MINE were unblinking, reptilian, and utterly calm. As I stared back, I heard a faint rattle that spoke to me of danger.

I was nowhere near a snake. I was a young police officer in the 1970s, standing in a hallway where I'd just arrested a burglar who had set off an alarm. He obeyed my commands, and I was able to handcuff him without incident. But I'm not ashamed to say that even though I'm 6 foot 1 and the suspect was secured, as he stared at me, I shook. There was something about that look that was unlike any I'd seen before. The sounds I heard were the bullets rattling in my service revolver as my brain and body instinctively recognized that I was in the presence of a human predator. When I checked his criminal record back at the office, it was all there: This man was a recently released convict who was a hardened criminal with a long track record of burglaries, robberies, and assault.

You can tell someone about evil; you can make scary movies; you can write about dangerous personalities. But until you're in the presence of evil, you don't really know it—not at a deep psychological level. That was what I experienced that day. It was a lesson I never forgot. My subconscious brain was warning me that this was not your average criminal. It was a lesson I later grew to appreciate—the effect predators have on us on a subconscious level.[1]

At some point in life, everyone reading this book will encounter someone like this: a person not bothered by being arrested or by committing a crime, who seems untroubled by the suffering they cause others. Of all the dangerous personalities, the predator causes the most harm. According to the renowned psychologist and psychopathy researcher Robert Hare, PhD, there are millions of these individuals out there.[2] This is why there's every reason to think you have been, are, or will be in contact with one at some point in your life.

Predators really have only one goal: exploitation. They do what we can't imagine, easily and repeatedly. They live to plunder, rob, victimize, or destroy. While most of us build our lives around relationships and achievements, predators focus on opportunities to use people, places, and situations for their own gain. This default setting governs much of their behavior.

These individuals don't think as we do. We care about others. They pretend to care or simply don't. We see each other as equals. They see us either as opportunities or as obstacles in fulfilling their needs. If they need a car, they steal one. If they need sex, they rape you. If they need money, they go after your grandparents' bank account. If you survive one of these individuals, a part of you still dies—be it trust, self-worth, dignity, or faith in others.

Our trusting nature puts us at a disadvantage with these personalities, as they're unfettered by emotional attachments, conscience, morals, laws, or ethics. For them, life has no stop signs. Rules, regulations, restrictions, locks, or fences are mere inconveniences to work around. And because you and I play by the rules, they view us as saps, losers, or objects of contempt, worthy of devaluation, derision, abuse, and perhaps elimination.

Thus while we engage in honest work to become successful, predators measure their success by how well they've exploited us. Exquisitely skilled at detecting weaknesses, they target the vulnerable, the injured, the struggling, the gullible, the susceptible, the young, or those who can't fight back. Then they pounce—sometimes with subtlety, at other times with feral ferocity.

Just from how someone moves or even looks, the predator knows whom to target. They select the helpful pedestrian who can be lured toward a car to give directions, the shopper laden with heavy packages, the child too trusting of an adult stranger, the lone teenager taking a shortcut, the naïve elderly couple, the homeowner who willingly opens her door. All this they can do without thinking about it; it's like software running constantly in the background, scanning for opportunities and weaknesses.

They know which chat rooms to enter to lure your child into their grip without breaking into your home. They know how to scam Medicare and Medicaid, costing us billions in fraud. They know which banks are easiest to rob and which stores are easy to shoplift from. They know how to hide in prestigious organizations—perhaps a hospital, a charitable organization, a police department, a school, an athletic program, or a church—aware that occupational legitimacy confers both access and cover for their predation.

Predators such as Ted Bundy, John Wayne Gacy, and Jeffrey Dahmer stand out because of their notoriety as serial killers, but such monsters are only a very small part of the picture.

Every serial rapist, pimp, pedophile, trafficker in humans, and mobster is a predator. So are those who target the elderly or children for abuse. Some we read about; some are so famous or notorious that they're immortalized in books and in the movies. Bank robber Jesse James, Butch Cassidy, Jack the Ripper, John Dillinger, Al Capone, Pablo Escobar, Ian Brady, James "Whitey" Bulger Jr., and the "Dapper Don" John Gotti are all predators. The only difference is their particular preference for exploitation or criminal behavior.

While prisons are full of these individuals, far more walk the streets. You don't have to be killed or raped to be severely harmed by predators. They beat their spouses, abuse patients, terrorize employees, embezzle money, prey on the faithful, corrupt public office, or, as heads of state, exterminate their own people. They carry briefcases, laptops, backpacks, Bibles, soccer balls, and babies. But they also carry knives, guns, machetes, ice picks, poison, and ropes. They may be your boss, your religious leader, your cube mate, your financial advisor, your child's camp counselor, your mother's caregiver, your babysitter, the next person you welcome into your bedroom, or your next-door neighbor.

George J. Trepal, a member of the high IQ society Mensa and a chemist by training, wasn't fond of his neighbor Peggy Carr or of her kids, who like most kids made noise when they played outside. So in 1988, he poisoned Peggy with cold indifference and nearly killed her children by placing thallium in Coke bottles while they were away. For a predator, apparently, this is a legitimate quick fix to a problem.

In 1978, near Quartzite, Arizona, John Lyons stopped the family car to help stranded motorists Gary Tison and Randy Greenawalt. They rewarded his good Samaritan generosity by killing him and his family. Why? Like Trepal, they needed a quick and efficient fix for their problem; after all, they had just escaped from prison, and they didn't want to be found.

The patients of Dr. Harold Shipman in Hyde, England, thought they were in a safe place in the hospital—the best place to be if you're seriously ill—but not if you were one of Dr. Shipman's patients. Between 1971 and 1998, he killed in excess of 200 of his patients, enriching himself by taking their jewelry and money or fraudulently naming himself in their wills.

For 2 decades, it was thought that Tim and Waneta Hoyt were an unlucky couple whose children had died from sudden infant death syndrome (SIDS)—until investigators looked closely and found Waneta was intentionally killing them one by one.[3] Those children, like Dr. Shipman's patients, were in a safe place, but not with a safe person—they were with a predator. They died simply because she did not want to deal with their crying, so she suffocated them, one at a time, usually within months of their birth.

As we can see, it's not the location (neighborhood, highway, hospital, or home) that makes us safe so much as whether or not there's a predator lurking nearby. It is these individuals' presence or access to you and their intrinsic callousness that increases your risk of being victimized. The outcome—whether or not someone will be tormented or victimized; live or die—is up to them.

This was a lesson learned by true crime writer Ann Rule, who worked at a crisis hotline in the 1970s and later wrote a fascinating book about working next to someone who, it turned out, was a predator—and not just any predator, but the infamous serial killer Ted Bundy. The only reason she lived to write *The Stranger Beside Me* is that he didn't target her.

When you think of predators, picture a hurricane or tornado—a massive force that can leave a giant debris field of human suffering behind. For every person this individual harms directly, many are harmed indirectly: Every relative, spouse, child, and friend of every victim suffers. Children abused by a predator may grow up to be traumatized adults or abusers themselves, and other generations may follow. The predator's family and friends can suffer public shame, scorn, or financial distress. Bernard Madoff's wife has been ridiculed, spat on, and ostracized as a result of his conviction for scamming investors of billions. Two years after Madoff's arrest, his son Mark hanged himself—he could not live with the "torment" of what his father had done and how he might be implicated.[4]

Look at how many have lost their faith in the Catholic Church because of the massive scandal of sexual predators cloaked in vestments. Neighborhoods haunted by predators become danger zones where people have to barricade themselves in their own homes because of muggings, robberies, and burglaries. New York City is considerably safer now than when I was stationed there in the early 1980s because Mayor Rudolph Giuliani and the New York City Police Department began to target predators at every level. Once predators were removed—even those involved in quality-of-life offenses such as aggressive panhandling or graffiti—honest citizens took back the streets.

I wish I could say there isn't a predator in your present or future, yet chances are there is or will be. But with a little knowledge, you stand a better chance of identifying these dangerous personalities who callously determine our future without our consent. I say this not to scare you but to make you aware—because they are certainly aware of you. Survival means knowing what they're like and how they behave so we can avoid them.

THE WAY OF THE PREDATOR

Predators can be nuanced and hard to detect if you don't know what to look for. They can be intelligent, friendly, attractive, quiet, reclusive, delinquent, or any of a number of other characteristics. Being successful, having friends, or holding a status position doesn't preclude someone from being a predator—a lesson that Penn State faculty, athletes, alumni, and students learned from Jerry Sandusky's multiple convictions for sexually abusing children, and that Bernie Madoff's friends and colleagues learned following his colossal swindle scheme.

These individuals are persistently calculating, manipulative, and aggressively predatory. When you read about someone who meticulously planned and executed a crime, who stalked and staked out his victim, who's been committing criminal acts for a long time, who traveled distances to achieve an illicit endeavor, or who's constructed elaborate Ponzi schemes, you're reading about predators. Similarly, when you hear of someone who's always in trouble with the law, is a serial sex offender, a recidivist, or someone who is scheming to cheat others of their money, you're hearing about a predator.

Expect predators to frequently change jobs, change plans, fail to repay loans, ruin or end relationships, disappoint or take advantage of others, and shirk responsibilities. Expect them to break laws, betray trust, take what isn't theirs, and leave others pained, victimized, maimed, or even dead. Expect it. Don't read this chapter and think someone like this will get better or won't harm you. We know they'll do harm. What we can't predict is whom or what they'll target.

Predators often have superficial knowledge of many topics, which they use to impress or ensnare their victims. They love controlling people like puppets: charming children with toys and candy, luring women online to meet, getting young girls or boys to "help" them, or manipulating people to part with their money. They're expert at getting others to have confidence in them, which is why we call them con men.

Like the other dangerous personalities in this book, the predator's behavior exists on a continuum or spectrum. Some start and stay at the low end: They do risky things, perhaps habitually breaking rules and regulations. They may be deceitful in their dealings with others. Or they may be in frequent trouble with the law for petty crimes.

Then there are those who are so pathological, so off the scale, that there's nothing they won't try or do, so long as it pleases them. John Edward Robinson is a renaissance man, if you will; a true entrepreneur of predation: a convicted con man, embezzler, forger, kidnapper, and sadistic serial killer, convicted in Kansas in 2003 of three murders. He's considered the first serial killer to use the Internet to lure his victims so he could sadomasochistically kill them. He's an example of the extreme predator—a polymath of sorts and a truly dangerous personality.

These are the extreme predators we read or hear about, but for the most part, predators go unnoticed because they're successful at what they do or simply because they don't get reported. But no matter where they are on the continuum or scale, low end or the high end, one trait they share with us is that they can learn from their mistakes and experiences and become emboldened to do even more. A case in point is Julian (I have changed his name), whose behavior I was able to track because his mother was a friend of my family.

Julian began, as far as we can tell, by taking money from his parents even before he was a teenager. In time, the amounts became larger and the thefts more frequent. His parents would confront him, he'd apologize, and he'd repeat the behavior each time slightly more proficiently. To avoid his parents' attention, he began to steal from his friends and playmates as well as from their parents.

As Julian got older, he pilfered bottles of wine and vodka. Prescription medications never seemed to last, disappearing completely, and at least once were replaced by aspirin. Accusations of theft were always met with ever more clever denials. His parents admittedly ignored his acts, were too accepting of his denials, bought into his explanations, or simply didn't want to be too accusatory; by their own account, they believed he'd outgrow these behaviors.

Julian got into all sorts of scrapes with the police once he learned to drive. The car repeatedly was scratched and dented. One day, it came home without a fender. About an hour later, the police showed up. There'd been a hit-and-run accident with injuries. Of course, Julian denied it. That would be his first felony. There would be others, but they seemed always to be pled down to misdemeanors.

By age 21, Julian had mastered how to extract money from his parents' bank account using forged checks or the ATM. He continued to steal ever-larger amounts, and as his parents got older, they were less challenging and in some ways more permissive—or maybe they were worn out by a son who was a predator, a thief, a liar, a con man, a drug user, and a danger to them as well as to society.

The final straw came when Julian stole his father's car and sold it for parts. Just like that. That same week, he took the last money they had in the house, claiming it must have been "eaten by rodents," since it was hidden in the rafters. My parents tell me that Julian's father was physically and psychologically tormented and depressed by all of this and a few months later died a "broken" man. I'm told that at the funeral Julian wanted to know if he could have his father's watch so he could pawn it and whether there was "any money left in the will."

Where does this story end? Not here. Julian was able to coerce his mother to give him access to her remaining retirement account and cleaned her out. In her early seventies, she was forced to go back to work—no retirement savings and no house (that had to be foreclosed), as there had been "other things" that he had done.

Talk about a debris field of human suffering. Julian hasn't killed anybody directly that I know of, but the suffering he's caused is significant to at least one family. He's been investigated many times but always escapes punishment. He's changed his criminal acts over time, but the result is always the same: He charmingly lies, cheats, and steals or lives parasitically off the hard work of others. If you run into him, he'll have a smile for you. And why not? Others have sacrificed their lives for him. Maybe you will, too.

So while predators may differ in scope, scale, and specifics, they all share some commonalities: They take but don't give, they put others at risk, they are callous and contemptuous, and they lack concern for others, even loved ones.

No Empathy, No Remorse, No Conscience

Watch a video of Dennis Rader, the BTK ("bind, torture, kill") serial killer, and listen to him talk about how he killed his victims. What you will notice is what psychologists call his flat affect. That cold, matter-of-fact quality of words and expression is seen in some predators, even when recounting their horrific crimes.

Predators don't feel emotion in the normal way. They don't understand others' suffering. Empathy is beyond them. Their emotions are usually superficial or contrived and self-serving. As Julian's example shows, they can victimize people who love, protect, and give to them. Our innocence or misfortune is their opportunity. An unhappy divorcée or grieving widow is a meal ticket. A trusting or unattended child is a sex toy to be lured with food and trinkets. Tourists and immigrants are easy targets for theft or protection money. Anyone who is naïve or in difficulty is wearing a "use me" sign. A natural disaster is an excuse to set up bogus donation sites. The list is endless.

These personalities know right from wrong and know what evil is, but they do it anyway. Case in point: Austrian Josef Fritzl placed his 18-year-old daughter in his cellar, where he imprisoned her for 24 years, raping her more than 3,000 times, fathering seven children, and never once taking her or the children to the doctor. He reportedly told a psychiatrist: "I simply have an evil streak."[5] Josef Fritzl knew what he was doing was wrong, and he had more than 8,000 days to stop his evil acts.[6] He simply chose not to.

If predators feel guilt, it's transitory and noninhibitive: It won't stop them, because they don't learn from the suffering they cause—they have no remorse. Feeling guilt requires accepting responsibility for one's actions. But predators live to take advantage, not to take responsibility, preferring to blame their upbringing, bad bosses, bad luck, pornography, or anything or anyone to get off the hook—including even the victim. Jodi Arias blamed her boyfriend for driving her to stalk him, call him habitually, seek him out, stab him repeatedly, shoot him, and nearly cut off his head. It just couldn't be because she's an unstable, selfish predator who couldn't face abandonment. No, it had to be, as is often the case with predators, the victim's fault. Fortunately, the jury didn't buy her lies.

Cold, Callous, Calculating, Controlling

Predators are coldly indifferent. It's why we liken them to reptiles and why so often at trial they seem impervious to emotions, in stark contrast to the grieving family of the victim. Notorious serial killer Henry Lee Lucas captured it this way: "Killing someone is just like walking outdoors. If I wanted a victim, I'd just go and get one." Only predators think this way.

For them, life's a game of "how much can I get away with?" So they plot and deceive. In the 1970s, John Wayne Gacy was involved in community politics and dressed up as "Pogo the Clown" to entertain neighborhood children not far from Chicago, but he also cunningly seduced boys into his home so he could sadomasochistically kill them—33, in fact. They'd plead for their lives, and he'd callously exterminate them.[7]

Harold Shipman, the well-loved and respected doctor in Hyde, England, mentioned earlier, hid his predation for decades—cool as a cucumber. For his own financial gain, he was callously killing those who needed his help the most. It was only when too many of his patients died that the truth came out; otherwise, he would have kept going. His criminal activity was not affecting him in the least; in fact, he was getting almost blasé about it.

Out of necessity, then, the predator lives by the calculated lie. While we use words to communicate, they use words to manipulate, compel, and connive. They know the phrases of pleasantry, persuasion, seduction, appeal, and apology as a craftsman knows his tools or the musician her notes. Promises to never cheat, steal, or hit again are empty. Their word is worthless, yet so many of us, even professionals such as law enforcement officers and judges, are bamboozled by them, persuaded by social convention to give them another chance. This is one reason recidivism rates are so high; predators lie to get out of prison promising to behave, and then they go right back to committing crimes.

Jack Henry Abbott, in prison for forgery and for stabbing a fellow inmate to death, became the darling of the writing glitterati when he wrote about his experiences being incarcerated (*In the Belly of the Beast: Letters from Prison*). He persuaded acclaimed writer Norman Mailer to argue for his early release. The parole board was convinced by Mailer's pleadings and acquiesced. Six weeks into his parole, Abbott stabbed a man to death at a café because, as he later said, the man "stared" at him for too long. All those who had advocated for Abbott's early release were shocked that someone so masterful with words could also kill. They shouldn't have been.

Words coupled with acts of kindness can be very appealing. Jerry Sandusky used this combination and an ever-ready smile to trap his victims. But when he was forcing his penis inside the anus of children (yes, that's the reality of what this venerated coach/predator did to his victims), he did so with callous disregard for the sanctity of those children.

Predators also know the words that intimidate. One word from notorious thugs John Gotti or James "Whitey" Bulger Jr. was enough to get people to pay them protection money or be killed. While in the FBI, I interviewed a "made" guy for the mob, and he related that to get protection money, they'd simply have a "conversation" with a store owner; otherwise, "who knows," expensive store windows might break overnight. Such little chats aren't just the stuff of the TV show *The Sopranos*—they fuel a multimillion-dollar extortion industry.

Even from death row, Ted Bundy manipulated investigators by holding out on revealing the names of all his victims. Just hours before execution, he released the name of one more as a ploy for a reprieve (no reprieve was given; he'd toyed long enough with the justice system). The name of the victim he identified was Sue Curtis, the young woman I mentioned in the Introduction who was abducted at Brigham Young University while I was on duty that tragic night.

Serial killer Clifford Robert Olson Jr. manipulated the Canadian government into paying him $10,000 per victim in return for identifying them and where he'd buried them. His wife received $100,000 as a result of his cooperation. He was gracious enough to throw in the 11th victim for free.[8] Such a gentleman.

One of the most notorious predators in history was Hermann Göring, field marshal and the second-highest ranking member of the Nazi party. Göring had helped to set up the Gestapo, and when he wasn't busy bombing London, he was stealing artwork and other property from Jews being sent to their deaths. After World War II ended, while he was in custody of the allied powers and awaiting trial by the Nuremberg court for war crimes, he repeatedly manipulated his American captors. In exchange for favors, he would sign autographs or have his picture taken. Most odiously, he manipulated at least one of his American captors into retrieving from his personal luggage a vial of poison that he then used to kill himself before his sentence (death by hanging) could be carried out—thus denying the court and millions of victims due justice.[9]

But this isn't just about pulling strings or manipulating others. It is worse. For many predators, it's about the godlike ability to have power over others, which can be intoxicating. Ted Bundy talked about feeling omnipotent, being able to decide who would live or die. Israel Keyes, who hid "kill kits" around the country filled with weapons and supplies to facilitate his crimes and who authorities think may have killed as many as 11 victims from Alaska to Vermont between 2001 and 2012, preferred to strangle his victims bare-handed so that he could enjoy watching them suffer as they died up close, eye to eye, in his self-appointed role as the final arbiter over their life.[10]

But their coldness is best exemplified by Charles Ng, who, on video-tape sometime in the 1980s, can be seen tormenting one of the women he and Leonard Lake killed in a home-built dungeon by telling her, "You can cry and stuff, like the rest of them, but it won't do any good. We are pretty—ha, ha—cold-hearted, so to speak."[11]

Many Urges, Few Controls, No Reflection

While these personalities like to control others, they themselves have no moral or ethical controls and can also be impulsive, adventure-seeking risk-takers. Clyde Chestnut Barrow, of Bonnie and Clyde fame, was just like that: a reckless thrill-seeker who became a bank robber and a murderer. Many modern bank robbers and serial shoplifters exhibit that lack of con-trols, as do street muggers. There's the thrill of the act, coupled with the attractive material reward—the very definition of a good day for a predator.

For many predators, acting on urges seems to dominate their lives, even when it means placing themselves or other people in danger. For example, Nushawn Williams was convicted of knowingly and intentionally infecting at least 13 women with the HIV virus. A career criminal also charged with rape, according to the courts, he intentionally jeopardized the lives of others just as surely as if he'd put a gun to their heads and played Russian roulette. Similarly, Anthony E. Whitfield, according to his own attorney, was a "methamphetamine-addicted 'sex machine' who bounced between women for shelter, money, and sex." He infected 17 women with the HIV virus before he was caught, with no apology or remorse—seemingly out of control.

Much like narcissists, predators may be highly reactive to the slightest provocation or perceived insult. They often lack any kind of inhibition or self-control. In prison, predators will avoid even looking at each other, knowing full well that an aggressive look in the hallway is enough to ignite an altercation or a lethal retribution.

As I write this, I'm reminded of Joe Pesci's memorable portrayal of Tommy DeVito in the film *Goodfellas*—temperamental, hypersensitive to slights, unforgiving, and with no conscience. Only in the movies, you say? No, there are real people like that. Richard Leonard "The Iceman" Kuklinski had a bad temper and took no prisoners when it came to insults. That's why the mob hired him as a contract killer. He told authorities after his arrest that he lost count of how many he had murdered; there were perhaps as many as 200 victims. He killed first—asked questions later. The real-life actions of predators are often worse than their movie portrayals. In this case, Kuklinski put the fictional Tommy DeVito to shame.

Predators frequently abuse alcohol and other illegal substances, which tend to make them more unstable, less inhibited, and more dangerous. Or they use alcohol and drugs to intentionally lower their own inhibitions or to seduce others. I examined numerous cases while in the FBI of stepfathers or even fathers using alcohol or drugs on underage young women, including their own daughters, to rape them. John Wayne Gacy was known to use alcohol to render his victims more pliant, especially just before he raped and sadistically killed them.

While predators are often driven by urges or say they couldn't help themselves, there's no excuse for what they do. If they engage in any kind of self-evaluation, it's to perfect their methods of predation. Don't ever expect them to introspectively ponder how to change for the better. They won't.

THEIR EFFECT ON YOU

Expect predators to turn your life upside down and derail your dreams or aspirations, as they come first and don't like people to get in their way. You may initially find them intelligent, charming, and interesting, but when

Words That Describe
THE PREDATOR

Here are the uncensored words of the victims. Notice how similar some words are to those describing the narcissistic personality (see Chapter 1): Abnormal, abusive, aggressive, aimless, amoral, animal, antisocial, arrogant, articulate, bad, badass, bad boy, barbaric, bastard, beast, beguiling, belittling, belligerent, bewildering, biker, black widow, boorish, bullshitter, bully, calculating, callous, charismatic, charming, cheat, cheater, clever, cold, cold blooded, con, con artist, con man, conniving, contemptuous, controlling, corrupt, corrupting, creep, creepy, criminal, crude, cruel, cunning, dangerous, deceitful, deceptive, degenerate, delinquent, demeaning, depraved, deranged, destructive, devilish, dick, discomforting, discordant, disgusting, dishonest, disingenuous, disruptive, domineering, egocentric, electrifying, empty, evil, exploitive, fire setter, forger, fraud, gangster, gigolo, glib, Godless, grandiose, grifter, guiltless, hasty, heartless, hellish, horrible, hostile, hustler, immoral, imposter, impulsive, incompatible, inconsiderate, incorrigible, indecent, indifferent, infidelity, inhuman, inhumane, insane, insatiable, insensitive, insincerity, intense, interesting, intimidating, irresponsible, irritable, irritating, killer, kleptomaniac, larcenous, lawbreaker, lecherous, leech, liar, loveless, Machiavellian, malevolent, manipulative, mean, mercurial, mesmerizing, mobster, monster, moody, mortifying, narcissistic, nomadic, notorious, noxious, nuisance, odd, parasite, parasitic, pedophile, perverted, picky, pimp, player, possessive, predator, predatory, prick, prickly, promiscuous, puppeteer, quick, rapist, risk-taker, robber, rubbish, rude, ruinous, sadist, sadistic, sarcastic, savage, scary, seducer, seductive, seductress, self-centered, selfish, shallow, shifty, shit, sleazy, smooth, superficial, swindler, tactless, temperamental, thief, thrill-seeker, thug, toxic, twisted, two-faced, tyrant, uncaring, undependable, unfeeling, unfettered, uninvolved, unreliable, unscrupulous, unsympathetic, untrustworthy, vandal, vile, vindictive, violent, volatile, vulgar, wicked, wild, witty.

you discover what they've done—or when they turn on you, which can happen at any moment—the shock and pain are indescribable.

They'll exhaust you because you must always be on guard, hiding what you treasure, trying to not antagonize, or struggling to survive. They can torment you or easily wear you down—it's their choice. Remember Julian's father?

Eleanor, a very nice woman I used to occasionally see at criminal profiling conferences, had been on guard against her son for years, to no avail. The last time I heard from her, she told me that her live-in, 40-year-old "good-for-nothing son" had taken all of her money. She was worn down from trying, as she said, to always be "one step ahead of that boy." Her son, the predator she'd harbored and sustained out of the goodness of her heart, had bankrupted her. At 60, this nearly retired nurse had to take on two jobs to meet her financial obligations—and she no longer has any faith in or affection for her son.

Some predators will get family and friends to cosign a loan or invest in something that has no future or prospects. They simply don't care what hardships they cause or what money you may lose, so long as it's not theirs. Ask a bail bondsman how many cases they know of where one of these career criminals has skipped on a bond and left the family impoverished after getting them to post tens of thousands of dollars in bail, or even the title to their homes. It's staggering.

These dangerous personalities think nothing of endangering you through their behavior. They're the kind who'll ask to borrow your car and then use it to rob a bank, or get you to drive them to a friend's house while, unbeknownst to you, they're carrying a backpack full of drugs. Or they'll ask you to lie and cover for them at work to conceal their criminal activities or even to provide alibis. Suddenly, you'll find yourself in trouble with the law because they asked you to do a favor, lie for them, or get involved in a criminal act.

Expect to feel uneasy at their intrusive looks, questions, or presence.

They unnerve us when they become too friendly too quickly and then latch on with too much familiarity. In the movie *The Talented Mr. Ripley*, Matt Damon plays the part of a predator who latches on to a victim and won't let go until he gets what he wants. In a similar way, predators place demands on us that we don't really want to fulfill, or they seek intimacy or trespass on our privacy without regard to our wishes or needs. This is no accident; it is intended.

With some predators, you may actually feel a physical reaction. You may shake or feel your hairs stand up, as I mentioned happened to me. The notable researcher and author J. Reid Meloy, PhD, found that even trained professionals have a visceral reaction to these predatory individuals.[12] Similarly, in his book *The Gift of Fear*, Gavin de Becker describes how these toxic individuals register with us on a very primitive (limbic) level—a subconscious warning system of sorts that we evolved to alert us to danger. Unfortunately, society tells us to turn off that warning system and assume everyone is good and kind. While you're busy trusting the predators, they're busy learning all your exploitable weaknesses, the better to take advantage of you. They'll steal your goodwill, your virtue, or your generosity as their due—that is what predators do.

As to reciprocity, they'll deliver it when and where they want, or not at all. In 2013, Michael Chadd Boysen's family eagerly awaited his release from incarceration for a burglary he committed. His grandparents readied a bedroom for him, picked him up when he was finally released, drove him to get a new ID card, even took him to his first meeting with his probation officer just to make sure everything went well. Sometime later that day, Boysen killed them.[13] That was their reward for their loving help.

When we help, give in to, or go along with these individuals, we enable and embolden them to take further advantage of us or of others. Thinking that they'll change or that "this time things will be different" is like expecting a snake to be less of a reptile just because you fed and stroked it. Don't expect goodness from those who can't deliver it. They can deliver kindness when they want, to get what they want. Kindness, however, can blind parents into letting their child spend time with the likes of Jerry Sandusky—the serial child molester.

Once they're done with you, not only will you feel violated or betrayed, but thanks to their profound treachery, you'll be reluctant to trust others. Posttraumatic stress disorder is often the net effect of victimization by a predator. Knowing that you or a loved one has been used is deeply scarring. I've talked to victims who years later remain unreconciled, traumatized, and untrusting. Some are still in therapy; others had to be medicated. I know parents who've had to seek medical treatment for anxiety because their daughter had run away with or was marrying a known predator.

As I've said, predators leave a large debris field of human suffering. The precise type and timing are really up to them. If you become involved with a predator, you're taking a big risk with your safety and that of your loved ones. You may be exposing others to unnecessary danger simply by granting a predator access. Please, don't take that chance.

THE PREDATOR IN RELATIONSHIPS

There's no equality in a relationship with a predator. These individuals target the trusting and the nurturing or act as parasites, living off a human host. They expect you to supply all their needs—but don't expect them to land a job or help around the house. They always have an excuse for not getting work: Their brilliance isn't appreciated; the job's beneath them; lousy boss; terrible hours; and on and on. They'll drain you till you have nothing more to give or they tire of you. Then they'll move on to another exploitable person or situation.

Elizabeth, whom I met while conducting behavioral training, is an accomplished, intelligent professional who had the misfortune to marry a parasitic predator. He looked good, sounded good, was always good for a beer, and was very athletic, but he did nothing. She tried arranging jobs, marriage counseling, career counseling, even handing out his résumé. By her account, he spent all day at home looking at porn while she worked. Those 3 years with him cost her nearly $40,000, as she paid for everything (clothes, jewelry, vacations, golf clubs, moving expenses, computers, cameras, etc.). When she finally had had enough and said it was time for him to go, incredibly, he demanded part of her retirement savings even though they'd been married for only 3 years. That's your parasitic predator: always looking for more.

The predator in relationships can be lethal. In all her published photos, Laci Peterson looks happy and effervescent, but in 2002, when she was pregnant and married to Scott Lee Peterson, he was seeing other women behind her back. On Christmas Eve, as the prosecutor proved at trial, Scott Peterson gutted Laci, killing her and her nearly 8-month-old fetus. As a predator, he had decided it was time for her to go.

In 2003, Stacy Ann Cales married Drew Peterson (no relation to Scott Peterson) shortly after he divorced his third wife, Kathleen Savio. A year later, Kathleen Savio would be found dead in an empty bathtub—her death initially ruled "an accident." Stacy was one of the first to defend her husband, Drew, when he came under suspicion for the death of his former wife. Her faith and allegiance were ill placed because she had married a predator, and for him, life was cheap. Four years later, Stacy herself disappeared, devastating her own family, who quite logically feared Drew Peterson. As a result of her disappearance and much pressure from both families, the police reinvestigated the death of Kathleen Savio and determined that it had been no accident. Drew Peterson's luck as a predator ran out in 2013 when he was convicted and sentenced to 38 years for the premeditated murder of Kathleen Savio.[14] Sadly, Stacy's body has never been found, leaving a family without closure or justice.

That is the stark reality of living with or marrying a predator. In fact, on average, three women die every day at the hands of an "intimate partner"—a predator in their midst. Intimate partner homicides account for 30 percent of the murders of women and 5 percent of the murders of men, according to the Bureau of Justice Statistics.[15] These are sobering statistics, and often there are clues beforehand that we are in the presence of danger, but we have to pay attention and know what we're looking for.

Drew Peterson's previous wives reported how abusive and callous he'd been to them—hints, perhaps, of things to come. Miss the cues or act too late and you and your loved ones may pay a heavy price. The clock is ticking. By this time tomorrow, according to the statistics above, three more women will lose their lives.

A predator may look good on paper, but he is still a predator. Colette Stevenson married a physician who was a Princeton graduate, US Army officer, and a Green Beret. But when her husband, Jeffrey Robert MacDonald, tired of Colette and their kids in 1970, he killed them all and then claimed that drug-crazed hippies had done it. Investigators didn't buy his story, and neither did the jury—the crime scene was "staged" to look like a home invasion, and his wounds were all superficial. Jeffrey MacDonald remains behind bars, still claiming his innocence, always seeking an appeal—cold as ice.

When you're in a relationship with a predator, you're poised somewhere between risky behavior, psychological abuse, or possibly losing your life. It is always that precarious. How often have we read of a wife or girlfriend who was so afraid that she either wrote in her journal or told friends and family that if she were to die or disappear, her husband or boyfriend was probably the culprit? They have premonitions because they see the predator's behavior up close.

Some predators live a double life: They prey outside the home and the family is kept in the dark—or if family members have suspicions, they're afraid to ask. Imagine finding out that Dad or Mom paid for the house where you grew up with stolen money. How do you love a parent who claims to love you but who has physically, emotionally, or financially hurt others? And if you do, what does that make you? These are just some of the ways these personalities damage their children without laying a finger on them.

Don't expect predators to always be there for their children. Do expect them to be absent or distant, to be brutal at times, or to expose their children to ridicule, harm, danger, criminal activity, and the potential of being incarcerated.

The worst situation occurs when the predator involves the whole family in criminal activity. Newspapers are full of stories of husbands who used their spouse to commit a crime. Brian David Mitchell and his wife, Wanda Barzee, abducted Elizabeth Smart in Utah in 2002 and held her for 9 months. Jaycee Lee Dugard was abducted at age 11 and held for 18 years in California by convicted sex offender Phillip Craig Garrido and his wife, Nancy Garrido. Take a deep breath and read Jaycee's book about her ordeal, *A Stolen Life: A Memoir*, but be prepared to cry.[16] It's a story of a remarkable human being's redemption following predation.

Predators are notorious for teaching their children to steal, cheat, lie, avoid responsibility, fight, and break social rules. Some of those I've studied or talked to punished their children not for committing crimes but for getting caught. John Walker, a US Navy communications specialist, spied for the Russians for decades. He not only put his nation at risk by giving away cryptographic secrets, he also got his son, Michael Walker, involved in his crimes. John Walker got life imprisonment for espionage; Michael got 25 years. Similarly, Mafia don John Gotti did his son John A. "Junior" no favor by introducing him into the life of a mobster. All that did was ensure that the federal government would focus its attention on him upon his father's death. That led to his pleading guilty to racketeering—loan sharking, bookmaking, and extortion—in 1999, for which he served 6 years in prison. Between 2004 (before he had left prison) and 2009, he was the defendant in four additional racketeering trials (these ended in mistrials), with all the attendant legal fees and stress. That is not the kind of life most people would want for their kids.[17] Unless, of course, you are a predator—then it doesn't matter what you bequeath your family.

Then there are those who turn on their own family. Who abuse their stepchildren and their own children. Or who go after their own parents, like brothers Lyle and Erik Menendez, two cold-blooded killers who in 1989 executed their parents with shotguns while the latter watched TV at home; they then went on a shopping and partying extravaganza until they were finally arrested.[18] These killers had the best of everything (school, money, clothes, cars, tennis lessons). But for predators, enough is never good enough.

Sometimes, the predator is very subtle, first testing to see how family members react. Carla, a Miami native, told me how her second husband almost immediately began to pay too much attention to her 14-year-old daughter after they married. Over time, she noticed that he was having more and more interactions with her daughter, including a lot of tickling and wrestling on the floor. Then there were the hugs and kisses that seemed to last too long. It was when she found out that he'd secretly taken her daughter to Victoria's Secret to buy her underwear that Carla began to sense something was wrong—especially when her daughter said that this had happened before.

Carla's gut feeling was confirmed when she found e-mails he'd sent her daughter from work. They weren't just playful missives. Carla questioned her daughter about what was going on. Her daughter had been reluctant to say anything, not wanting to rock the boat or spoil her mom's happiness.

As it turns out, the husband had tried to do more than just hug her; he had reached between her legs while driving and touched her in other ways that were progressively more intimate and vile.

Carla confronted her new husband. He, of course, had one explanation after another: He was trying to fit in and be more of a father to his stepdaughter; the touching inside the legs was accidental or it never happened. Nothing was his fault. He callously brought Carla's daughter into the conversation, asking, "Haven't I been nice to you? Don't I buy you things? Please tell your mom this is all a mistake." What was her daughter—who Carla told me was shaking like a leaf—supposed to say? His conclusion: "You see? Everything is fine."

With mobile phone in hand, Carla said to him, "You have an hour to pack and leave, or I am calling the sheriff's office." She took her daughter outside and told her to wait with a neighbor while family came to get her.

He tried to reason with her. She pointed at the clock. Carla told me that by this time the hairs on her neck were standing up and her skin was "crawling" as she thought about how much time he'd spent alone with her daughter and those messages she'd read. But what was really getting to her were his attempts to "bullshit" her and make her think it was all in her head—a common tactic of the predator. At that moment, she knew she was in the presence of a predator. And it made her angrier because, as she said, "he was just trying to con me again into closing my eyes."

Stepchildren are often the targets of sexual abuse by an intimate of the parent. I admire Carla, who did the right thing, and quickly. But the cost was still tremendous in time, money, court depositions, divorce proceedings, attorney fees, and more. There were trust issues that caused her nightmares and psychological damage to her daughter, who felt betrayed that her mother had brought a dangerous person into their home. Years later, there were still issues for everyone involved. That's the debris field left by a predator.

Fortunately, Carla prevailed. Many women don't. Not all can get away or see the warning signs in time. And in some cases, the victim is too young, helpless, or trusting to escape. All of Marybeth Tinning's children (nine in all) died over the years under her care—unfortunately, the government was only able to prove that she murdered one of them.[19] Diane Downs felt her three kids were keeping her from attracting a man who didn't want children. In 1984, she was convicted of shooting her three children, killing one.[20] What a horror story that is for those children to have experienced.

In 1999, Crista Decker, mother of three, whom I helped to investigate in Tampa at the request of the Hillsborough County sheriff, told investigators that her 6-month-old baby boy had been taken from her vehicle while she went to get a shopping cart at a store.

During my interview with her, just hours after she alleged her son had been abducted, I told her I was interested in knowing what her children were like. It was startling to see the difference in how she talked about them. She spoke in warm terms about the two older children. But there was a certain coldness in her manner as she spoke about her missing son. We as investigators were already suspicious of her story, but what gave her away was the fact that even though her baby had been missing for only a few hours, she referred to him in the past tense. "He *was* always a good baby," she told me. Her two living kids, she said, "*are* good kids." [The italics in these statements are mine for emphasis.]

The coldness of her tone and her use of the past tense ("*was*") led us to conclude that the child was already dead and she knew it. And he was. Eventually, she admitted that she had suffocated her baby (fathered by someone other than her husband) in a plastic garbage bag because "he wouldn't stop crying."[21] Yes, predators are that cold.

There is a lesson here for all of us, and it is this: No relationship or family is safe if one of the parties is a predator.

ENCOUNTERS WITH THE PREDATOR

Most encounters with predators tend to be transient. We can meet one at a sporting event, at a bar, at work, or at a concert, or someone introduces us. They come and they go; after all, they have agendas that may not include us. Others, however, we encounter because they target us or because of our occupation or situation in life. Those are the individuals we especially want to be vigilant of.

There are embezzlers, bank robbers, pickpockets, car thieves, and many more. But there's a reason why we have the Adam Walsh Child Protection and Safety Act, Megan's Law, and Jessica's Law, among others: because there are so many predators out there who prey on minors. Some are in and out of prison. Each time they get out, they strike again. Others operate undetected for decades—remember the Catholic priest child abuse scandal?

We're fortunate to have those laws, and they're helpful. But even with such laws in place, we still have men like Jerry Sandusky prowling for children. Sexual predation will always be a considerable challenge for society. After all, who in England would have imagined Jimmy Savile, famous BBC TV personality and host of a children's show, raping children? But he did, for decades; yet all such allegations were dismissed because of his status and popularity.[22] It is axiomatic that it is never healthy for children to be near predators—no matter who they are.

Women are also often predators' targets. In the 1960s, Albert Henry DeSalvo, known as the Boston Strangler, traveled the city creating opportunities for himself. Women would let him into their homes and apartments on a multitude of pretenses (he represented a model agency; his car had broken down; he needed to make a call, etc.). Women encountered him at home where they felt safe—but as I've mentioned, you'll never be safe with a predator.

Sometimes, we unwittingly enter the predator's familiar hunting ground, where they can more easily target us. Natalee Holloway went to Aruba on holiday with her high school friends in 2005. Within hours of meeting Joran van der Sloot, she disappeared and most likely was killed soon thereafter; her body was never found.

On the surface, van der Sloot looked handsome, charming, and fun. Unfortunately, Natalee had little time to discover what a terrible person he really is. Five years to the day after Natalee's disappearance, van der Sloot robbed and murdered Stephany Tatiana Flores Ramírez, whom he met in Peru while playing cards at a casino. Why would he do that, you ask? That is the kind of question the parent of a missing child asks. Unfortunately and tragically, it is really not about why predators do these things; it is simply that they can.

Sometimes, all it takes is to live near a predator. The very week I started this chapter in May 2013, Ariel Castro was arrested in Cleveland for abducting three girls and holding them hostage for 10 years, fathering at least one child with one of them.[23] Unfortunately, the girls had been unlucky enough to live in the same neighborhood as this vile predator, who later hanged himself in his jail cell rather than face trial. Castro defeated justice by committing suicide before his trial.

Then there are industry-specific predators who tailor their predation to where they're working or what they're doing. Charles Cullen, for instance, was a night shift nurse who admitted killing at least 40 patients, though there may have been many more.[24] He did his worst at work and nowhere else.

In the 1980s, Clyde Lee Conrad, too, tailored his activities to his environment. As a US Army sergeant stationed in Germany, he pilfered military supplies when he could, sold gasoline and cigarette ration booklets on the black market, and when that wasn't enough, he stole military secrets and sold them to Soviet Warsaw Pact countries. He put tens of thousands of soldiers and millions of civilians at risk in Europe with his betrayal—all for money.

Some predators are pillars of the community—veterans, churchgoers, volunteers, scout leaders, coaches, public officials. Rita Crundwell was the comptroller of Dixon, Illinois, and a renowned American quarter horse breeding enthusiast. She also embezzled $53 million over a 22-year career. The "BTK killer" Dennis Rader was a church leader and a reliable city employee who used his knowledge of the city and the mobility his job afforded him to target his victims.

Then there are the corporate predators, who can be found in large institutions as well as in two-person operations. Some say that today's business climate, particularly the high-stakes, cutthroat world of finance, attracts and rewards predatory behavior. These individuals may be charismatic and interesting, but they can also place a company at risk through their impulsive, aggressive behavior. That's exactly what Kenneth Lay and Jeffrey Skilling are famous for having done at Enron. They were charged with fraud, and Enron's 2001 bankruptcy was the biggest corporate bankruptcy of its time, where many people lost their livelihood as well as their life savings.[25] The Enron case is a reminder that predation often takes place at the highest levels of the corporate world if unethical individuals are in charge. The financial meltdown of 2008 was in part created by predators within the financial industry who created risky lending practices and then hedged against those ventures, knowing they were highly unstable if not toxic.

Aggressiveness and toughness in business are one thing, but criminal acts and intentional fraud are quite another. Businesses are learning that having a predator on the books is hazardous to the organization, investors, and employees. They can do risky things or they can be disruptive, destabilizing, or dangerous to the business.

While working with a predator is bad enough, living under the thumb of one when they lead a government can be horrific. Just ask anyone who experienced the torment of Adolf Hitler, Pol Pot, or Joseph Stalin. The alleged "Butcher of Bosnia" Radovan Karadžić was, according to the victims, no better; neither was Iraqi president Saddam Hussein, who used torture and poisonous gas weaponry on his own Kurdish minority.[26]

As I write this chapter, we're reading and hearing about Syria, where Bashar Hafez al-Assad, no friend of human rights, has turned his military loose on his own countrymen, using poisoned gas, causing millions to flee and tens of thousands of casualties.

Predators as leaders have one mission: staying in power by any means. To them, suffering and deaths are insignificant. The saying often attributed to Joseph Stalin summarized best how predators view mass killings: "Kill one person and it's a national tragedy; kill a million people, it is a statistic." Yes, they are that cold.

I hope this chapter has demonstrated that encounters with a predator are always dangerous. Sometimes, we encounter them because we're in the wrong place at the wrong time. Or they're our boss or the person at the desk next to ours. Nevertheless, we can still work at being safe by knowing how these individuals act. We can look for behaviors to see if this person is toxic, is recklessly irresponsible, thinks only of him- or herself, is dangerously intrusive, or is a mortal threat. That is our responsibility to ourselves and our loved ones.

YOUR DANGEROUS PERSONALITIES CHECKLIST

Warning Signs of the Predator

As I noted in the Introduction, I developed various behavior-based checklists during my career to help me assess individuals to see if they were dangerous personalities. This particular checklist will help you determine if someone has the features of the predator and where that person falls on a continuum or spectrum (from calculating and opportunistic to cold and callous—or, at the extreme, lacking conscience and utterly dangerous). This will help you decide more precisely how to deal with this person, determine his or her toxicity, and assess whether he or she may be a threat to you or others.

This checklist, as well as the others in this book, was designed to be used in everyday life by you and me—people who are not trained mental health professionals or researchers. It is not a clinical diagnostic tool. Its purpose is to educate, inform, or validate what you have witnessed or experienced.

Read each statement in the checklist carefully and check the statements that apply. Be honest; think about what you have heard an individual say or seen him or her do, or what others have expressed to you. Obviously, the best evidence is what you yourself have observed and how you feel when you are around or interact with this person.

Check only the statements that apply. Don't guess or include more than meet the criteria exactly. *If in doubt, leave it out.* Some items seem repetitive or appear to overlap—that is intentional, to capture nuances of behavior based on how people typically experience or describe these personalities.

It is very important that you complete the entire checklist, as designed, to increase its reliability. Each complete checklist covers very subtle yet significant issues that you may never have thought about. Some items may help you remember events you'd forgotten. Please read each statement, even if you feel you've seen enough or that the first few items don't seem to apply.

Gender pronouns (he, she, etc.) are used interchangeably in the statements. Any statement may be applicable to any gender.

We'll evaluate scores when you're done, but for now, check off each item below that applies.

☐   1. Disregards the rights of others by abusing them or taking advantage of them.

☐   2. Is manipulative and all too often gets people to do things for him.

☐   3. Was arrested and adjudicated as a child in the courts or had a juvenile record expunged.

☐   4. Is self-absorbed and feels entitled to do as he or she pleases, even if it hurts others.

☐   5. Proudly flaunts violations of law or rules—brags about crimes committed or people she has duped.

☐   6. Is deceitful, enjoys lying, or lies when he doesn't have to.

☐   7. Feels that rules or laws are for others to obey, not for him.

☐   8. Repeatedly violates laws or breaks rules of custom or decency.

☐   9. Recognizes weaknesses in others quickly and seeks to exploit their weaknesses.

☐   10. Has shoplifted in the past both in youth and as an adult.

☐   11. Lacks remorse and is indifferent to the suffering of others.

☐   12. Avoids or has bragged about not paying restaurant bills.

☐   13. Blames life, circumstances, parents, others, even victims, for her actions.

☐   14. Habitually tries to dominate others—control and dominance play a big part in this person's life.

☐   15. Is referred to as "heartless," "toxic," "obnoxious," "without morals," or lacking "scruples" or "decency."

☐   16. Has on several occasions written forged checks or checks with insufficient funds.

☐   17. Takes delight in duping others.

☐ 18. Likes to provoke people by bumping into them, staring at them, or saying things.

☐ 19. Has abundant self-confidence—but it is reckless or of little practical utility.

☐ 20. Doesn't take criticism well—lashes out at others with anger, rage, or threats of revenge.

☐ 21. Is or was considered a bully in school or at work, frequently hurting feelings.

☐ 22. Is skilled at gaining the trust of others for the sake of taking advantage of them.

☐ 23. Uses family, friends, co-workers, and loved ones to provide money, to lie for her, or to provide an alibi.

☐ 24. Has started fires that have placed people, animals, or property in danger.

☐ 25. Has no hesitation in putting others at financial, physical, or criminal risk.

☐ 26. Sees life as a matter of survival of the fittest.

☐ 27. Committing crimes comes easily; is known to have a very long rap sheet (criminal history) with the police.

☐ 28. Is at times callous and cold, while at other times is charming and seductive.

☐ 29. Falsely claims to be a doctor, professor, or some other professional.

☐ 30. Has conned others out of money, property, or valuables.

☐ 31. Has sabotaged bicycles, cars, or other things where someone could or did get hurt.

☐ 32. Schemes and plans to take advantage of others.

☐ 33. Has been cruel to animals as a child or as an adult.

☐ 34. Is cynical and contemptuous of others.

☐ 35. Is haughty and opinionated and often comes across as arrogant—some think he is a "legend in his own mind."

☐ 36. Has been described as being extremely cocky or pushy.

☐ 37. Fails to keep appointments, is unreliable or irresponsible, and always has an excuse for failing responsibilities.

☐ 38. Plays psychological head games to keep others down, make them feel inferior, or harass them.

☐ 39. Considers being respected and having power very important and lets you know that these things are important.

☐ 40. Has used force or intimidation to obtain sex.

☐ 41. Values you one minute and devalues you the next with callous disregard and indifference to past kindness.

☐ 42. Overvalues herself and her own abilities while devaluing others easily.

☐ 43. As a leader or manager, sees workers as minions or lemmings, not as equals.

☐ 44. Has lived or lives day to day by committing thefts or other crimes.

☐ 45. Encourages others to do things that put them at risk or may be illegal.

☐ 46. Seeks to dominate one of these for personal gain: your space, time, body, mind, or what you value.

☐ 47. Has destroyed others' property for fun or to "get back at them."

☐ 48. Trouble seems to follow him everywhere—often called a troublemaker.

☐ 49. Has little regard or respect for the property of others or institutions.

☐ 50. Has a history of intimidating others to get her way.

☐ 51. Often complains of being bored or lacking excitement.

☐ 52. As a child, frequently ran away from home.

☐ 53. Holds grudges and then acts on them in a mean way.

☐ 54. Expressions of remorse seem insincere or contrived when attempted.

☐ 55. As a child, was suspended from school multiple times for fighting.

☐ 56. Loyalty and care are reserved principally for herself.

☐ 57. Fails to accept responsibility for personal acts—tends to blame others.

☐ 58. Thought of as "smooth," "slick," "a charmer," or "too good to be true."

☐ 59. As a child, repeatedly disobeyed parents, stayed out late, broke rules.

☐ 60. Parasitically uses others to provide lodging, food, money, or sex.

☐ 61. Claims to have accomplished more than is humanly or logically possible or believable.

☐ 62. Had a father or mother who was physically abusive, tyrannical, or indifferent or was a felonious criminal.

☐ 63. Has led an irresponsible lifestyle (e.g., can't hold down a job; relationships repeatedly fail; financial obligations are ignored).

☐ 64. Has unexplained possessions or wealth.

☐ 65. Has a sense of entitlement and thinks he is above others or he can do as he pleases.

☐ 66. Displays of emotion appear contrived, performed, or insincere.

☐ 67. Is contemptuous of others, especially of those in authority.

☐ 68. Has arrogant, condescending attitude with an air of superiority that offends people.

☐ 69. People hate working with or for this individual or have become physically or psychologically sick as a result of working with this person.

☐ 70. Stares at you like a reptile: unflinching, unwavering, cold, having little to say.

☐ 71. Uses gaze to stare down, intimidate, or dominate others (makes you or others very uncomfortable).

☐ 72. Has superficial charm—which is attractive at first.

☐ 73. Rationalizes stealing from, hurting, or mistreating others ("they deserved it").

☐ 74. Has had run-ins with the law in youth and as an adult.

☐ 75. Intentionally has asked workers or others to bend rules, ignore laws, alter or destroy important records or evidence, or hide information.

☐ 76. Has little fear of acting out criminally.

☐ 77. Uses aliases, changes identities, or intentionally hides portions of his past.

☐ 78. Is impulsive—suddenly, on a lark, will act out or commit crimes of opportunity.

☐ 79. Fails to plan for the future or to take the future into consideration (example: spends all the rent or food money or buys gifts for herself and not for the family).

☐ 80. Is irritable or aggressive when challenged, reprimanded, or rejected.

☐ 81. Seeks to or has kept you or others from associating with or contacting friends, family, or loved ones.

☐ 82. Easily bullies or fights with others.

☐ 83. Targets the weak, the elderly, children, the gullible, or women for abuse, to gain sexual favors, or to take advantage of them financially.

☐ 84. Has a reckless disregard for his own safety or that of others (e.g., speeding; driving while intoxicated).

☐ 85. Has or is currently intimidating or abusing (physically or psychologically) family, parents, workmates, or friends.

☐ 86. Takes advantage of parents by stealing from them, conning them, or selling or pawning their property without their consent.

☐ 87. Claims to be in the CIA, Navy SEALS, or other secret or elite service, with no verifiable evidence to prove such claims.

☐ 88. Has been rejected for employment or by the military because of failure to pass psychological tests.

☐ 89. This person causes a physical reaction in others: People feel their skin react (goose bumps; hairs stand up; "makes skin crawl") or feel their stomach ache or become acidic.

☐ 90. Is aggressively narcissistic—toxic in dealing with others, puts them down, belittles them, or makes them feel bad.

☐ 91. Has a history of criminal activity, including extortion, and has gotten away with criminal acts.

☐ 92. Is inquisitive about pain, punishment, or torture or how to effectively kill someone.

☐ 93. Has spent time in criminal institutions, detention facilities, jail, prison, halfway houses, etc.

☐ 94. Has a history of raping, robbing, or assault with a deadly weapon.

☐ 95. Has committed burglary or property crimes or has stolen cars multiple times.

☐ 96. Talks about women with derision, seeing them as objects or "whores."

☐ 97. Has sexually molested children (touching; exposing self) or thinks about having sex with children.

☐ 98. Seems to have poor behavioral self-control.

☐ 99. Had a mother who was a prostitute or was in the sex trade.

☐ 100. Has sexual preference for children.

☐ 101. Practices irresponsible sex, exposing others to sexually transmitted diseases or the HIV (AIDS) virus.

☐ 102. Has fathered children in various relationships, taking no responsibility (emotionally, custodially, or financially) for those children.

☐ 103. Justifies cruelty or criminal behavior as something that the other person had "coming to them."

☐ 104. Has jumped bail, leaving family or friends financially responsible.

☐ 105. Disappears for days, even months; then reappears without explanation or any accountability.

☐ 106. People have commented they feel "uncomfortable" around him or "don't trust him."

☐ 107. Expects others to provide alibis, hide, or harbor her from justice.

☐ 108. Has broken into someone's car, business, or home or has stalked someone.

☐ 109. Rarely, if ever, pays money back to friends or associates.

☐ 110. Beats or abuses spouse or children with frequency.

☐ 111. Children or spouse avoids or dreads being around him.

☐ 112. Has spoken or written about having fantasies or thoughts of committing criminal acts or raping someone.

☐ 113. Has repeatedly defaulted on loans or credit cards or failed to pay child support.

☐ 114. Has or claims to have killed someone but is not bothered about it or brags about it.

☐ 115. Has used someone else's credit card to pay without approval.

☐ 116. Seeks to obtain power, sex, or money by other than legal or moral means.

☐ 117. When it's time to pay, repeatedly claims to have forgotten wallet or that his money is "tied up" in investments.

☐ 118. At work, is mean or cruel—yells or screams at subordinates in public.

☐ 119. As a parent, is irresponsible, inattentive, uninvolved, callous, or reckless when it comes to children (failure to nurture, feed, bathe, take to school or to the doctor, etc.).

☐ 120. Seems detached from others, never really gets close to them.

☐ 121. Has left or moved out of state to avoid prosecution, the police, or financial responsibilities.

☐ 122. Targets the elderly or the senile specifically for abuse or to con them out of money.

☐ 123. Has engaged in producing child pornography.

☐ 124. Had behavioral problems even in youth.

☐ 125. Is or has been described as sexually sadistic.

☐ 126. Has been dishonorably discharged from the military.

☐ 127. Love has little meaning; confuses sex with love.

☐ 128. Has rationalized abuse of children with simplistic sayings such as "She wouldn't stop crying" or "It'll make him tough."

☐ 129. Lives on the "wild side," has "bad friends" or criminal associates (gang members, drug dealers, prostitutes, pimps, mobsters).

☐ 130. Possesses contraband, child pornography, or weapons for criminal use.

☐ 131. Is a gang enforcer or leader.

☐ 132. Belongs to a criminal syndicate or organization (drug dealer, mobster, crime family), traffics in humans, or is a pimp.

☐ 133. Has repeatedly been fired or let go from jobs, even menial tasks, for underperformance, failure to comply, arguing, or for not showing up.

☐ 134. Has tattoos or flaunts signs or flags espousing racial hatred, criminal acts, or misogyny.

☐ 135. Hates to be disrespected or made fun of—gets very angry and mean when this happens.

☐ 136. Doesn't seem to learn from mistakes or experience.

☐ 137. Repeatedly takes things of value from others without asking or steals from stores (shoplifting).

☐ 138. Rarely says, "I'm sorry," or only does so when forced to.

☐ 139. Rejects apologies of others and holds grudges, which he violently acts on.

☐ 140. Has or is working in an illegal, terroristic, or criminal enter-
prise such as running numbers, gambling, selling drugs,
stealing cars, etc.

☐ 141. Has had significant periods of unemployment throughout
life, despite available jobs, or because of incarceration.

☐ 142. Has mistreated (malnourished, failed to provide adequate
clothing), incarcerated, or assaulted children under his or
her care.

☐ 143. Has used ropes, handcuffs, reinforced room, or other
restraining devices to control someone against his or
her will.

☐ 144. Derives pleasure from the suffering or pain of others.

☐ 145. Appears to enjoy creating psychological discomfort or
fear in others.

☐ 146. Seems to always be angry or hostile or resents the world.

☐ 147. Has told others about having a "dark, mean, or evil" side,
which may be dismissed by others as just talk.

☐ 148. His thinking is very rigid and inflexible; things must be
done his way or he lashes out.

☐ 149. Women in his life either have grown to detest or mistrust
him or have disappeared mysteriously.

☐ 150. Those who associate with him feel anxious, unsafe,
victimized, tormented, cheated, or betrayed.

SCORING

☑ Count how many statements apply to this individual based on
the criteria discussed at the beginning of this checklist.

☑ If you find that this individual has at least 25 of these features,
this is a person who will occasionally take an emotional toll on
others, is taking advantage of others, may be difficult to live or
work with, or may be placing you in financial jeopardy.

☑   If the score is 26 to 75, this indicates that the individual has all
the features of and behaves as a predator. You have to be very
cautious, especially if you are in an intimate or prolonged relationship with this individual or there are matters of trust at
stake (e.g., loans, financial transactions, investments, lending
of property, access to children).

☑   *Warning:* If the score is greater than 75, this person has a
preponderance of the major features of a predator and is an
emotional, psychological, financial, or physical danger to you
and others. Immediate action should be taken to distance
yourself from this individual.

IMMEDIATE ACTIONS

Predators are notoriously resistant to change—or if they change, it's to
improve their predatory prowess. In his book *Fatal Flaws*, Stuart C.
Yudofsky, MD, notes the difficulty of finding mental health professionals
who are highly knowledgeable and well trained in dealing with antisocial
personalities such as these. If that's the case with the pros, what are the rest
of us to do? We're left with little recourse but to try to distance ourselves
from these dangerous personalities.

In my experience and that of many other professionals, you really need
to extricate yourself from individuals like this and seek competent and
qualified professional help if it is needed. I subscribe to the wisdom of the
Buddha when he wisely said, "People should learn to see and avoid all danger. Just as a wise man keeps away from mad dogs, so one should not make
friends with evil men."

For those of us who are not mental health professionals, our best strategies are awareness and distancing. If these predatory individuals don't harm you directly—physically, emotionally, financially, or all of the above—they'll harm you indirectly by harming people you care about or by compromising your community. They can and do devastate body, mind, and spirit. They can ruin you financially or destroy your life with absolutely no concern for what happens to you.

You may feel obligated to someone like this because you're married to him, because she's family, or because he gave you a job. Just be aware, however, that your loyalty will not keep you from being victimized, tormented, or financially ruined, no matter what the relationship. That is the nature of the predator. For additional strategies, see Chapter 6, Self-Defense against Dangerous Personalities.

I will close with the warning words of one who intimately knew the ways of the predator:

We serial killers are your sons, we are your husbands, we are everywhere. And there will be more of your children dead tomorrow.

—Theodore "Ted" Bundy

CHAPTER 5

ONE IS BAD, TWO IS TERRIBLE, THREE IS LETHAL

COMBINATION PERSONALITIES

THUS FAR, WE'VE LOOKED AT the different personality types in isolation. The benefit of that has been to more clearly understand these dangerous personalities. However, in reality, dangerous personalities are often composed of more than one personality type. In the medical literature, this is referred to as comorbidity, and it should come as no surprise; after all, we all contain different personality traits—it's what makes us complex and interesting. But when individuals possess features from two or more dangerous personality types, your risk increases, sometimes dramatically. And while the risk increases, as most clinicians will tell you, recognizing the specific personality type can be a real challenge. So to assist the reader, I have used examples from real-life cases to shed some light on the comingling of personality traits among dangerous personalities. The complexity of comingling traits is also why we emphasize reviewing each and every checklist thoroughly in order to assess fully the danger these personalities pose.

Additionally, just as our behavior may change depending on life circumstances, so a dangerous personality's behavior can change: Instead of perennially yelling at the child who's acting out, the emotionally unstable personality may one day suddenly shake that child violently or throw the child against a wall. Similarly, the aloof, narcissistic bachelor may marry and become a dominating and dictatorial husband who is increasingly critical and disparaging. Just as we may change over time, so many factors can contribute to these individuals becoming more unstable, more toxic, and ever more dangerous. The key for us is to habitually assess others for these traits and recognize them for what they are. What we can't assume or naïvely hope for is that a dangerous personality will, on his or her own, get suddenly better over time.

Analyzing the intricacies and nuances of human personalities can get very complicated, and a complete discussion of all personality types is outside the scope of this book. This is where the Dangerous Personalities Checklists can help. As we assess others for their potential for toxicity, instability, or danger, we have to remind ourselves not to get rigidly fixated on one personality type. We must not ignore the possibility that the person in question may fit comfortably into multiple personality categories. This, too, is part of the process—seeing what behaviors fit where. Doing so will give us a better picture of the individual we're dealing with, keeping in mind that certain personality traits, when combined, can potentiate each other, sometimes with horrible results.

We see examples daily in crisis situations around the world. I'm sure when accused cop killer and former police officer Christopher Dorner was on the run in early 2013, the Los Angeles Police Department profilers and psychologists were asking: "What kind of personality is he? What will he do next?" Fortunately, Dorner had written a lengthy manifesto that gave us insight beyond what was in his official personnel file. That manifesto revealed:

- An individual full of emotional wounding, with a need to dispose of his enemies (paranoia), coupled with

- His view that he felt entitled to take violent action against fellow police officers and their families to fix what he deemed needed to be fixed (narcissistic grandiosity)

Dorner's manifesto provided critical information: It helped to explain his behavior and to a certain extent predicted how he would behave in the future. When you're trying to apprehend a highly paranoid individual who narcissistically devalues fellow law enforcement officers, a shootout is the most likely outcome—and indeed it was.[1]

NOT SO RARE: COMBINATION PERSONALITIES

From the Dangerous Personalities Checklist instructions in previous chapters, you've learned important essentials about how to be alert to dangerous personalities: Observe the persons in question and note their behaviors, the things they say, how they make us feel, what's known about their past, and what others who've interacted with them have experienced and noted. As we'll discuss in Chapter 6, this is part of doing due diligence: objectively assessing what you and others observe, looking for significant indicators that someone may be toxic, unstable, or dangerous. This is our responsibility, and it's both wise and judicious.

Now let's expand on this foundation by seeing whether the information we gather might be placed in more than one of the four Dangerous Personalities Checklists. In this way, we'll gain a better sense of the individual's personality type and his or her potential for danger.

For instance, suppose we note that Harry talks and acts as if he thinks he's really somebody special. That characteristic potentially fits in three checklists: the narcissistic personality, the paranoid personality, and the predator. But this is just one behavior. So we carefully continue to collect information (How does he treat us? How does he make us feel? What specific behaviors do we see?), and we place those actions or behaviors in the specific checklist that applies.

Let's say we also note that Harry displays a need to control others and he has a nasty habit of being vindictive. These added behaviors narrow down his personality type further, and over time we may see a preponderance of features that fit the checklist for the paranoid personality as well as the checklist for the predator.

If, through enough interaction with him or through your observations, you eventually find that this fictional Harry has, let's say, 45 or more behavioral characteristics in each of two of the Dangerous Personalities Checklists, this is significant. A person who scores this high on the paranoid personality checklist and the predator checklist can be not just nasty but downright dangerous.

The key to a more complete picture is not to try to pigeonhole someone from the beginning, but rather to let the behaviors speak for themselves. Otherwise, you might find yourself blinded to important information— something that can happen even to professionals. And so as I have said from the beginning, we focus on behaviors, not on statistics or probabilities, and we allocate behaviors to the Dangerous Personalities Checklists wherever they may apply.

Suppose we meet someone who's charming, highly confident, and full of grand ideas and plans but who has accomplished little—and we quickly decide that he fits the narcissistic personality category. Okay, now let's step back and assess that decision for a moment. He may indeed have those characteristics, but slotting him too quickly into a single category may mean that we stop being alert to other information—such as his sudden appearance in town, his apparent lack of verifiable work history and credentials, his transient lifestyle, and his lack of discernible income—all things that fit the predator checklist and could point to a personality with the potential to do serious harm (see Chapter 4). It's that kind of mistake we want to avoid. It's what pilots call target fixation: They get so focused on one target that they miss all the other targets nearby, or they're so fixated on a particular task, landmark, or issue that they plow straight into a mountain.

There are, of course, all sorts of possible combinations among the four dangerous personality types. For instance, you can have someone who's highly intelligent but who is paranoid and narcissistic. Look at the behavior of John McAfee (founder of McAfee, Inc., the world's largest antivirus software company) in Belize; one wonders, is that what we're seeing? Someone who moves to a foreign country and, according to one interview, felt the necessity to clean up the place as if the gods had anointed him to that responsibility—that is a characteristic of narcissism. But he also irrationally feared the national police force and his neighbors—that is a common trait of paranoia.[2] So we may be looking at narcissism and paranoia, but we can't be sure because we don't have all the facts. So we collect information and place it where it belongs in the Dangerous Personalities Checklist that applies, and we add to each list as information becomes available.

Eventually, we begin to get a sense of who this individual is, based on his behaviors. Maybe a little of this, maybe more of that at this time, recognizing that the mix may change and vary because we're dealing with characteristics that apply to more than one personality type—we are, after all, dealing with humans. They may be more grandiose and self-centered one day, while another day, they display more of the characteristics of a preda-tor. That is what makes humans interesting to study: We act upon life, and life acts upon us. We are never rigidly in one place, and neither are danger-ous personalities.

Does it matter which personality traits are strongest? Yes and no—it depends on the individual person and that person's traits. But keep in mind that we're not criminal profilers or researchers; we are merely inter-ested in determining how dangerous this person really is. So if someone scores high (above 50) on two or more Dangerous Personalities Checklists, determining precisely which pathology is more prominent isn't essential compared to realizing that a critical threshold has been crossed, and we can say that this person is likely to be very toxic, very unstable, or even dangerous and a threat to you.

For example, someone who's highly unstable emotionally and highly paranoid is an extremely difficult person to live with: forever suspicious and lashing out with fearsome regularity. Whether the paranoia or the instabil-ity is driving the outbursts is less important than securing your safety.

A woman I'll call Amanda wrote me that her husband initially displayed "little quirks," as she called them. He'd lash out sometimes, especially if he'd had a bad day. Over the years, according to her, both the instability and the paranoia increased, for no reason at all. He became so hypersuspicious that he'd search her mobile phone for activity and would even check the message pad at home for latent indentations by rubbing a pencil across the surface to see what messages she had written down. Even-tually he became "unbearable," especially when the violence toward her escalated from pushing to shoving to slapping to choking. Yes, choking.

So what was the predominant feature here—the unstable emotional side or the paranoid side? It's an intriguing question, and one that a researcher or a therapist might find of interest. But I can tell you this: Amanda didn't care, and neither do I—nor should you. We don't live in a laboratory where we can safely experiment, leisurely debate, or validate with absolute precision. We live in a world where spousal abuse is rampant, children disappear and are raped or killed, personal safety is an issue, time is of the essence, and our decisions need to made quickly in the moment, based on what little information is available to us. In essence, we want to be accurate without having to be perfectly precise. If we have to wait to be perfectly precise, it may be too late (as you'll see later in this chapter with what happened to a woman named Susan Powell).

Just as Amanda had to deal with her present reality of abuse and, as she described it, "the craziness" of her immediate situation, so we must deal with our own reality. Amanda's role became one of survival, not one of metrics, measurements, and experimentation. Her immediate concern was not "Is my husband 80 percent of this or 20 percent of that?" Leave such analysis to others, if they so desire. The most important question for you, as it was for her, was: Am I in danger? That is the sole purpose of this book and where the Dangerous Personalities Checklists will help.

As you do your due diligence, remember that all of these personality types reside on a broad spectrum that goes from light to dark, low to high, irritating to impossible, difficult to toxic and even dangerous—and that their place on this spectrum can vary depending on circumstances, life stressors, opportunities, or moods. One way to think about this is to imagine a radio. Play it softly and the music may be almost unnoticeable. Turn it up slightly and you can hear the music more clearly. Turn it up loud and it becomes annoying; even louder and it's painful and almost intolerable to your ears. Turn it to maximum volume and you may damage your eardrum—it is, in fact, dangerous. That's one way to consider these dangerous personalities: How high is the volume right now? Down low, showing few signs? In the middle, annoying or irritating us? Or turned up high where they're dangerous to our well-being—a risk to our health?

But to hear anything, you have to tune in. It bears repeating: Most people who are toxic or dangerous live under the radar, mostly undetected, with limited or no contact with law enforcement and even less with clinicians. Usually, friends and family, lacking any road map for deciphering dangerous personalities, are clueless, don't know what to look for, or are biased in their favor. For example, when asked, a friend of Timothy McVeigh said, "If you don't consider what happened in Oklahoma City, Tim is a good person."[3] And that says it all. There are people who refuse to see what is in front of them, or they're so biased as to be blind. Dangerous personalities thrive in that environment. In the end, there are two truths that you need to keep in mind about all dangerous personalities: We see only what we are prepared to see, and most people will mask who they really are.

From doing both criminal profiling and behavioral profiling on national security matters for the FBI, I know that personality types can be challenging to study, especially when dealing with someone who's a complex mixture of two or more personality types. This is where the Dangerous Personalities Checklists will be most useful, helping you to decipher what traits stand out, in which personality type, so you can more precisely understand whom you are really dealing with.

NOTABLE COMBINATIONS OF DANGEROUS PERSONALITIES

Perhaps the best way to understand those who have major features of two or more dangerous personality types is to look at examples from history and the headlines, since both are filled with the chaos these individuals leave behind.

"There Are Enemies Out There, But I Have the Answers": Paranoid + Narcissistic

Let's start with the last century, as that was the century of mass media, giving us a better accounting of historical figures than perhaps at any other time. The first person who stands out has to be Joseph Stalin. Stalin narcissistically craved power and adoration—in Chapter 1, you learned about the many titles he claimed for himself, some of which verged on the ridiculous—and he had whole cities named after himself. But in addition to being narcissistic, Stalin had a darker side driven by paranoia, and both pathologies were at the extreme, more virulent (acute) end of the spectrum, making him highly toxic and dangerous.[4]

Given his totalitarian control of his people, security services, and the military, the consequences of this combination were therefore of epic proportions. Imagine killing every human being living in California. That's pretty much what he achieved, killing more than 30 million people—the exact numbers are unknown.[5] His hypersuspicion led him to shift entire populations, especially the minorities he distrusted. He also had up to one-quarter of his top military staff after World War I killed because he didn't trust them—a blindly self-defeating move that put every Russian citizen at risk when World War II broke out and their skills were most needed.

Is Stalin a horrifying rarity? Not really. Adolf Hitler (more than 5 million killed) was also pathologically narcissistic and paranoid. So was Pol Pot in Cambodia, known for his "killing fields" and forced labor (more than 1.2 million killed).

Or let's talk recent history: How about Slobodan Milosević in the 1990s and his xenophobic view of ethnic minorities, especially Muslims and Croats? Or Ratko Mladić, also called the Butcher of Bosnia, accused by the International Criminal Court for the former Yugoslavia in the ethnic killing of more than 7,500 Bosnian Muslim men and boys in Srebrenica in 1995? What all of these individuals have in common is that they were personalities that were both narcissistic (all had grand, violent solutions to problems) and paranoid (they saw enemies everywhere). That made them dangerous enough. But they also had access to security forces and the military, making for the most destructive mixture of all: a dangerous personality with unfettered power.

Then there's Anders Behring Breivik, responsible for bombing a government building in Oslo, Norway, on July 22, 2011, killing 8, followed by a mass shooting, killing 69 teenagers. He, too, as the court found, was narcissistic and paranoid. He saw himself as the only person capable of saving his country (narcissism) from foreigners and Muslims (paranoia), so he murdered the innocent in protest.[6] Breivik demonstrated that you can still do a lot of damage even without a standing army if you're a narcissistic and paranoid personality and you have access to improvised explosives or high-powered weapons.

Unfortunately, we have seen this personality type before: Those who are small bit players on life's stage but who want to make a name for themselves in history. Their high valuation of themselves, coupled with their paranoia, drives them to extremes—but when no one will listen to them or if they are rejected, they seek ways to make themselves or their cause known, just as Breivik did.

They become large players, perhaps even on the world stage, by the quickest means known—through violence. Long before Breivik shocked Norway, one other highly stubborn, rigid-thinking, and difficult individual with all the features of paranoia and narcissism we have described made a name for himself. First, he tried to do it in April 1963 by attempting to assassinate Major General Edwin Walker, the man who ran against John Connally for Texas governor the previous year, while Walker was reading at home in Dallas. When that failed (he only slightly injured Walker), his next opportunity would clinch it. This would be the big leagues, as he always told his wife he wanted to be in.[7] His next target of opportunity fortuitously would, according to the route published by the local papers, drive by his place of work on November 22, 1963, in an open limousine. His target: John F. Kennedy, president of the United States. His name: Lee Harvey Oswald, a man who had all the features of the paranoid personality as well as those of the narcissistic personality in abundance.

For most of us, the danger from the narcissist + paranoid personality is of special concern when the person self-isolates. Over and over, we've seen that when these individuals self-isolate, there's no outside dampening of their outlandish ideas. In isolation, they can fixate on an issue or on perceived wounds, marinating in their passions, hatred, and fears. Unfortunately, their trajectory is usually the same: violence against those they devalue or fear.[8]

For example, when Timothy McVeigh was turned down for the Green Berets and was discharged from the US Army, he made the decision to isolate himself in Arizona so he could focus his hatred on the federal government. In that isolation, he planned the bombing of the Alfred P. Murrah Federal Building in Oklahoma City. Decades earlier, Theodore Kaczynski (the Unabomber), narcissistic and paranoid like McVeigh, similarly went to live in a remote Montana cabin, where he further refined his hatred of technology and from where he could build his bombs that eventually killed 3 and injured 23.[9]

"Pay Attention While I Do As I Please": Narcissist + Predator

In 2003, I was asked by the US State Department to help the government of Colombia set up its first criminal profiling unit. It was an honor to assist in that endeavor, and the *Unidad Especial de Comportamiento Criminal de Colombia* remains very active in solving the most atrocious criminal cases in Colombia. One of the first cases I was asked to analyze was that of Luis

Alfredo Garavito Cubillos, known as the Butcher of Colombia. Most Americans have never heard of Garavito Cubillos, yet he's the most prolific serial killer in this hemisphere, having killed more than 240 children in a 7-year period (140 bodies were found—he could not remember where the rest were buried).

As we sat down to analyze the case, there was something about the way he looked in one particular photo that sparked my attention. My counterpart from the Colombian government, Luis Alfonso Forero-Parra, a brilliant officer and psychologist who now heads the Colombian criminal profiling unit, noticed me pausing over the photo. "Do you see that narcissistic glee on his face?" I asked. "He's just been arrested, and he appears to enjoy the attention he's getting from the media."

"Funny you should say that," Dr. Forero-Parra replied. "As he was being led into the jail, he asked, 'How does my hair look?'" Sometimes, predators are palpably narcissistic. This was one of those times.

Indeed, we often see some of the features of the predator with the narcissist. Bernard Madoff, mastermind and architect of the largest Ponzi scheme in US history, who took advantage of his own family and friends, appears to have many of the features of the narcissist, whose behaviors say, "I can do anything, by any means, without restraint" and the predator, whose behaviors say, "I will take advantage of whom I can, when I can, without remorse." The grandiose scale of the plan, the audacity of its implementation, the aloofness and willingness to hurt others—all speak volumes about this multifaceted dangerous personality.[10]

Many experts believe that aggressive narcissism is at the core of social predation—in other words, in order to prey mercilessly on others, you have to be able to overvalue yourself and devalue others.[11] It makes sense. To be a Ted Bundy, one has to have a tremendous sense of entitlement and a keen ability to devalue others without any kind of conscience. So when we see a predator with a prevalence of narcissistic features, we can say we're dealing with a highly dangerous individual, a topic we'll discuss further in Chapter 6, Self-Defense against Dangerous Personalities.

Like Ted Bundy, Charles Manson also met the criteria of the narcissist and the predator. From an early age, Manson was a petty criminal, burglar, thief, sexual predator, and a liar who enjoyed manipulating others.[12] He saw himself as a gifted musician (which he was not) and cult leader, but his real gift was exercising God-like control (narcissism) over others, taking advantage of them and getting them to commit crimes for him (predator).[13] He was found guilty of conspiracy to commit the murders of Sharon Tate and Leno and Rosemary LaBianca, along with their companions, which were carried out, at his instruction, by members of his cult. After 40 years, thankfully, he remains behind bars, a testament to how dangerous he is. If you ever doubt the danger posed by the narcissistic predator, read *Helter Skelter* by Vincent Bugliosi or *Manson* by Jeff Guinn; then you will understand.

COMBINING THREE OR MORE DANGEROUS PERSONALITY TYPES

Now let's consider individuals with three or more traits. When I look at the behaviors of Jim Jones, the cult leader of Jonestown, Guyana, I find that he certainly had narcissistic traits. His need to be worshipped is clearly narcissistic. But he also had paranoid features and elements of the predator. His need for isolation and his fear of outsiders are clearly paranoid. His narcissistic self-elevation gave rise to inflated notions of the number of his enemies.[14] His taking of people's money and the Draconian punishments he meted out are the behaviors of a predator. Ultimately, that punishment included the drinking of cyanide-laced Kool-Aid, which killed more than 900 of his followers, a testament to how profoundly dangerous (narcissistic + paranoid + predator) he really was.[15]

Sad to say, it isn't that uncommon to identify someone with multiple personality types, especially when studying leaders in hate groups or cults. Recent history gives us several. David Koresh, leader of the Branch Davidians, was similar in many ways to Jim Jones: narcissistic and paranoid, with traits of the predator. But then so is polygamist cult leader Warren Jeffs. Until his arrest, Jeffs's cult had been a personal breeding ground that permitted him to have sex with underage girls, with the assistance of their complicit mothers. He fits the criteria for the key features of narcissism in believing that God called him to do this and that "earthly" laws don't apply to him, and he has no remorse for the despicable things that he does, much as the predator believes. Last, he shunned outsiders or anyone who would compete or disagree with him (paranoia).[16] He typifies individuals who have all three personality types (narcissistic + predator + paranoid)—selfish, manipulative, abusive, and fearful.

Perhaps no discussion of this personality triad would be complete without mentioning al-Qaeda founder Usama bin Laden, whose extreme narcissism and severe paranoia, with flavorings of the predator, resulted in the 9/11 terror attacks on the United States.[17] It's difficult to overstate the global economic, social, and political impact this single individual had in a remarkably short time (though, like many of the most dangerous predators, he planned his 9/11 campaign for years with single-minded intent). With terrorists possessing this level of grandiosity, one tends to find few terrorist acts, but those that do happen are huge, i.e., events they feel are worthy of them.[18] If they're charismatic and intelligent, they can construct elaborate plans and recruit other dangerous personalities to carry out the work according to their particular abilities: vicious predators who get a thrill from killing, or paranoid personalities whose fear and hatred make them pliant and susceptible to being called into becoming suicide bombers.

THE FULL MONTY: FOUR DANGEROUS PERSONALITIES

It's possible to meet someone who has the core characteristics of all four dangerous personalities to varying degrees. As you can probably imagine, this makes for a highly destructive, unstable individual. Stress and other factors can push this individual to the more extreme and dangerous ends of the spectrum within any of the four pathologies. Hitler certainly exhibited many of the features of the predator, the narcissist, the paranoid, and the highly emotionally unstable personality as the tide turned against him in World War II and he neared the end of his life.[19]

You may think it's rare to find someone who combines all four types, but you'd be amazed at how many people are like that. They sometimes do their damage in a neighborhood, in an office, or in a nearby town, and we don't hear about it. Or if we do hear about it after they've wrought their particular brand of mayhem, rarely does someone do a psychological postmortem and conclude, "So-and-so did these things because they were a combination of these personality types." It's too bad, because while we routinely perform autopsies to establish the manner and cause of death, rarely are psychological postmortems done on these cases, which could educate us about the real dangers out there.

If someone claims it's unlikely that a person could have the acute features of all four dangerous personality types, remember Ugandan dictator Idi Amin. He had all of the acute features we're describing here in varying quantities. Was he always like that?[20] I don't know. And once again, does it matter, if that's what he became in the end? The tens of thousands of Ugandans he tortured or killed and their surviving family members don't care, either. What matters is that at some point, something clicked and those behavioral traits became the essence of his personality, and the damage he did was horrific.

But these personalities don't have to kill or hurt hundreds or thousands to be dangerous. This type of personality can live in your neighborhood, quite close to you. In her diary, Utah wife and mother Susan Powell detailed some of the things that her husband, Josh Powell, was doing that troubled her. In 2008, she even noted that if she died, it would be no accident. She felt that she was in peril, but she acted too slowly for fear that her husband would take away her children.[21] She was a good observer, but she was hesitant and reluctant to clearly see the danger because she had little to help validate her observations. She hoped that her faith and the church would make things better.[22] Her pious hope did not and would not save her, nor will it save you from a dangerous personality.

In the end, Susan Powell mysteriously disappeared in 2009. She is, as she herself predicted, presumed dead. Husband Josh immediately came under investigation and rightly so, as it's mostly spouses who hurt spouses. When the investigation became more intense and focused on him, Josh moved away.[23] Finally in 2012, when social workers came to the house, Josh killed his children with a hatchet and later himself by setting the house on fire.[24]

From what witnesses have said and from the writings of Susan Powell in her diary, Josh had features of both a paranoid and emotionally unstable personality as well as those of a predator and a narcissist. She could not do anything without his permission; he was entitled to do as he pleased; he would lash out at her at will, unfazed by his cruelty toward her; and he would keep tabs on her and question whom she talked to. It was so bad that she had to call family and friends from work, so he wouldn't know.

Unfortunately, no one had told Susan that she was married to a man with these dangerous personality traits. As far as I can tell, she received little or no guidance about dangerous personalities and what you can expect from them. Still, somehow, she perceived that she was dealing with a dangerous personality, because she began to write about it in her journal, sensing that her life was in danger.

Susan Powell's whereabouts remain unknown. Most likely she was killed at the hands of her husband. Susan perceptively had an inkling of how dangerous her husband was based on his behaviors; she just didn't have reliable confirmation and an authoritative guide to tell her to run, get out, get help, *now*. But you do.

WHEN DANGEROUS PERSONALITIES JOIN FORCES

Ever wonder why prisoners, when they are released, are forbidden to associate with other convicted felons? It's because experience has taught us that when dangerous personalities associate with other dangerous personalities, the risk to society (and themselves) increases. Here are some historical examples of what happens when dangerous personalities buddy up:

- Frank and Jessie James were notorious train and bank robbers in the 1860s who wantonly killed and murdered their way to infamy.

- Like the James brothers, Robert LeRoy Parker (Butch Cassidy) and Harry Alonzo Longabaugh (Sundance Kid), along with the Wild Bunch gang, were train robbers and murderers in the late 1800s and early 1900s.

- Bonnie Parker and Clyde Barrow (Bonnie and Clyde) were bank robbers and murderers—and nowhere near as nice as they're portrayed in films.

- Charles Manson and his collection of sycophants he called his "family" stole, robbed, and killed without hesitation or remorse.

■ Angelo Buono Jr. and Kenneth Bianchi (the Hillside Stranglers) were two cousins who raped, tortured, and murdered women and girls ranging in age from 12 to 28 in the late 1970s in California.

■ Charles Ng and Leonard Lake in Wilseyville, California, sadistically killed somewhere between 11 and 25 victims, including two babies, in the 1980s. Some of these events were videotaped inside the torture chamber they had built.

■ Henry Lee Lucas and Ottis Toole together killed perhaps more than 100 individuals throughout the United States in the early 1980s and over a 7-year period. It was Toole who admitted killing 6-year-old Adam Walsh in 1981 with a machete. Adam's father, John Walsh, became the host of the noted television crime-solving show *America's Most Wanted,* and the Adam Walsh case raised awareness about the risks posed by dangerous personalities and spurred passage in the United States of the Adam Walsh Child Protection and Safety Act of 2006, which led to the creation of the National Sex Offender Registry, among other advances in the effort to protect children from predatory personalities.[25]

■ Eric Harris and Dylan Klebold killed 12 students and a teacher and wounded 23 others before committing suicide at Columbine High School.[26]

■ John Muhammad and Lee Boyd Malvo randomly shot and killed 13 people in the Washington, Virginia, and Maryland area in 2002 using a sniper rifle and while concealed in the trunk of their car.

And that's just a few. It's bad enough when these personalities act alone, but when they collaborate, they truly put us in danger, as they tend to feed and nurture each other to do even more harm. In the case of Muhammad and Malvo, they catalyzed each other into a 3-week killing frenzy that terrified one of the most well-protected capitals in the world—Washington, DC—and for a while they seemed unstoppable.

PUTTING IT ALL TOGETHER

I hope this chapter has helped you understand how to use the checklists in combination to assess those whose behavior gives you pause or is causing you or others to suffer—whether you're hearing it on the news or experiencing it in your life.

Bottom line: When someone has features of more than one dangerous personality, these combined characteristics potentiate one another, making this person much more complex, much more unstable, and potentially more dangerous. The higher such individuals score on the checklists, the greater their complexity, instability, and dangerousness. Even if a person scores low across the board, you're still talking about someone who will aggravate, irritate, frustrate, frighten, or otherwise drain your cup—in short, a dangerous person you want to avoid if you value your psychological, mental, emotional, physical, or financial health.

While the checklists won't predict precisely what someone will do, they give you an idea of the trajectory of that person's behavior. No one's behavior can be predicted—we're all too complex for that. But remember, the best predictor of future behavior is past behavior. And since dangerous personalities are flawed in character as well as in personality, chances are they're not going to take steps to improve themselves. So the trajectory of their behavior is likely to remain the same or worsen, depending on circumstances.

If the checklists aren't handy and you need to assess someone quickly, ask yourself the following five questions:

❶ Do they affect me emotionally in a negative way?

❷ Do they do things that are illegal, erratic, unethical, or defy social norms?

❸ Do they do things that are exploitative or manipulative?

❹ Do they do things that are dangerous?

❺ Do they do things impulsively with little control or with unwillingness to delay gratification?

The more yes answers you have, the more likely it is that you're dealing with someone who combines traits of more than one type of dangerous personality. The checklists will then help you pinpoint more specifically the type of person you're dealing with and where this individual falls on the spectrum of severity.

Another tip: Turn to the "Words That Describe . . ." sections in Chapters 1 through 4 and circle the words that feel like the right match for this personality. Those words alone have helped many people validate that what they're experiencing is similar to what other victims have experienced.

In his landmark work *The Gulag Archipelago*, Aleksandr I. Solzhenitsyn, who shed so much light on the ghastly abuses of the Soviet empire and its leaders, cautioned that there can come a point where a human crosses the line into what he called "evil."[27] There was a time when Ted Bundy wasn't interested in killing college students, but at some point, he crossed that line, and he never returned. Many may ask how or why it happened. Some may remember when this person was not that way. These are valid points of curiosity; but you and I live in the present, and all that matters is what this person is like now and whether he or she presents a danger to you and your loved ones. That is all I care about, and that is my purpose in writing this book.

SELF-DEFENSE AGAINST DANGEROUS PERSONALITIES

YOU PROBABLY KNOW THE STORY of how to boil a frog. If you put it in boiling water, it'll leap out. But if you put it in tepid water and slowly increase the temperature, the frog won't even know it's slowly boiling to death.

At the FBI, when we interviewed people who'd been victimized by a dangerous personality, I heard versions of this refrain over and over: "By the time I realized what was going on, it was too late."

Our ability to adapt is a powerful survival mechanism. But with dangerous personalities, we may boil to death before we realize we're in hot water.

Fortunately, we're a lot smarter than those frogs. We can learn how to be alert to those who can hurt us and take steps to protect ourselves. Still, I have to be honest, until I attended the Utah Police Academy and the FBI Academy, I really didn't know how criminals behaved. Television had given me limited insight, but it certainly didn't look into all four of the dangerous personalities we've explored in these chapters and how those personalities behave.

I wrote this book to share what I've learned from experience through decades of training and study and from talking to victims. I wanted to share this with you because I know that you are not going to have the training I received, nor will you have a police officer or mental health professional constantly at your side to help you. None of us do.

There are thousands of suicide call centers around the country, and there are many battered spouse centers. But there's no center you can call when you have suspicions of a dangerous personality. Just as it's up to us to "look before we cross," so it's up to us, individually and as parents or managers, to be vigilant, to have situational awareness, to assess for threats and danger, to take appropriate action to prevent dangerous individuals from entering our lives, and to deal with them if they do. I don't want you to be that frog that thinks everything's fine, not realizing that the temperature's rising by 1 degree every hour.

This book is just part of the equation. There are other great books out there, including J. Reid Meloy's classic, *Violence Risk and Threat Assessment*; *Fatal Flaws* by Stuart Yudofsky, MD; *The Criminal Personality* by Samuel Yochelson and Stanton E. Samenow; *Without Conscience* by Robert Hare; and *The Gift of Fear* by Gavin de Becker; along with others listed in the Bibliography. Many people can help, and I hope you'll turn to the Selected Resources section that follows to see some of the various organizations prepared and willing to assist you. The more you learn and the more you reach out for support, the better equipped you'll be.

What follows are my personal insights based on decades of law enforcement and criminal profiling experience. Please consider these ideas, keeping in mind that my perspective is that of a former law enforcement officer and criminal profiler—it is not the same perspective as that of a mental health professional. You are wise to consider what they have to say also. This is my contribution to the literature and my opinions; this is not, and cannot be, the last word on the subject.

FIRST THINGS FIRST: REALITY

When people are dealing with a dangerous personality, the usual well-meaning advice they hear is generally some version of "Try to talk to him; try to get her some help; try to work things out together; give him another chance." Nicole Brown Simpson, former wife of O. J. Simpson, did all of that. She's dead. I think this is fine advice when you're dealing with run-of-the-mill interpersonal problems. But when it comes to the four dangerous personalities in this book, things are a little different.

First of all, as mentioned in previous chapters, these personalities usually don't think there's anything wrong with them. So your efforts to introduce them to that reality usually get this kind of reaction: "I don't have a problem; you're the problem" or "You don't know what you're talking about" or "Who told you I have a problem? I'm fine" or "Who've you been talking to? What have you told them?" There are other reactions; these are a few of the nicer ones.

I'm not saying you shouldn't try to talk. Maybe they're low enough on the behavioral spectrum that they may be willing to seek help without lashing out at you. But don't be surprised if they say they'll seek help but then they don't, or if they go once and never go back. I say this because I've talked to scores of people who tell me this is what happened.

Remember, these individuals are flawed in character and personality, so narcissists may explode at you with rage because they see themselves as perfect and you are suggesting otherwise. The emotionally unstable will lash out because that is this individual's nature. The predator definitely doesn't see anything wrong with himself and may become violent on a whim at the mere suggestion that he seek help, while the paranoid personality may now see you as a confirmed "enemy" and trust you even less. This is why I say that offering the suggestion to seek help from mental health professionals or a counselor is a good approach for most troubled people, but with dangerous personalities, you really have to be careful, because doing so can be very dicey.

For example, if you choose to confront them and suggest that they see a professional, know that this will have to be done delicately, minimizing any offense, and be aware that there may be serious repercussions. I think it's worth trying only if you believe you can do it safely. Only you know your situation. Don't let anyone cavalierly talk you into doing it—and then you're the one who gets her face punched or you have to live in hell for the next month.

There are professionals who specialize in dealing with personality disorders and criminal behavior. Some are listed in the Selected Resources chapter. Always remember that fixing people is both an art and a science best left to professionals, but even they can't fix some people. Dangerous personalities, as I've described, lack introspection and dedication to improving their behaviors, so it will be an uphill battle that should be fought by the pros—mental health professionals, not you or me—and even then, there are no guarantees of success, as these dangerous personalities are practically immune or resistant to change.

Be especially careful with personalities who have crossed the line from irritating and noxious to the more virulent, unstable, or criminal side of the spectrum. People like Ted Bundy, Henry Lee Lucas, John Wayne Gacy, or Jerry Sandusky don't line up at the local mental health clinic wanting to confront their demons. They don't because they don't think they have any, even as they kill or rape. It's a whole different ball game when it comes to getting them some help. Once they've crossed into the criminal arena or they are irrational or unstable, it's time for you to distance yourself, get out, and get away. It sounds harsh, but it's the best advice I can give you from a lifetime of experience.

THINGS WE CAN DO EVERY DAY

Over the years, I've talked to experts about what we can do every day to protect ourselves. That's one of the most important questions we can ask. The list below is not all-inclusive, and there are many books out there that go into greater detail about dealing with toxic or dangerous personalities. Nevertheless, I hope you'll find some guidance here and that these tactics will help you as they have helped others in similar situations to stay safe.

Gain Knowledge

Louis Pasteur, the French chemist and microbiologist who among other things gave us pasteurization, said with some authority, "Chance favors the prepared mind." He was right. By now, you've read the previous chapters and are familiar with the four dangerous personalities and the accompanying checklists. (And many times I've heard people say, "Wow, I know someone exactly like that!") Now that you've been sensitized to the personality traits of these dangerous personalities, you're better prepared to deal with these individuals and improve your chances of staying safe.

These checklists were created not just to help you assess those individuals in your life that cause you concern; they're also there to educate. They can serve as reminders of how these individuals manipulate; pull emotional strings; insinuate themselves into peoples' lives against their will; abuse others physically or mentally; lie, cheat, steal, or engage in risky behaviors that wreak havoc; or place others in danger or actually victimize them. Even if you never reread this book in its entirety, at least periodically review the four Dangerous Personalities Checklists to remind yourself that these are the people to avoid and why.

Don't Just Look: Observe

When I was young, I went to the beach every weekend in Miami. There were many tourists there from Europe, and their toddlers often bathed naked on the beach, as was their custom. Often I'd see a man nearby, dressed in street clothes, taking photographs. I thought he was a professional photographer, with his big bag of lenses and 35 millimeter film. He took a keen interest in photographing the tourists, but often he'd come closer to photograph their children as they played in the surf or built sand castles. I didn't think anything of it at the time; I was more interested in his cameras, which I knew my parents couldn't afford.

What I was seeing, at age 11, was a photographer. What I was not observing was a pedophile in action. I was blind to what was going on because no one had taught me what to look for; no one had pointed out that this is how a sexual predator or child pornographer behaves. It wasn't until years later while I was studying sex crimes that I realized what I had seen, but not observed, because I was mentally unprepared.

After some horrible crime occurs, how many times have we seen a reporter ask a neighbor of the accused "what kind of person" this individual was, only to hear some variation of "He was a nice guy"? Nearly 40 years ago, when investigators were digging up the 26th body from under John Wayne Gacy's house in Illinois, his neighbor, true to form, told reporters what a "great guy he was."[1] Nothing has changed. People see, but they don't observe. In fact, it may be getting worse. The next time you're in a public space, look around you: People now have their faces buried in their smartphone screens, often to the point of bumping into others, and their ears are obstructed by headphones or earpieces. It's tough to see or hear a stalker as you're walking to your car if your eyes are glued to a screen, you're on a call, or you've got music cranked up. But look how many people do precisely that. And the predators out there know it.

Let this book and the checklists serve as your informal training to prepare you to observe. Your powers of observation can go a long way toward keeping you and your loved ones safe. As the renowned 19th-century French criminologist and biometrician Alphonse Bertillon said, "One can only see what one observes, and one observes only things which are already in the mind."

Trust Your Feelings: How Does This Person Make You Feel?

In Chapter 4, I wrote about hearing my gun rattling as my body shook in recognition of a social predator. We have an internal alerting system that tells us we're in danger, if only we will listen to it. Be alert to how others make you feel—this is a key criterion often missed even by experts. Tune in to your physical reactions to people and situations: gut clenching, hairs prickling, skin flushing, queasiness, anxiousness, or just a vague unease. Be grateful for these feelings, because they're messages from our brain to our body: "Be careful—this person could be a dangerous personality." Be thankful for that "gift of fear" that Gavin de Becker so eloquently wrote about in his book of the same title—a book we should all read.

Know the Difference between Niceness and Goodness

Serial killer Ted Bundy offered to help young women carry their groceries. Sexual predator and serial murderer John Wayne Gacy literally clowned for neighborhood kids. Convicted pedophile Jerry Sandusky held sports programs for troubled youth. They could all act nice (these individuals usually know how to do that well), but behind closed doors they were not nice or good; they were evil.

One problem with society is that we're inclined to attribute goodness to people who don't deserve it. As I've mentioned in previous chapters, dangerous personalities know how to be nice, but they're not good.

When I was very young, my mother taught me a Spanish version of this wisdom: "*Ventajeros no son buenos*," which means: Those who do nice things for advantage or for gain (opportunists) are not really good or nice people. Years later, I appreciated Gavin de Becker's variant: "Niceness is not goodness."[2] We need to recognize the difference and teach our children this valuable lesson.

Niceness comes and goes and can be displayed for selfish reasons. Goodness comes from the heart and is part of a person's essential nature. It's the ability to consistently think and care about the needs of someone else, as a good parent does for a child. Good people can sometimes have a bad day—but then they return to their baseline of goodness in thought, word, and deed. Niceness is really about actions anyone can perform. Goodness is about character and intentions. When we assess for goodness, we're assessing the intentions behind behaviors. Teach your children the difference.

Control Space and Distance

Use distance as a barrier to keep you and yours safe. Walls, fences, gates, doors, car windows, parental settings on a computer—all are there to help keep you safe. Sometimes, we ourselves have to create that distance and barrier. You don't want a person too close to you at the ATM machine or following you to your car. Nor do you want your intimate partner arguing with you 3 inches from your face. Space and distance, as well as barriers, can help keep you safe. Remember, predators try to control your space, body, mind, money, or emotions. Space and distance can help keep them from achieving that.

Control Time—Slow Things Down

Dangerous personalities use time to take advantage of you. They create urgency or want you to act quickly to draw you in—to get married, hire them, sign the contract, write the check, let them in the door, or adopt their beliefs. Slow things down. Create time buffers so that you can think and reflect without pressure. This is a clue: If time is being used to pressure you, if you feel you are being rushed, then something is wrong. When people really care, they don't want you to hurry.

Dangerous personalities may also use time to wear you down, using persistence, repeated arguments, or even incrementally more serious threats. If you sense someone is trying to wear you down, distance yourself or put a more definitive stop to your interaction. This is where empathetic allies you can trust can be of assistance to rally around you, if need be (see "Make Supportive Alliances," discussed later in this chapter).

Cut the Emotional Strings

If you are around a person who is pulling your emotional strings (or trying to), something's wrong. Caring people don't do that. Dangerous personalities are social puppeteers: They know what to say and do to tug at your emotions. They may threaten to leave or to commit suicide, or will tell you that they'll be devastated if you don't do this or that. Or, toddlerlike, they may sulk and cry and whine, trying to get you to do what they want. Just stop and remind yourself: When your emotions are being pulled, it means that someone is intentionally pulling those strings. This is manipulation. You don't want to spend your life being manipulated by someone. Take control of your life away from dangerous personalities who act as puppeteers. Recognize what they are doing, set boundaries, and walk away from those who do not respect you by pulling your emotional strings.

Assess How Much/How Often

When it comes to dangerous personalities, what behaviors we observe and how those behaviors are displayed often give us clues as to where people are on their individual dangerous personality continuum or spectrum as well as provide insight into how dangerous they are or whether they are a combination of dangerous personality types (see Chapter 5). This means everyone gets a pass if they have one or two behaviors that stand out once in a great while. After all, as I've mentioned, anyone can have a bad day. But if the behaviors noted in the checklists happen repeatedly, if these behaviors increase over time, or if they are affecting you emotionally or physically, take heed. Remember: When it comes to dangerous personalities, permissiveness on your part is seen as either weakness or as a green light to continue doing more of the same.

Know That Time and Location Matter

I once worked a case in Tampa where a young woman was found raped and strangled in the bushes just 12 feet from a major road. Analysis of her modus vivendi (how she lived) revealed the following: At some point during the night she disappeared, she ran out of cigarettes (we found all the cigarette boxes in her apartment empty). She walked to an all-night convenience store 2 blocks away, where she bought cigarettes and left at around 11:10 p.m.—the store surveillance camera captured her making the purchase and exiting alone. Sometime after that, while walking home, she was attacked (defense wounds on her arms), raped (semen on and in her), and killed (ligature around neck). According to the convenience store clerk who had served her, she had gone to the store to buy cigarettes or other items many times in the past. What was different this time was the time of day: Usually, she went to the store around 5:30 p.m. after work when it was still light out and there were plenty of people and cars going by. This single change altered her situation from hard-working young woman running an errand after work to murder victim.

You can go from being a low-risk victim to being a high-risk victim just by changing the time of day and your location. Interpersonal violence increases between the hours of 8:00 p.m. and 2:00 a.m. When alcohol and drugs are involved, violence escalates. We've known these facts since the 1960s, yet people seem oblivious to this reality.

This doesn't mean you shouldn't go out after 8:00 p.m., but it does mean you have to be extra careful. A simple act at 11:00 in the morning can turn deadly at 11:00 at night.

Make Yourself Uninviting to Dangerous Personalities

Predators often pick their targets by how they walk. When you're out and about, look around; pay attention; look at people directly; let them know you see them—or even that you're onto them. Walk with purpose and decisively (good arm swing), not passively—predators love passive, inattentive walkers. Face traffic; don't let traffic come up behind you. When walking to your car, avoid being on the phone, and try to keep one hand free. You should avoid alleys or being too close to the street if walking alone. In rural areas or where there's a lot of vegetation, look for places someone can hide.

Check 'Em Out

Due diligence is a term used in business that entails verifying whether people are who they say they are, whether they're trustworthy, or whether there are any issues. Whether we call it due diligence, "checking them out," "verifying trustworthiness," or seeing if they are "on the up and up," we need to do this with those we meet in our own lives. It's amazing how many people bring someone home, let a stranger babysit their child, or allow someone to handle their finances without checking references. People get married only to find out later that their spouse is still married to someone else, is a wanted criminal, or (as we saw in the "Clark Rockefeller" story in Chapter 1) is a complete impostor.

People should spend more time getting to know whom they're dating or marrying than they do researching their next kitchen appliance. Does this individual's personal information (name, where she grew up, where she went to school) check out? Have you met her family? Does she really work where she says she does? Has she been married before? It seems like a lot to do, but by now you've heard many stories of how trusting people have been taken advantage of or violated. If you fail to do due diligence, to actually get to know people, then you do so at your own peril.

Don't Wait Too Long

Don't wait too long to act. If you sense something negative, even early on, act on it. Maybe Natalee Holloway sensed something was wrong toward the end of the evening in Aruba, but if she did, it came too late—by then her friends had left and she was in a foreign country surrounded by male strangers she had just met. As you'll recall, she was never found. Maybe Travis Alexander felt something was wrong early in his relationship with Jodi Arias, but he delayed taking action for too long also.

When it comes to dangerous personalities, you may not have much time to act. If you don't know what to do, distancing yourself is probably the best course of action.

DEALING WITH DANGEROUS PERSONALITIES

Obviously, the best thing we can do is avoid them, but sometimes we can't. Perhaps they find us or we find ourselves with them for a variety of reasons, including travel, marriage, and work, or maybe one is a relative. Whatever the reason, if you think you're in the presence of a dangerous personality, take care of yourself first and foremost. I hope these strategies will help.

Who Is This?

Use the Dangerous Personalities Checklists to get a better feel for whom you're dealing with. If you can't do that, then at least run through your memory of the checklists and try to see where this individual fits. Doing this will give you insight into how bad your situation really is and what protective measures you should take. Having said that, however, never delay if you feel you're in danger. If you see a man with a gun in a hallway, you don't need these checklists—just run. But sometimes, as I've noted in previous chapters, it isn't so obvious—for example, when smooth-talking swindlers get your grandmother's bank account information.

Complex Situations

You may know that your husband is a liar and a cheat and that he's abusive, but issues such as family and finances can really complicate matters. Yes, he's a dangerous personality and he scores high on two of the Dangerous Personalities Checklists, but perhaps you find it hard to leave for valid reasons. If it's a work situation, maybe you need the money, maybe the nasty boss is a relative, or maybe you can't leave until you can save some more money. I have heard all of these things many times, and I understand. Be realistic about your situation so that you can deal with it.

Frankly, the more complex the situation is, the more help you will need. It may also take longer to extricate yourself, but if things escalate, especially the threat level and the violence, you may have no choice. Every military pilot I know wants to save his aircraft, but at some point there's nothing more a pilot can do and he has to eject to save himself. The same can happen to us in life.

If it's an employment issue, see if you can transfer or work a different shift. Talk to HR or management and build supportive alliances; but in the end, you may have to quit. Incidentally, these are all things that some people who worked for Apple's cofounder Steve Jobs eventually were forced to do. Read Walter Isaacson's biography *Steve Jobs* and you will appreciate that while Jobs was a visionary, he was also mercurial and pathologically nasty to his own people—for decades. He made many of his own employees emotionally distressed and others physically sick. Even his long-term partner, Steven Wozniak, finally had to quit; he couldn't take Jobs's nastiness anymore.[3] That may be something you'll have to do also because, as these Apple employees found out, making millions wasn't worth their mental and physical health—nothing is.

Quitting a job is obviously easier than quitting a marriage where there are kids and finances involved. Or what if you're a teenager and you actually want to be emancipated from your parents because they are toxic, involved in drugs, or clearly fit any of the dangerous personality descriptions we've discussed? Getting out can become really complicated—but there are ways.

If your situation is complex, you truly will need help, and more than any book can give you. You need professionals to step in and guide you, assist you, and lend a hand. Or maybe things are so bad that social services or the police need to intervene.

By all means, use the checklists to confirm and validate what you're experiencing. Then it's time to talk to a professional and get them involved. Don't ever hesitate to go to a mental health professional or even to the police with this book in hand and say, "Please take a look at this checklist, because my intimate partner/my husband/my wife/my parents/my friend/ my child does all these things." It is so much harder to ignore someone who comes in prepared with documentation.

And while we're on the subject of documentation . . .

Catalog the Behaviors

While I was stationed in Puerto Rico, I had a boss who was verbally abusive to everyone below him. He screamed and yelled at me and just about everyone else. After he lashed out at me a couple of times, I learned my lesson. So every time he came to my office or called me into his office, I made sure I had my personal journal with me. As soon as he started yelling, I would begin to write. Soon he stopped, because he knew I was writing down what he said and how he said it. I learned that for some people, writing down their words and actions can often change their behavior or prevent further harassment.

But some people aren't just screamers—some are more combustible or violent. In those cases, I have the same recommendation. Write down everything they do by date and time, especially if these are recurring events. You are doing yourself a favor, and it may save you later on— whether the situation's happening at home or at work. Something so simple as e-mailing details of the event to yourself preserves a record that may assist you in the future.

If someone lashes out at you, slams a door in your face, slaps you, hits you, lets the air out of your tire, stalks you, or begins to harass you over the phone, write it down somewhere (time, day, what happened). I always go back to the example of Nicole Brown Simpson. If only she had kept a private journal of how many times O. J. harassed her, called her, broke into her apartment, slapped her around, threw her to the floor, beat her, and on and on.[4] What if Nicole had gone to the police or the state prosecutors with a journal full of entries and said, "Please do something about this"? I would like to think that things would have turned out differently for her. Don't ever assume that police or law enforcement records will be enough—they won't; we have a responsibility in building a case also.

I've talked to many women who were saved in their divorce proceedings because they walked in with a journal full of entries of how their husbands abused or stole from them. Remember: A written journal will always trump someone's memory in any court or a formal proceeding. The last thing an attorney on the opposing side wants to see is a spouse, worker, or businessperson who dutifully wrote down all the details—case over.

Make Supportive Alliances

The more features you see on the Dangerous Personalities Checklists, the more you need to reach out to others to make or deepen supportive alliances. Make sure that everyone in your family knows how you're being mistreated or what kind of person you are dealing with. Tell your neighbors, tell your bartender, talk to your coach or gym teacher, make sure your friends know what it's like to be tormented or mistreated by this individual. You want people on your side calling, checking in, visiting, being vigilant, and validating your experience. There may come a time when they may actually have to step in to help.

Remember the story I shared in Chapter 1 of the woman who was compelled to sit on the floor with her children? Incredible as it seemed, it was finally validated when a friend who had been clued in visited and witnessed it firsthand.

Resist Isolation

Any person who seeks to isolate you physically is a potential danger. If you enter into a relationship, a group, an organization, or a cult and you sense that this person is trying to isolate you from family, friends, co-workers, or people you feel comfortable with, you are dealing with a dangerous personality. If people care for you, they want you to flourish and be happy, to be with your friends. If they want to keep you from others (and they have all sorts of ways of achieving that, including using guilt or shaming your friends and family), just be aware that dangerous personalities use isolation for control. Everyone from Jim Jones to Ted Bundy used isolation to control their victims. Avoid it if possible.

This also includes avoiding getting into vehicles with strangers or with those whose intentions may be in question. Once you are in a car, the potential for danger increases dramatically, while your chances of escape decrease significantly. Any attempt to force you into a vehicle should be resisted with screaming, yelling, kicking, biting, and scratching by any means, even if the person has a handgun or a knife. The greater danger awaits you in the vehicle, not on the outside, and I repeat, even if the person has a gun, you should avoid getting into that vehicle. As a former law enforcement officer and FBI Special Agent, I cannot stress this enough.

Set Boundaries

My father worked for years at a hardware store where the owner was a bully (narcissistic and emotionally unstable). He screamed at the staff, berated them, threw things against the wall, and even screamed at customers. But he never treated my father that way. When I asked my father why not, he said, "Because I told him on the first day, 'Don't ever talk to me like that.' " People will often do what you let them get away with. Set boundaries that are rigid and not up for modification. A "no" must be absolute with these individuals. Give them an inch; they'll take 10 miles. You must set clear boundaries about what is and isn't permissible and persistently defend them. Interestingly, the emotionally unstable personality actually does well with structure, rules, and routines, so boundaries may be helpful there.

Once you've established those boundaries, live by them. They are your red line never to be crossed. If the person repeatedly crosses those boundaries, you will have to take action at some point; otherwise, he or she will continue as before to abuse you, drain you of energy, try your patience, make you emotionally or physically sick, or place you in danger.

Avoid Manipulation

Often, people focus on setting boundaries against victimization but fail to set them against manipulation. Yet manipulation is frequently the prelude to victimization, as these personalities will up the ante repeatedly, wearing you down, asking for special treatment or favors. They will be late; they will make you wait; they will ask you to change your schedule; they will want you to accommodate them over and over. Don't reward bad behavior. When the narcissist finds out that the meeting started without him and he is ignored when he finally comes in, he'll arrive early next time. But if everyone waits for him and fawns over him once he's there, he'll repeat the behavior.

Some will say, "Isn't this like tough love?" No, not really. True love, altruistic love, has healthy boundaries imbued with respect. There's nothing tough about it. It's only "tough" for the dangerous personality who doesn't like boundaries, who has no sympathy, and who doesn't respect others. It's only "tough" because for the selfishly narcissistic, the emotionally unstable, or the predator, everything that respects boundaries and dignity is tough.

Give Children Respite and Positive Outlets

These innocent souls must be protected as much as possible from dangerous personalities, and that includes parents or partners. If children can't be removed from the situation, the best hope is to give them opportunities to be away from home and in places where they can escape, excel, and feel safe and happy.

They need the opportunity to spend time with a loving relative or caregiver in whom they can confide; get therapy if possible; get involved in activities at school; play sports; work with animals; or immerse themselves in the creative worlds of art, reading, or music. Let them see what normal life is like: a life without constant fighting, bickering, or threats.

I dealt with a family where the children were schooled at home and the father had features of the predator and narcissist. It wasn't until those kids were 15 or so that they realized what "normal" was. That is not fair to them. It's our job to help children understand that abuse in all its forms (physical or psychological) is not normal or acceptable.

WHEN IN DANGER, ACT

Sometimes, a dangerous personality exhibits such a high level of toxic, unstable, risky, or criminal behavior that those close by or who are involved with them are in serious danger. Whether it's financial, emotional, psychological, or physical danger, once these individuals have crossed into that mode (the dangerous side of the continuum or spectrum), immediate action is necessary. At this point, it really doesn't matter how you got into the situation. You have to distance yourself immediately or extricate yourself somehow from that relationship.

Here are some strategies for dealing with that immediate threat.

ACT. If your body, your gut, or your mind is saying get away, then do so. If apologies are needed later, you can make them if need be—but if you feel threatened in the moment, try to get away. Don't wait. Any threats of physical harm or any attempt on the part of a dangerous personality to control your body, mind, space, money, or those you love should be a warning to act immediately. Be cautious; don't attract their attention if possible, but get away.

THINK. If this is a highly dangerous personality, you may be safer not talking to this person about what's happening and focusing instead on getting to safety. As I've said, these personalities can lash out at you. If you sense a high degree of danger, telling them they need help or confronting them to the point of escalation is not in your best interest. They may become violent, come after you, destroy property, clean out your bank account, take the children and vanish, show up at the office with a gun, take hostages, attempt suicide, or any number of other violent actions. So think first about how you can leave, exit, or extricate yourself safely. If you must talk to them, do so calmly; try to do it near a door or exit.

ALERT YOUR NETWORK OF FAMILY MEMBERS AND FRIENDS. If things escalate, if you feel increasingly threatened, or if the situation is deteriorating, activate your network. Have them stop by and visit unannounced with greater frequency. Let them know they are to call you every day and if you don't answer the phone, they should stop by or call the police—yes, it gets that bad sometimes.

SEEK HELP FROM PROFESSIONALS. If you haven't reached out to support agencies, faith-based organizations, clergy, therapists, attorneys, police, crisis centers, social services, or help lines, do so now. Now! You need a supportive team and a safety net. Please don't be embarrassed and don't wait. The 911 emergency services (police, fire department, ambulance) were created precisely because all of us at some point need immediate help.

DON'T FACE THEM ALONE. If you must talk with an abuser or a criminal but fear the person might unleash on you, get a mental health professional, family member, or friend to be there with you, with cell phone in hand. Or call the police and tell them you want them standing by just in case. They will come—most police agencies have learned that domestic violence is a critical issue that needs to be addressed promptly.

PLAN YOUR EXIT STRATEGY. Ensuring safety is paramount. I've talked to people who've spent months planning their exit from a relationship with a highly dangerous personality, camouflaging it completely; for example, they might set things up so it seems like a normal dinnertime, telling the person they need to run out to buy something—and not coming back (or they may come back at some point later with a friend to pick up belongings). When it comes to your safety and that of your children, do what you have to do to safely get away from a dangerous personality.

RAISE ESCAPE MONEY. You need funds to draw on if you must leave quickly. If you sense things are bad and going to get worse, prepare financially for the escape. Do what you have to do, including selling personal items to get enough money to get you out of danger. A woman I know in Colombia did this by taking pennies—*pennies!*—every day from her abusive husband until she could afford a bus ticket for herself and her daughter to return to her own family.

ADDRESS FINANCIAL MATTERS. If you feel there's something fishy about a financial deal or something doesn't seem right financially, start asking questions and delay decision making or issuing that check or revealing that credit card number. Whatever you do, don't move forward alone. Get others (preferably a qualified professional such as a banker, an accountant, or an attorney) to assess the situation or look at what you're investing in or contemplating doing and ask them if it is a good deal. Spending $400 on an attorney is far better than losing $40,000 to a dangerous personality.

EXPECT THE GREAT AWAKENING. One thing that happens to those involved with a dangerous personality is what I've come to call the Great Awakening. People often give up years to these individuals. Most are disappointed. But they're so invested that they just continue to try to work things out—until finally they realize that their hopes for this relationship will never be fulfilled. That is the Great Awakening: that moment when you finally realize nothing more can be done for this individual, you are suffering, and it is time to let go.

REMEMBER THAT YOU AREN'T ALONE. I've been there. People feel foolish—like they've been used, are living a lie, or can't trust anyone. Some turn their pain inward, blaming themselves. That's why therapy is always useful at this point, if you can get it. But please don't feel that you're alone. All of us, in one way or another, have experienced something like this.

CLAIM AND MAINTAIN DISTANCE. By now you've probably sensed a theme in my advice, and it is that distance can be very effective. You are correct—and I make no apology, as I am mainly concerned with victims and their loved ones. Experience has taught me that rarely do dangerous personalities get better and that they can have devastating psychological, emotional, financial, and physical effects on us. More often than not, when we distance ourselves from danger or from those who hurt us, we stop hurting. This is where I differ from many others. I have talked to too many victims to prattle, as others do, about trying to work things out when your well-being is at risk. I am persuaded by the wise words of the late Swedish diplomat, author, and second Secretary-General of the United Nations Dag Hammarskjöld, who, having lived through the carnage of World War II, said: "He who wants to keep his garden tidy doesn't reserve a plot for weeds."[5] If the weeds won't go away, it's time to move to a new garden.

A SPECIAL NOTE: IF YOU THINK YOU MAY BE A DANGEROUS PERSONALITY

Over the years, I've written articles about dangerous personalities. Invariably, someone will write in and say, in essence, "I recognize many of those features and behaviors in myself." If that's the case, I want to be the first to congratulate you on your honesty. Now that you see those features, seek help from a mental health professional who is an expert in dealing with your particular behaviors and who can help you. Learn to cognitively distance yourself from your own behaviors that, in the end, also put you at risk.

WHERE DO WE GO FROM HERE?

I hope that reading this book has given you insight into dangerous personalities and some tools for keeping them from hurting you. Life is a gift to be treasured, not spent with a yoke around your neck, catering to a toxic person. When we lived in small villages where everyone pretty much knew each other, it was easier to spot these personalities. When we migrated to cities, doing this became harder. But it's not impossible.

We have an obligation to ourselves, to our families, and to our community to be safe. We achieve that with education, with vigilance, and by sharing information. But first we must help ourselves. By reading this book, you have taken a great step forward toward your own safety and that of those you love. There are many more books out there that will also help and educate you; I hope you'll avail yourself of them through the Bibliography.

I believe in treating others with dignity and respect. I've always tried to do that, even those I put in prison for terrible crimes. We should all treat each other with respect, but that doesn't mean allowing others to abuse or victimize us.

This book was written, in part, to help you validate when you're not being respected, when you're being abused, when you're being violated, and when you're in danger. You are now better equipped to spot these individuals before they hurt you.

Fortunately, most of the people you'll meet and interact with in your daily life aren't dangerous personalities. For the most part, people mean well and care. But I know that in time, you will run into a dangerous personality, because there are millions of them out there. When you do, please remember my final words to you:

**You have no social obligation to be tormented
or to be victimized—ever.**

SELECTED RESOURCES

THE WEB HAS CERTAINLY MADE it easier to find help. Below are some organizations that can provide assistance if you know someone who has mental health issues or who has been victimized. This list is, of course, not all-inclusive. Many states have very supportive groups that can be of great assistance—most are listed in the phone book, and they can also be found online. Never think you are alone or that you are the only one going through problems such as what you may be experiencing. All of us have had our share of troubles, and there are plenty of organizations to assist us.

Children/Child Abuse

National Center for Missing and Exploited Children
missingkids.com
Victim and Family Support: missingkids.com/Families
800-843-5678
Call immediately after calling 911 if your child is missing

National Child Abuse Hotline
childhelp.org
800-422-4453
Crisis counselors available 24/7

National Runaway Safeline
1800runaway.org
800-786-2929

US Department of State
International Parental Child Abduction
United States Department of State, Bureau of Consular Affairs, Office of
    Children's Issues, SA-29, 2201 C Street NW, Washington, DC 20520
childabduction.state.gov
888-407-4747; 202-501-4444
202-736-9132 (fax)
AskCI@state.gov (e-mail)

Crisis Hotlines

Domestic Abuse Helpline for Men and Women (DAHMW)
dahmw.org
888-743-5754 (888-7HELPLINE)
Provides crisis intervention and support services to victims of intimate
    partner violence (IPV) and their families

National Domestic Violence Hotline
thehotline.org
acf.hhs.gov/programs/fysb/help
800-799-7233 (800-799-SAFE)
800–787–3224 (TTY)
Resource center for domestic violence
Department of Health and Human Services provides assistance and will take
    your calls 24/7

National Resource Center on Domestic Violence (NRCDV)
nrcdv.org
800-799-7233 (hotline)
800-787-3224 (hotline TTY)
A comprehensive source of information for those wanting to educate
    themselves on the many issues related to domestic violence

Domestic Violence Assistance

Futures without Violence
futureswithoutviolence.org
Education and professional training programs designed to end violence
    against women, children, and families around the world

Gavin de Becker, Incorporated
11684 Ventura Boulevard, Suite 440, Studio City, CA 91604
gavindebecker.com/main/

National Center for Victims of Crime
ncvc.org
Information includes materials on domestic violence, stalking, and sexual
    assault

National Center on Domestic Violence, Trauma & Mental Health
nationalcenterdvtraumamh.org
312-726-7020
312-726-4110 (TTY)
312-726-7022 (fax)

National Clearinghouse on Families & Youth
ncfy.acf.hhs.gov
301-608-8098
ncfy@acf.hhs.gov (e-mail)

National Coalition against Domestic Violence
ncadv.org
800-799-7233 (800-799-SAFE)
800-787-3224 (TTY)
Anonymous and confidential help 24/7

National Resource Center on Domestic Violence (NRCDV)
nrcdv.org

National Online Resource Center on Violence against Women
vawnet.org
800-537-2238

Womenslaw.org
womenslaw.org
womenslaw.org/index.php?lang=es (in Spanish)
Legal information Web site, including referrals and detailed protective/
    restraining order information, state by state

Elder Abuse Prevention

Center of Excellence on Elder Abuse & Neglect
centeronelderabuse.org
800-677-1116
Information and resources for preventing elder abuse

General Psychological/Mental Health

American Psychiatric Association
psych.org
888-357-7924; 703-907-7300
apa@psych.org (e-mail)

American Psychological Association
apa.org
800-374-2721; 202-336-5500
202-336-6123 (TDD/TTY)

MedLine Plus en Espanol
nlm.nih.gov/medlineplus/spanish/
Un servicio de la Biblioteca Nacional de Medicina de EE.UU

Mental Health America (MHA)
mentalhealthamerica.net
800-969-NMHA (6642); 703-684-7722

National Alliance on Mental Illness (NAMI)
nami.org
800-950-6264 (helpline); 703-524-7600
703-524-9094 (fax)
888-999-6264 (member services)
Resource center for a variety of issues dealing with mental illness, including
    education, support, and advocacy—also offers a helpline

National Institute of Mental Health
nimh.nih.gov/index.shtml
866-615-NIMH (6464) toll-free; 301-443-4513
866-415-8051 (TTY toll-free); 301-443-8431 (TTY)
301-443-4279 (fax)
nimhinfo@nih.gov (e-mail)

PsychCentral
psychcentral.com

Psychology Today magazine
psychologytoday.com
Useful for finding a mental health professional in your area—just type in your zip code

Psychology Today Spycatcher Blog by Joe Navarro
psychologytoday.com/blog/spycatcher

Overseas Crime/Victimization

If you are victimized overseas, contact the local law enforcement authorities. If it is a serious crime and you need assistance, you can go to the nearest US Embassy or Consulate. You can also contact the FBI, which has representatives in all major embassies.

Department of Justice Office for Victims of Crime Overseas
    Crime Assistance
810 Seventh Street NW, Eighth Floor, Washington, DC 20531
ovc.ncjrs.org/findvictimservices/

FBI Legal Attachés World Wide
fbi.gov/contact-us/legat

Federal Bureau of Investigation (FBI)
fbi.gov

State Department Overseas Citizens Services
travel.state.gov
888-407-4747
202-501-4444 (from overseas)
Before you travel and if you have difficulties while abroad, this is where you can find a lot of valuable assistance

Research/Crime Statistics

Bureau of Justice Statistics
bjs.gov

FBI Uniform Crime Reports (FBI-UCR)
fbi.gov/about-us/cjis/ucr/ucr

Suicide Prevention

National Suicide Prevention Lifeline
suicidepreventionlifeline.org
800-273-8255 (800-273-TALK) (24/7 hotline)
888-628-9454 (Spanish)
800-799-4889 (TTY)
No matter what issue or problem you are facing, hurting yourself is not the
solution; please call if you need help or you just want to talk

Victim Assistance

National Association of Crime Victim Compensation Boards
PO Box 16003, Alexandria, VA 22302
nacvcb.org
703-780-3200
If you have been victimized, they can help you receive compensation for your
injuries or to cover hospital or mental health counseling, lost wages, even
funeral expenses. State victim compensation boards can be located here
by zip code

National Organization for Victim Assistance
trynova.org
The oldest national victim assistance organization of its type in the United
States

The National Center for Victims of Crime
victimsofcrime.org

LAST—AND THIS IS IMPORTANT: Go to your own local phone book, if available, and write down here or place in your mobile phone the phone number of your local police department, mental health professional, or other victim assistance numbers you think you might need. It will save you time when you need it the most, and it will remind you that help is nearby.

_____

_____

_____

Introduction

[1] Cloud, "Preventing Mass Murder," 28–29.
[2] FBI Uniform Crime Reports, 2011.
[3] Walsh and Wu, "Differentiating Antisocial Personality Disorder, Psychopathy, and Sociopathy."
[4] Pearce, "Cleveland Suspect Ariel Castro."
[5] Goforth, Ortiz, and McShane, "Kidnap Victims Released from Cleveland Hospital Reunite with Families."
[6] Kreisman and Straus, *I Hate You—Don't Leave Me.*

Chapter 1

[1] Cox, *Cinderella.*
[2] Kilduff and Javers, *Suicide Cult.*
[3] Ibid.
[4] Chan, "Remembering Leona Helmsley."
[5] Quinn, interview.
[6] Martinez, "Charges in Rebecca Sedwick's Suicide."
[7] Durando, "BP's Tony Hayward."
[8] Karas and O'Neill, "Ex 'Mrs. Rockefeller.'"
[9] Suddath, "Top 10 CEO Scandals"; Lipman-Blumen, *Allure of Toxic Leaders.*
[10] Kilgannon, "Hedda Nussbaum Promotes Her Memoir"; Russo, "Faces of Hedda Nussbaum."
[11] Yaccino, "Former Official Pleads Guilty."
[12] Radzinsky, Stalin, 276–77.

Chapter 2

[1] Kashner and Schoenberger, *Furious Love.*
[2] Spoto, *Marilyn Monroe;* Taraborrelli, *Secret Life of Marilyn Monroe.*
[3] Kreisman and Straus, *I Hate You—Don't Leave Me.*

[4] Sutton, *No Asshole Rule,* 183.
[5] Navarro, "Are You Being Manipulated by a Social Puppeteer?"
[6] Moore et al., "Actor Phil Hartman, Wife Killed in Murder-Suicide Tragedy."
[7] Guinn, *Manson.*
[8] Spoto, *Marilyn Monroe;* Taraborrelli, *Secret Life of Marilyn Monroe.*
[9] Coscarelli, "Jodi Arias Found Guilty of First-Degree Murder."
[10] Van Horn, "Read Transcripts from Jodi Arias Trial Closing Arguments."
[11] de Becker, *Gift of Fear,* 209–10.
[12] Ibid., 218–19; Bugliosi, *Outrage.*
[13] Dickinson, "He Lied to Me When We First Met."
[14] Hedges, *Devil Wears Prada.*
[15] Epstein, *Lincolns.*

Chapter 3

[1] Associated Press, "Neighbors of Ala. Man Suspected of Holding Child in Standoff Say He Was Threatening, Violent"; Brown and Robertson, "Standoff in Alabama Ends in Boy's Rescue and Kidnapper's Death."
[2] Hoffer, *True Believer.*
[3] Ibid., 93–94.
[4] Navarro, "Lessons from the Oslo Terrorist Attack."
[5] Robins and Post, *Political Paranoia,* 24–29.
[6] Kantor, *Understanding Paranoia.*
[7] Navarro, *Hunting Terrorists.*
[8] Ibid.
[9] Dawson, "Children's War."
[10] Ibid.
[11] Navarro, *Hunting Terrorists,* 49.
[12] Kilduff and Javers, *Suicide Cult,* 83–127.
[13] Kantor, *Understanding Paranoia.*
[14] Robins and Post, *Political Paranoia,* 19.

Chapter 4

[1] Meloy and Meloy, "Autonomic Arousal in the Presence of Psychopathy," 21–34.
[2] Hare, *Without Conscience.*
[3] Keefe, "Did a Murderer in Waiting Go Undetected?"
[4] Madoff Mack, *End of Normal.*
[5] " 'I Was Born to Rape,' " *Austrian Times.*

6 *The WEEK,* March 21, 2009, 20; Connolly, "I Was Born to Rape."

7 Cahill, *Buried Dreams.*

8 Vitello, "Clifford Olson, Canadian Serial Killer, Is Dead at 71."

9 Pool, "Former GI Claims Role in Goering's Death."

10 Callahan, "Hunt for the Perfect Serial Killer."

11 Greig, *Evil Serial Killers,* 94.

12 Meloy and Meloy, "Autonomic Arousal in the Presence of Psychopathy," 21–34.

13 Esser, "Michael Chadd Boysen, Accused of Killing Grandparents, to Be Extradited."

14 Tarm, "Drew Peterson Sentenced to 38 Years for Murder."

15 Rennison, *Bureau of Justice Statistics Crime Data Brief: Intimate Partner Violence 1993–2001;* Bureau of Justice Statistics, *Intimate Partner Violence in the U.S. 1993–2004.*

16 Dugard, *A Stolen Life.*

17 Ehrenfreund, "Prosecutors Investigating Reported Stabbing of John Gotti, Jr. on Long Island"; Rogers, "Ill Suited Life as a Crime Boss."

18 Davis, *Bad Blood.*

19 Bovsun, "14 Years and Nine Tiny Corpses Later."

20 Rule, *Stranger Beside Me,* 129–36, 155, 213; Baker, "Diane Downs."

21 Mabe, "Questions Elicit Tale of Baby's Death."

22 Gibson, "Scotland Yard Report Reveals Details of Jimmy Savile's Crimes."

23 Fantz, "Ariel Castro Agrees to Pleas Deal."

24 Graeber, "Tainted Kidney."

25 Suddath, "Top 10 CEO Scandals."

26 *U.S. News & World Report,* April 4, 1988, 11.

Chapter 5

1 Winter and Leinwand Leger, "Dorner Charged with Murder, Attempted Murder of Cops."

2 Davis, "Dangerous"; McGinnes, "Millionaire on the Run."

3 Will, *With a Happy Eye but . . . ,* 57.

4 Radzinsky, *Stalin;* Robins and Post, *Political Paranoia.*

5 Radzinsky, *Stalin.*

6 Navarro, "Lessons From the Oslo Terrorist Attack."

7 Bugliosi, *Reclaiming History,* 513–70.

8 Navarro, *Hunting Terrorists.*

9 Ibid.

[10] Madoff Mack, *End of Normal.*
[11] Kernberg, *Borderline Conditions and Pathological Narcissism*, 18, 228; Meloy, *Mark of Cain*, 315–18.
[12] Bugliosi, *Helter Skelter;* Sanders, *Family.*
[13] Guinn, *Manson.*
[14] Kantor, *Understanding Paranoia*, 4–89.
[15] Kilduff and Javers, *Suicide Cult.*
[16] Bentley and Durante, "Polygamist Paedophile Warren Jeffs 'in a Coma."
[17] Navarro, *Hunting Terrorists*, 39, 57, 63.
[18] Ibid., 38–41.
[19] Robins and Post, *Political Paranoia;* Langer, *Mind of Adolf Hitler.*
[20] Kyemba, *State of Blood;* Avirgan & Honey 1982).
[21] Moses, "Desperately Seeking Susan Powell."
[22] Associated Press, "Susan Powell's Diary Foreshadows Family Tragedy."
[23] Mcfarland, "Josh Powell's Lasting Identity: Murderer."
[24] Baker and Johnson, "Josh Powell Dead."
[25] Msnbc.com news services, "Police: 1981 Killing of Adam Walsh Solved"; Adam Walsh Child Protection and Safety Act of 2006.
[26] Brooks, "Columbine Killers."
[27] Solzhenitsyn, *Gulag Archipelago*, 175.

Chapter 6

[1] Cahill, *Buried Dreams.*
[2] de Becker, *Gift of Fear*, 67.
[3] Isaacson, *Steve Jobs,* 192–218.
[4] Bugliosi, *Outrage.*
[5] Hammarskjöld, *Markings*, 15.

BIBLIOGRAPHY

Adam Walsh Child Protection and Safety Act of 2006. 109th Congress Public Law 248, July 27, 2006. Washington, DC: US Government Printing Office. Accessed December 3, 2013. DOCID: f:publ248.109.

American Psychiatric Association. *Diagnostic and Statistical Manual of Mental Disorders*, 5th ed. Arlington, VA: American Psychiatric Association, 2013.

———. *Diagnostic and Statistical Manual of Mental Disorders*, 4th ed. Text rev. Washington, DC: American Psychiatric Association, 2000.

Arrigo, Bruce A. *Introduction to Forensic Psychology*. San Diego: Academic Press, 2000.

Associated Press. "Neighbors of Ala. Man Suspected of Holding Child in Standoff Say He Was Threatening, Violent." *Washington Post*, January 30, 2013. Accessed February 2, 2013. http://www.startribune.com/188985031.html.

———. "Susan Powell's Diary Foreshadows Family Tragedy, Detailing Fears of Controlling Husband." Foxnews.com. Accessed July 1, 2013. http://www.foxnews.com/us/2013/05/26/susan-powell-diary-foreshadows-family-tragedy-detailing-fears-controlling/.

Athens, Lonnie. *The Creation of Dangerous Violent Criminals*. Urbana, IL: University of Illinois Press, 1992.

Avirgan, Tony, and Martha Honey. *War in Uganda: The Legacy of Idi Amin*. Westport, CT: Lawrence Hill & Co. Publishers, 1982.

Babiak, Paul, and Robert D. Hare. *Snakes in Suits: When Psychopaths Go to Work*. New York: Regan Books, 2006.

Baker, Mark. "Diane Downs." *Register-Guard*, May 19, 2008, A1.

Baker, Mike, and Gene Johnson. "Josh Powell Dead: Missing Woman Susan Powell's Husband, 2 Sons Killed in Home Explosion." *Huffington Post*, February 5, 2012. Accessed November 19, 2013. http://www.huffingtonpost.com/2012/02/05/josh-powell-susan-powell-home-explosion_n_1256113.html.

Bancroft, Lundy. *Why Does He Do That? Inside the Minds of Angry and Controlling Men.* New York: Berkley Publishing Group, 2002.

Beck, Aaron. *Prisoners of Hate: The Cognitive Basis for Anger, Hostility, and Violence.* New York: Harper Collins Publishers, 1999.

Bentley, Paul, and Thomas Durante. "Polygamist Paedophile Warren Jeffs 'in a Coma after Going on Hunger Strike in Solitary Cell.'" *Daily Mail,* August 29, 2011. Accessed August 1, 2013. http://www.dailymail.co.uk/news/article-2031483/Polygamist-paedophile-Warren-Jeffs-coma-going-hunger-strike-solitary-cell.html.

Berke, J. H. *The Tyranny of Malice: Exploring the Dark Side of Character and Culture.* New York: Summit Books, 1986.

Blackburn, R. "Psychopathology and Personality Disorder in Relation to Violence." In *Clinical Approaches to Violence.* K. Howells and C. R. Hollins, ed. New York: Wiley, 1989: 187–205.

Blair, James, Derek Mitchell, and Karina Blain. *The Psychopath: Emotion and the Brain.* Malden, MA: Blackwell Publishing, 2006.

Bohm, R. M. *A Primer on Crime and Delinquency Theory.* Belmont, CA: Wadsworth, 2001.

Bovsun, Mara. "14 Years and Nine Tiny Corpses Later, Authorities Finally Took Action on Murderous Mother." *New York Daily News,* March 20, 2011. Accessed August 20, 2013. http://www.nydailynews.com/news/crime/14-years-tiny-corpses-authorities-finally-action-murderous-mother-article-1.122089.

Brooks, David. "The Columbine Killers." *New York Times,* April 24, 2004. Accessed June 1, 2013. http://www.nytimes.com/2004/04/24/opinion/the-columbine-killers.html?pagewanted=print&src=pm.

Brown, Robbie, and Campbell Robertson. "Standoff in Alabama Ends in Boy's Rescue and Kidnapper's Death." *New York Times,* February 4, 2013. Accessed May 8, 2013. http://www.nytimes.com/2013/02/05/us/boy-is-safe-after-alabama-hostage-standoff.html?_r=0.

Browning, C. *The Path to Genocide.* Cambridge: Cambridge University Press, 1992.

Brussel, James A. *Casebook of a Crime Psychiatrist.* New York: Grove Press, 1968.

Bugliosi, Vincent. *Helter Skelter: The True Story of the Manson Murders.* New York: W. W. Norton & Company, 1994.

———. *Outrage: The Five Reasons Why O. J. Simpson Got Away with Murder.* New York: W. W. Norton & Company, 2008.

———. *Reclaiming History: The Assassination of President John F. Kennedy.* New York: W. W. Norton & Company, 2007.

Bureau of Justice Statistics. *Intimate Partner Violence in the US. 1993–2004.* Washington, DC: US Department of Justice, 2006.

Butcher, James N., ed. *Clinical Personality Assessment.* New York: Oxford University Press, 1995.

Cahill, Tim. *Buried Dreams: Inside the Mind of a Serial Killer.* New York: Bantam Books, 1986.

Callahan, Maureen. "The Hunt for the Perfect Serial Killer." *New York Post,* December 30, 2012. Accessed November 19, 2013. http://nypost. com/2012/12/30/the-hunt-for-the-perfect-serial-killer/.

Campbell, Andy. " 'Whitey' Bulger Verdict: Boston Mobster Guilty of Federal Racketeering, Some Murders." *Huffington Post,* August 12, 2013. Accessed August 12, 2013. http://www.huffingtonpost.com/2013/08/12/whitey-bulger-verdict-guilty-racketeering_n_3712706.html?view=print&comm_ref=false.

Chan, Sewell. "Remembering Leona Helmsley." *New York Times,* August 20, 2007. Accessed July 1, 2013. http://cityroom.blogs.nytimes. com/2007/08/20/leona-helmsley-is-dead-at-87/.

Chapman, Alexander L., and Kim L. Gratz. *The Borderline Personality Disorder Survival Guide: Everything You Need to Know about Living with BPD.* Oakland, CA: New Harbinger Publications, 2007.

Christie, Richard, and Florence L. Geis, eds. *Studies in Machiavellianism.* New York: Academic Press, 1970.

Cialdini, Robert B. *Influence: The Psychology of Persuasion.* New York: William Morrow and Company, 1993.

Cloud, John. "Preventing Mass Murder." *Time,* August 6, 2012, 28–29.

Coleman, James C., et al. *Abnormal Psychology and Modern Life,* 7th ed. Glenview, IL: Scott, Foresman and Company, 1984.

Connolly, Kate. "I Was Born to Rape, Fritzl Tells Doctor." *Guardian,* October 22, 2008. Accessed August 9, 2013. http://www.theguardian.com/world/2008/oct/23/josef-fritzl-trial.

Coscarelli, Joe. "Jodi Arias Found Guilty of First-Degree Murder." *New York,* May 8, 2013. Accessed July 20, 2013. http://nymag.com/daily/intelligencer/2013/05/jodi-arias-guilty-verdict-first-degree-murder.html.

Cox, Marian Roalfe. *Cinderella: Three Hundred and Forty-Five Variants of Cinderella, Catskin, and Cap O'Rushes.* London: Folk-Lore Society, 1893. Google Books. Accessed February 15, 2013.

BIBLIOGRAPHY

Crompton, Vicki, and Ellen Zelda Kessner. *Saving Beauty from the Beast: How to Protect Your Daughter from an Unhealthy Relationship.* New York: Little, Brown and Company, 2003.

Davis, Don. *Bad Blood: The Shocking True Story behind the Menendez Killings.* New York: St. Martin's Press, 1994.

Davis, Joshua. "Dangerous: An In-Depth Investigation into the Life of John McAfee." *Wired,* March 2, 2013. Accessed July 27, 2013. http://www.wired.co.uk/magazine/archive/2013/02/features/dangerous/viewall.

Dawson, Pat. "The Children's War." *Time,* June 11, 2001, 30.

de Becker, Gavin. *The Gift of Fear.* New York: Dell Publishing, 1997.

Dees, Morris, and James Corcoran. *Gathering Storm: America's Militia Movement.* New York: Harper Collins, 1996.

Dickinson, Debbi. "He Lied to Me When We First Met and I Married Him Anyway." *Huffington Post,* April 14, 2012. Accessed February 17, 2013. http://www.huffingtonpost.com/debbi-dickinson/mr-wrong_b_1421712.html?ncid=edlinkusaolp00000008.

Dreeke, Robin. *It's Not All about "Me": The Top Ten Techniques for Building Quick Rapport with Anyone.* Robin K. Dreeke, 2011.

Dugard, Jaycee Lee. *A Stolen Life: A Memoir.* New York: Simon & Schuster, 2011.

Durando, Jessica. "BP's Tony Hayward: 'I'd like my life back.' " *USA Today,* June 1, 2010. Accessed November 18, 2013. http://content.usatoday.com/communities/greenhouse/post/2010/06/bp-tony-hayward-apology/1#.UotkOZG9zKc.

Dyer, Joel. *Harvest of Rage: Why Oklahoma City Is Only the Beginning.* Boulder, CO: Westview Press, 1998.

Ehrenfreund, Max. "Prosecutors Investigating Reported Stabbing of John Gotti, Jr. on Long Island." *Washington Post,* November 11, 2013. Accessed November 17, 2013. http://www.washingtonpost.com/national/prosecutors-investigating-reported-stabbing-of-john-gotti-jr-on-long-island/2013/11/12/f7129d62-4bb1-11e3-ac54-aa84301ced81_story.html.

Emerson, Steven. *American Jihad: The Terrorists Living among Us.* New York: Free Press, 2002.

Epstein, Daniel Mark. *The Lincolns: Portrait of a Marriage.* New York: Ballantine Books, 2009.

Erikson, Erik H. *Identity: Youth and Crisis.* New York: W. W. Norton & Company, 1968.

Esser, Doug. "Michael Chadd Boysen, Accused of Killing Grandparents, to Be Extradited to Washington State." *Huffington Post*, March 14, 2013. Accessed August 8, 2013. http://www.huffingtonpost.com/2013/03/14/michael-chadd-boysen-extradited_n_2875068.html.

Evans, Patricia. *The Verbally Abusive Relationship: How to Recognize It and How to Respond.* Avon, MA: Adams Media Corporation, 2010.

Fantz, Ashley. "Ariel Castro Agrees to Plea Deal to Avoid Death Penalty." CNN, July 28, 2013. Accessed August 1, 2013. http://www.cnn.com/2013/07/26/justice/ohio-castro/.

Federal Bureau of Investigation. *Uniform Crime Reports: Crime in the United States 2010.* Washington, DC: United States Department of Justice.

———. *Uniform Crime Reports: Crime in the United States 2011.* Washington, DC: United States Department of Justice. Accessed July 8, 2013. http://www.fbi.gov/about-us/cjis/ucr/crime-in-the-u.s/2011/crime-in-the-u.s.-2011.

Ford, Charles V. *Lies!, Lies!, Lies!: The Psychology of Deceit.* Washington, DC: American Psychiatric Press, 1996.

Fox, James Allen, and Jack Levin. *Extreme Killing: Understanding Serial and Mass Murder.* Thousand Oaks, CA: Sage Publications, 2005.

Frank, Gerold. *The Boston Strangler.* New York: New American Library, 1966.

Gabbard, Glen O. *Psychodynamic Psychiatry in Clinical Practice*, 4th ed. Washington, DC: American Psychiatric Publishing, 2005.

———. *The Psychology of the Sopranos: Love, Death, Desire, and Betrayal in America's Favorite Gangster Family.* New York: Basic Books, 2003.

Gardner, D. L., and R. W. Cowdry. "Suicidal and Parasuicidal Behavior in Borderline Personality Disorder." *Psychiatric Clinics of North America* 8, no. 2 (1985): 389–403.

Giannangelo, Stephen J. *The Psychopathology of Serial Murder: A Theory of Violence.* Westport, CT: Praeger, 1996.

Gibbs, Nancy. "Tracking Down the Unabomber." *Time*, April 15, 1996, 38–46.

Gibson, Megan. "Scotland Yard Report Reveals Details of Jimmy Savile's Crimes." *Time World*, January 11, 2013. Accessed August 1, 2013. http://world.time.com/2013/01/11/scotland-yard-report-reveals-details-of-jimmy-saviles-crimes/.

Glover, Barry. Interviewed by Joe Navarro, April 7, 2000.

Goforth, Candace, Erik Ortiz, and Larry McShane. "Kidnap Victims Released from Cleveland Hospital Reunite with Families; 3 Brothers Arrested in Shocking Case." *New York Daily News*, May 7, 2013. Accessed November 18, 2013. http://www.nydailynews.com/news/crime/castro-brothers-arrested-connection-missing-cleveland-women-article-1.1337032.

Goleman, Daniel. *Emotional Intelligence*. New York: Bantam Books, 1995.

———. *Social Intelligence*. New York: Bantam Books, 2006.

Graeber, Charles. "The Tainted Kidney." *New York*, October 24, 2007. Accessed May 18, 2013. http://nymag.com/news/features/30331/.

Greig, Charlotte. *Evil Serial Killers: In the Minds of Monsters*. New York: Barnes & Noble, 2005.

Guinn, Jeff. *Manson: The Life and Times of Charles Manson*. New York: Simon & Schuster, 2013.

Gunderson, John G., and Paul S. Links. *Borderline Personality Disorder: A Clinical Guide*. Arlington, VA: American Psychiatric Publishing, 2008.

Gunderson, John G., and Perry D. Hoffman. *Understanding and Treating Borderline Personality Disorder: A Guide for Professionals and Families*. Arlington, VA: American Psychiatric Publishing, 2005.

Hammarskjöld, Dag. *Markings*. New York: Alfred A. Knopf, 1964.

Hare, Robert D. *Without Conscience: The Disturbing World of the Psychopaths among Us*. New York: Pocket Books, 1993.

Hare, Robert D., et al. "Psychopathy and the DSM-IV Criteria for Antisocial Personality Disorder." *Journal of Abnormal Psychology* 100, no. 3 (1991): 391–98.

Haroun, Ansar M. "Psychiatric Aspects of Terrorism." *Psychiatric Annals* 26, no. 6 (1999): 335–36.

Harris, Grant T., et al. "Criminal Violence: The Roles of Psychopathy, Neurodevelopment Insults, and Antisocial Parenting." *Criminal Justice and Behavior* 28, no. 4 (2001): 402–26.

Harris, Judith Rich. *The Nurture Assumption: Why Children Turn Out the Way They Do*. New York: Touchstone Books, 1998.

Hedges, Peter (revisions by Howard Michael Gould, Paul Rudnick, Don Roos; current revisions by Aline Brosh McKenna). *The Devil Wears Prada*, screenplay, March 10, 2005. Accessed April 21, 2013. http://www.dailyscript.com/scripts/devil_wears_prada.pdf.

Hoch, Paul H. *Differential Diagnosis in Clinical Psychiatry*. New York: Science House, 1972.

Hoffer, Eric. *The True Believer: Thoughts on the Nature of Mass Movements*. New York: Harper & Row, 1989.

Horowitz, Mardi J., ed. *Hysterical Personality*. New York: Jason Aronson, 1977.

Hotchkiss, Sandy. *Why Is It Always About You? The Seven Deadly Sins of Narcissism*. New York: Free Press, 2003.

Hyde, Maggie, and Michael McGuinness. *Introducing Jung*. New York: Totem Books, 1998.

Iadicol, Peter, and Anson Shupe. *Violence, Inequality, and Human Freedom*. New York: General Hall, 1998.

Isaacson, Walter. *Steve Jobs*. New York: Simon & Schuster, 2011.

"'I Was Born to Rape,' says Josef Fritzl." *Austrian Times*, October 24, 2008. Accessed August 21, 2013. http://austriantimes.at/news/General_ News/2008-10-24/9273/I_was_born_to_rape,_says_Josef_Fritzl.

Jones, Stephen A. "Family Therapy with Borderline and Narcissistic Patients." *Bulletin of the Menninger Clinic* 51, no. 3 (1987): 285–95.

Kantor, Martin. *Understanding Paranoia: A Guide for Professionals, Families, and Sufferers*. Westport, CT: Praeger Publishers, 2008.

Karas, Beth, and Ann O'Neill. "Ex 'Mrs. Rockefeller': 'I Had a Pretty Big Blind Spot.'" CNN Online, June 2, 2009. Accessed July 1, 2013. http:// www.cnn.com/2009/CRIME/06/02/massachusetts.rockefeller.trial/index. html?eref=rss_mostpopular.

Kashner, Sam, and Nancy Schoenberger. *Furious Love: Elizabeth Taylor, Richard Burton: The Marriage of the Century*. New York: Harper Collins, 2010.

Keefe, Patrick Radden. "Did a Murderer in Waiting Go Undetected Because She Was a Woman?" *New Yorker*, February 14, 2013. Accessed February 17, 2013. http://www.newyorker.com/online/blogs/newsdesk/2013/02/ did-a-mass-murderer-in-waiting-go-undetected-because-she-was-a-woman.html.

Kernberg, Otto F. *Borderline Conditions and Pathological Narcissism*. Northvale, NJ: Jason Aronson, 1985.

———. *The Psychopathology of Hatred: In Rage, Power and Aggression*. New Haven, CT: Yale University Press, 1993.

Kiernan, B. *How Pol Pot Came to Power: History of Communism in Kampuchea, 1930–1975*. London: Verso Press, 1985.

Kilduff, Marshall, and Ron Javers. The *Suicide Cult: The Inside Story of the Peoples Temple Sect and the Massacre in Guyana*. New York: Bantam Books, 1978.

Kilgannon, Corey. "Hedda Nussbaum Promotes Her Memoir on Life with an Abuser." *New York Times*, April 6, 2006, NY/Region. Accessed February 11, 2013. http://www.nytimes.com/2006/04/06/nyregion/06hedda.html?_ r=1&.

Kreisman, Jerold J., and Hal Straus. *I Hate You—Don't Leave Me: Understanding the Borderline Personality*. New York: Avon Books, 1989.

Kyemba, Henry. *A State of Blood: The Inside Story of Idi Amin.* New York: Ace Books, 1977.

Langer, Walter C. *The Mind of Adolf Hitler: The Secret Wartime Report.* New York: Basic Books, 1972.

Laqueur, Walter. *Voices of Terror: Manifestos, Writings and Manuals of al Qaeda, Hamas, and Other Terrorists from around the World and throughout the Ages.* New York: Reed Press, 2004.

Lawson, Christine Ann. *Understanding the Borderline Mother: Helping Her Children Transcend the Intense, Unpredictable, and Volatile Relationship.* Northvale, NJ: Jason Aronson, 2000.

LeDoux, Joseph E. *The Emotional Brain: The Mysterious Underpinnings of Emotional Life.* New York: Touchstone, 1996.

Levin, Jack, and Jack McDevitt. *Hate Crimes: The Rising Tide of Bigotry and Bloodshed.* New York: Plenum, 1993.

Levine, Sol. "Psychiatric Aspects of Terrorism: Youth in Terroristic Groups, Gangs, and Cults: The Allure, the Animus, and the Alienation." *Psychiatric Annals* 26, no. 6 (1999): 342–49.

Linehan, Marsha. *Cognitive-Behavioral Treatment of Borderline Personality Disorder.* New York: Guilford Press, 1993.

Lipman-Blumen, Jean. *The Allure of Toxic Leaders: Why We Follow Destructive Bosses and Corrupt Politicians—And How We Can Survive Them.* New York: Oxford University Press, 2005.

Luhrmann, T. M. *Of Two Minds: The Growing Disorder in American Psychiatry.* New York: Random House, 2000.

Mabe, Logan D. "Questions Elicit Tale of Baby's Death." *St. Petersburg Times,* August 30, 1999. Accessed May 11, 2013. http://www.sptimes.com/News/83099/TampaBay/Questions_elicit_tale.shtml.

Madoff Mack, Stephanie. *The End of Normal: A Wife's Anger, a Widow's New Life.* New York: Blue Rider Press, 2011.

Maguire, Daniel C., and A. Nicholas Fargnoli. *On Moral Grounds: The Art and Science of Ethics.* New York: Cross Roads Publishing, 1991.

Maguire, John, and Mary Dunn. *Hold Hands and Die: The Incredible True Story of the People's Temple.* New York: Dale Books, 1978.

Martinez, Michael. "Charges in Rebecca Sedwick's Suicide Suggest 'Tipping Point' in Bullying Cases." CNN, October 28, 2013. Accessed November 18, 2013. http://www.cnn.com/2013/10/25/us/rebecca-sedwick-bullying-suicide-case/.

Masterson, James F. *The Search for the Real Self: Unmasking the Personality Disorders of Our Age.* New York: Free Press, 1988.

Mcfarland, Sheena. "Josh Powell's Lasting Identity: Murderer." *Salt Lake Tribune,* February 6, 2012. Accessed November 20, 2013. http://www. sltrib.com/sltrib/faith/53450298-78/powell-josh-sons-susan.csp.

McGinnes, Jamie. "Millionaire on the Run: How the Man Who Founded Software Giant McAfee Lost His Fortune and Ended Up Hiding from Police in Belize after They Rousted Him from the Bed of a 17-Year-Old and Shot His Dog Because He's Running a Meth Lab.'" *Daily Mail,* May 25, 2012. Accessed June 10, 2013. http://www.dailymail.co.uk/news/article-2149904/John-McAfee-arrested-Belize-police-claim-running-meth-lab.html.

Meloy, J. Reid. *The Mark of Cain: Psychoanalytic Insight and the Psychopath.* Hillsdale, NJ: Analytic Press, 2001.

———. *The Psychopathic Mind: Origins, Dynamics, and Treatment.* Northvale, NJ: Jason Aronson, 1998.

———. *Violence Risk and Threat Assessment.* San Diego: Specialized Training Services, 2000.

———. *Violent Attachments.* Northvale, NJ: Jason Aronson, 1997.

Meloy, J. Reid, and M. J. Meloy. "Autonomic Arousal in the Presence of Psychopathy: A Survey of Mental Health and Criminal Justice Professionals." *Journal of Threat Assessment* 2, no. 2 (2002): 21–34.

Millon, Theodore, and Roger D. Davis. *Disorders of Personality: DSM-IV and Beyond.* New York: Wiley and Sons, 1996.

Monahan, John. *Predicting Violent Behavior: An Assessment of Clinical Techniques.* Beverly Hills, CA: Sage, 1981.

Moore, Solomon, et al., "Actor Phil Hartman, Wife Killed in Murder-Suicide Tragedy: The Comedian Is Apparently Shot by Spouse in Their Encino Home." *Los Angeles Times,* May 29, 1998. Accessed July 20, 2013. http://articles.latimes.com/1998/may/29/news/mn-54521.

Moses, Jeanette. "Desperately Seeking Susan Powell: A Best Friend's Quest." *Time,* February 10, 2012. Accessed November 20, 2013. http://content.time.com/time/nation/article/0,8599,2106632,00.html#ixzz2lVKNFYHm.

Msnbc.com News Services. "Police: 1981 Killing of Adam Walsh Solved." Crime & Courts, NBC News.com, updated December 16, 2008. Accessed December 3, 2013. http://www.nbcnews.com/id/28257294/#.Up4f9RzPZCc.

Muller, Rene J. *Anatomy of a Splitting Borderline: Description and Analysis of a Case History.* Westport, CT: Praeger Press, 1994.

Munro, Alistair. *Delusional Disorder: Paranoia and Related Illnesses.* New York: Cambridge University Press, 1999.

Murray, Jill. *But I Love Him: Protecting Your Teen Daughter from Controlling, Abusive Dating Relationships.* New York: Harper Collins, 2001.

Myers, David G. *Exploring Psychology,* 2nd ed. New York: Worth Publishers, 1993.

Navarro, Joe. "Are You Being Manipulated by a Social Puppeteer?" *Spycatcher* (blog). *Psychology Today,* January 7, 2013. Accessed February 21, 2013. http://www.psychologytoday.com/blog/spycatcher/201301/are-you-being-manipulated-social-puppeteer.

———. *How to Spot a Psychopath.* Kindle edition, 2010.

———. *Hunting Terrorists: A Look at the Psychopathology of Terror.* Springfield, IL: Charles C. Thomas Publishers, 2005.

———. "Lessons from the Oslo Terrorist Attack." *Spycatcher* (blog). *Psychology Today,* July 30, 2011. Accessed May 4, 2013. http://www.psychologytoday.com/blog/spycatcher/201107/lessons-the-oslo-terrorist-attack.

———. *Narcissists Among Us.* Kindle edition, 2012.

———. "The Psychopathology of Terror." Lecture before the FBI National Academy graduates, Key West, FL, July 28, 2003.

———. "Wound Collectors." *Spycatcher* (blog). *Psychology Today,* April 7, 2013. Accessed July 20, 2013. http://www.psychologytoday.com/blog/spycatcher/201304/wound-collectors.

Navarro, Joe, and John R. Schafer. "Universal Principles of Criminal Behavior: A Tool for Analyzing Criminal Intent." *FBI Law Enforcement Bulletin* (January 2003): 22–24.

Nicholi, Armand M., Jr., ed. *The Harvard Guide to Modern Psychiatry,* 3rd ed. Cambridge, MA: Harvard University Press, 1987.

O'Brien, D. *Two of a Kind: The Hillside Stranglers; The Inside Story.* New York: Signet, 1985.

O'Connor, Anahad. "Government Ends Case against Gotti." *New York Times,* January 13, 2010. Accessed July 20, 2013. http://www.nytimes.com/2010/01/14/nyregion/14gotti.html?ref=johnagotti&gwh=4773BDA2194941569DFECA25576B1987.

Ohlin, Lloyd, and Michael Tonry, eds. *Family Violence: Crime and Justice: A Review of Research,* 2nd ed. Chicago: University of Chicago Press, 1990.

Oldham, John M., and Lois B. Morris. *The New Personality Self-Portrait: Why You Think, Work, Love, and Act the Way You Do.* New York: Bantam Books, 1995.

Panksepp, Jaak. *Affective Neuroscience: The Foundations of Human and Animal Emotions.* New York: Oxford University Press, 1998.

Payson, Eleanor D. *The Wizards of Oz and Other Narcissists: Coping with the One-Way Relationship in Work, Love, and Family*. Royal Oak, MI: Julian Day Publications, 2002.

Pearce, Matt. "Cleveland Suspect Ariel Castro: A Troubling Portrait Emerges." *Los Angeles Times*, May 9, 2013. Accessed November 18, 2013. http://www.latimes.com/news/nation/nationnow/la-na-nn-castro-abuse-history-20130509,0,1600490.story#axzz2l3Qm5YEs.

Pennebaker, James W. *Emotion, Disclosure, and Health*. Washington, DC: American Psychological Association, 1995.

———. *Opening Up: The Healing Power of Expressing Emotions*. New York: Guilford Press, 1990.

Pinker, Steven. *The Blank Slate: The Modern Denial of Human Nature*. New York: Penguin Books, 2002.

Pool, Bob. "Former GI Claims Role in Goering's Death." *Los Angeles Times*, February 7, 2005. Accessed July 1, 2013. http://articles.latimes.com/2005/feb/07/local/me-goering7.

Post, Jerrold M. "It's Us against Them: The Group Dynamics of Political Terrorism." *Terrorism* 10 (1987): 23–36.

———. *Leaders and Their Followers in a Dangerous World: The Psychology of Political Behavior*. Ithaca, NY: Cornell University Press, 2004.

———. "Terrorist Psycho-Logic: Terrorist Behavior as a Product of Psychological Forces." In *Origins of Terrorism: Psychologies, Ideologies, Theologies, States of Mind*. Walter Reich, ed. Cambridge: Cambridge University Press, 1992: 25–40.

———. "The Mind of the Terrorist: Individual and Group Psychology of Terrorist Behavior." Testimony before the Senate Armed Services Committee, November 15, 2001.

———. *The Psychological Assessment of Political Leaders*. Ann Arbor, MI: University of Michigan Press, 2003.

President's Commission on Law Enforcement and Administration of Justice. *The Challenge of Crime in a Free Society*. Washington, DC: US Government Printing Office, 1967.

Quartz, Steven R., and Terrence J. Sejnowski. *Liars, Lovers, and Heroes: What the New Brain Science Reveals about How We Become Who We Are*. New York: HarperCollins, 2003.

Quinn, Phil. Interview by Joe Navarro, November 7, 2001.

Radzinsky, Evard. *Stalin: The First In-Depth Biography Based on Explosive New Documents from Russia's Secret Archive*. New York: Anchor Books, 1996.

Raine, Adrian. *The Anatomy of Violence: The Biological Roots of Crime.* New York: Pantheon Books, 2013.

Reeser, Marc. Interview by Joe Navarro, April 13, 2003.

Reich, Walter, ed. *Origins of Terrorism: Psychologies, Ideologies, Theologies, States of Mind.* Cambridge: Cambridge University Press, 1992.

Rennison, Callie Marie. *Bureau of Justice Statistics Crime Data Brief: Intimate Partner Violence 1993–2001.* Washington, DC: US Department of Justice, 2003.

Ressler, Robert H., and Tom Shachtman. *Whoever Fights Monsters.* New York: St. Martin's Press, 1992.

Rhodes, Richard. *Why They Kill: Discoveries of a Maverick Criminologist.* New York: Vintage Books, 1999.

Robins, Robert S., and Jerrold M. Post. *Political Paranoia: The Psychopolitics of Hatred.* New Haven, CT: Yale University Press, 1997.

Roche, Mike. *Face 2 Face: Observation, Interviewing and Rapport Building Skills: An Ex-Secret Service Agent's Guide.* Kindle edition, 2012.

Rogers, Patrick. "Ill-Suited for Life as a Crime Boss, John Gotti Follows His Father into Federal Prison." *People,* September 27, 1999. Accessed November 20, 2013. http://www.people.com/people/archive/ article/0,,20129328,00.html.

Roth, Kimberlee, and Freda B. Friedman. *Surviving a Borderline Parent: How to Heal Your Childhood Wounds and Build Trust, Boundaries, and Self-Esteem.* Oakland, CA: New Harbinger Publications, 2003.

Roy, Joe. *False Patriots: The Threat of Antigovernment Extremists.* Montgomery, AL: Southern Poverty Law Center, 1996.

Rule, Ann. *Small Sacrifices.* New York: Signet, 1987.

———. *The Stranger Beside Me: Ted Bundy; The Shocking Inside Story.* New York: Signet Printing, 2001.

Russo, Francine. "The Faces of Hedda Nussbaum." *New York Times Magazine,* March 30, 1997. Accessed February 11, 2013. http://www. nytimes.com/1997/03/30/magazine/the-faces-of-hedda-nussbaum. html?pagewanted=all&src=pm.

Samenow, Stanton E. *Inside the Criminal Mind.* New York: Crown Publishers, 1984.

Sanders, Ed. *The Family.* New York: Thunder's Mouth Press, 2002.

Schafer, John, and Joe Navarro. "The Seven-Stage Hate Model; the Psychopathology of Hate Groups," *FBI Law Enforcement Bulletin* (March 2003): 1–9.

Schechter, Harold, and David Everitt. *The A to Z Encyclopedia of Serial Killers.* New York: Simon & Schuster, 1997.

Schouten, Ronal, and James Silver. *Almost a Psychopath: Do I (or Does Someone I Know) Have a Problem with Manipulation and Lack of Empathy?* Center City, MN: Hazelden, 2012.

Seigel, L. J. *Criminology: The Core,* 2nd ed. Belmont, CA: Wadsworth, 2005.

Shapiro, Ronald M., and Mark A. Jankowski. *Bullies, Tyrants, and Impossible People: How to Beat Them without Joining Them.* New York: Crown Business, 2005.

Siever, L. J., and H. W. Koenigsberg. "The Frustrating No-Mans-Land of Borderline Personality Disorder." *Cerebrum, The Dana Forum on Brain Science* 2, no. 4 (2000).

Simmons, D. "Gender Issues and Borderline Personality Disorder: Why Do Females Dominate the Diagnosis?" *Archives of Psychiatric Nursing* 6, no. 4 (1992): 219–23.

Simon, George K. *In Sheep's Clothing: Understanding and Dealing with Manipulative People.* Little Rock, AR: A.J. Christopher & Co., 1996.

Singer, Margaret Thaler, and Janja Lalich. *Cults in Our Midst: The Hidden Menace in Our Everyday Lives.* San Francisco: Jossey-Bass Publishers, 1995.

Sluka, Jeffrey A., ed. *Death Squad: The Anthropology of State Terror.* Philadelphia: University of Pennsylvania Press, 2000.

Soloff, P. H., et al. "Self-Mutilation and Suicidal Behavior in Borderline Personality Disorder." *Journal of Personality Disorders* 8, no. 4 (1994): 257–67.

Solzhenitsyn, Aleksandr I. *The Gulag Archipelago 1918–1956: An Experiment in Literary Investigation,* parts I–II. New York: Harper & Row, 1974.

Spitz, Vivien. *Doctors from Hell: The Horrific Account of Nazi Experiments on Humans.* Boulder, CO: Sentient Publications, 2005.

Spoto, Donald. *Marilyn Monroe: The Biography.* New York: Cooper Square Press, 1993.

Stanton, Bill. *Klanwatch: Bringing the Ku Klux Klan to Justice.* New York: Grove Weidenfeld, 1991.

Stern, Kenneth S. *A Force upon the Plain: The American Militia Movement and the Politics of Hate.* New York: Simon & Schuster, 1996.

Stout, Martha. *The Sociopath Next Door.* New York: Broadway Books, 2005.

St-Yves, M., and P. Collins. *The Psychology of Crisis Intervention for Law Enforcement Officers.* Toronto: Carswell Publisher, 2012.

St-Yves, M., C. Baroche, and J. Renaud. "Personality Disorders and Crisis Intervention." In *The Psychology of Crisis Intervention for Law Enforcement Officers*, M. St.-Yves and P. Collins, eds. Toronto: Carswell Publisher, 2012, 167–98.

Suddath, Claire. "Top 10 CEO Scandals." *Time*, August 10, 2010. Accessed June 4, 2013. http://www.time.com/time/specials/packages/article/0,28804,2009445_2009447_2009502,00.html.

Sutherland, E. H., and D. R. Cressey. *Principles of Criminology*. Philadelphia: Lippincott, 1978.

Sutton, Robert I. *The No Asshole Rule: Building a Civilized Workplace and Surviving One That Isn't*. New York: Business Plus, 2007.

Swanson, Charles R., Neil Chamelin, and Leonard Territo. *Criminal Investigation*, 11th ed. New York: McGraw-Hill Companies, 2011.

Swartz, M., et al. "Estimating the Prevalence of Borderline Personality Disorder in the Community." *Journal of Personality Disorders* 4, no. 3 (1990): 257–72.

Taraborrelli, J. Randi. *The Secret Life of Marilyn Monroe*. New York: Rose Books, 2009.

Tarm, Michael. "Drew Peterson Sentenced to 38 Years for Murder." Associated Press, February 21, 2013. Accessed November 20, 2013. http://news.yahoo.com/drew-peterson-sentenced-38-years-murder-214735862.html.

Thomas, M. E. *Confessions of a Sociopath: A Life Spent Hiding in Plain Sight*. New York: Crown Publishers, 2013.

Twenge, Jean M., and W. Keith Campbell. *Living in the Age of Entitlement: The Narcissism Epidemic*. New York: Simon & Schuster, 2009.

U.S. News & World Report, April 4, 1988, 11.

Van Horn, Charisse. "Read Transcripts from Jodi Arias Trial Closing Arguments, Videos." Examiner.com, May 14, 2013. Accessed July 20, 2013. http://www.examiner.com/article/read-transcripts-from-jodi-arias-trial-closing-arguments-videos-photos.

Verplaetse, Jan, et al., eds. *The Moral Brain: Essays on the Evolutionary and Neuroscientific Aspects of Morality*. New York: Springer, 2009.

Vitello, Paul. "Clifford Olson, Canadian Serial Killer, Is Dead at 71." *New York Times*, October 4, 2011. Accessed August 9, 2013. http://www.nytimes.com/2011/10/05/world/americas/clifford-olson-canadian-serial-killer-is-dead-at-71.html?_r=0.

Waldinger, Robert, and John Gunderson. *Effective Psychotherapy with Borderline Patients: Case Studies*. New York: Macmillan, 1987.

Walsh, Anthony, and Huei-Hsia Wu. "Differentiating Antisocial Personality Disorder, Psychopathy, and Sociopathy: Evolutionary, Genetic, Neurological, and Sociological Considerations." *Criminal Justice Studies* 21, no. 2 (2008): 135–52.

WEEK, The, March 21, 2009, 20.

Will, George F. *With a Happy Eye but . . . : America and the World, 1997–2002.* New York: Free Press, 2002.

Wilson, K. J. *When Violence Begins at Home: A Comprehensive Guide to Understanding and Ending Domestic Abuse.* Alameda, CA: Hunter House, 2006.

Winter, Michael, and Donna Leinwand Leger. "Dorner Charged with Murder, Attempted Murder of Cops." *USA Today,* February 11, 2013. Accessed June 22, 2013. http://www.usatoday.com/story/news/nation/2013/02/11/los-angeles-murder-charges-dorner/1910643/.

Yaccino, Steven. "Former Official Pleads Guilty to Defrauding Illinois Town of $53 Million." *New York Times,* November 14, 2012. Accessed July 13, 2013. http://www.nytimes.com/2012/11/15/us/former-official-pleads-guilty-to-defrauding-illinois-town-of-53-million.html?_r=0.

Yochelson, Samuel, and Stanton E. Samenow. *The Criminal Personality.* New York: Jason Aronson, 1989.

Yudofsky, Stuart C. *Fatal Flaws: Navigating Destructive Relationships with People with Disorders of Personality and Character.* Washington, DC: American Psychiatric Publishing, 2005.

INDEX

<u>Underscored</u> references indicate boxed text.

A

Abbott, Jack Henry, 138
Alexander, Travis, 75–76
American Beauty (film), 93–94, 109
Amin, Idi, 182
Appearance, overvaluing, 19–20, 33–34
Argumentativeness, 102–3, 124, 125
Arias, Jodi, 75–76, 136–37
Aristotle, 16
Arrogance, 18, 22
Assad, Bashar Hafez al-, 155

B

Barrett, James, 102
Barrow, Clyde Chestnut, 72, 140, 184
Barzee, Wanda, 148
Bertillon, Alphonse, 194
Bianchi, Kenneth, 185
Bin Laden, Usama, 104, 181
Boss, Sandra, 25
Boundaries
    personalities lacking, 26–27, 64–65
    setting, 92, 204–5
Boysen, Michael Chadd, 144
Breivik, Anders Behring, 100, 104, 177
Britton, John, 102
Buddha, the, 166
Bugliosi, Vincent, 180
Bulger, James Jr. "Whitey," 138
Bullying
    by narcissist, 18, 20–21, 30–35, 38–39
    reporting, 39
    setting boundaries, 204–5
Bundy, Theodore "Ted," 2, 131, 138–39, 167, 179–80, 187, 194–95
Buono, Angelo Jr., 185

C

Calculating nature, 132–33, 137–38
Cales, Stacy Ann, 146–47
Carr, Peggy, 130
Cassidy, Butch, 184
Castro, Ariel, 10, 153
Charisma and charm, 25, 29, 32–33, 34
Checklists. *See* Dangerous Personalities Checklists
Combined personalities, 168–87
    all four types, 182–84
    in association, 184–86
    changeability of, 169
    emotionally unstable/paranoid, 173–74
    identifying, 169, 170–75, 186
    narcissist/paranoid, 97, 170, 172, 176–78
    narcissist/predator, 178–80
    quick identification of, 187
    risk increased with, 168
    three or more types, 180–81
Conrad, Clyde Lee, 153–54
Conscience, lack of, 136–37
Controlling others, 27, 29, 133
Crawford, Christina, 75
Crawford, Joan, 75
Criminal Personality, The, 189
Crundwell, Rita, 41, 154
Cullen, Charles, 153
Cults, 41–44, 71, 181
Curtis, Susan "Sue," 1–3, 139

D

Dangerous personalities. *See also specific personality types*
    additional resources for, 15, 189
    checklists, about, 11–14
    as flawed characters, 7
    gender bias avoided for, 14

238

labels chosen for, 8–9
mass killings by, 3–4
news coverage of, 3, 4
normal surface of, 6, 7, 10
number of crimes committed by, 4
often unrecognized, 7–10
percentage incarcerated, 5
perspective of this book on, 14–16
professional help for, 124–25, 190–91
repeat crimes by, 4, 5
responsibility for safety from, 10–11, 16
seeing features in yourself, 210
statistics avoided for, 13
types of harm caused by, 5
Dangerous Personalities Checklists
    author's compilation of, 11–12
    combined types, 169, 170–75, 186
    as descriptive, not diagnostic, 14
    as education tools, 192
    emotionally unstable type, 82–91
    length and detail of, 13
    narcissistic type, 45–55
    paranoid type, 114–24
    predators, 155–66
    for understanding, 12, 200, 201–2
De Becker, Gavin, 144, 189
Decker, Crista, 151
DeSalvo, Albert Henry, 152
*Diagnostic and Statistical Manual of Mental
    Disorders* (DSM-5), 13–14
Disney, Walt, 18
Distancing yourself, 56, 126, 166–67, 201, 210
Dorner, Christopher, 97, 169–70
Downs, Diane, 151
Dugard, Jaycee Lee, 148
Dykes, Jimmy Lee, 99, 126

E

Effect on you
    emotionally unstable personality, 59–60,
        61, 73–76
    narcissistic personality, 29–32
    paranoid personality, 106–8
    predators, 141–45
Egocentricity, 19–20
Emotionally unstable personality, 57–92
    allure of, 58
    changeability of, 57–58, 64, 65
    checklist, 82–91
    combined with others, 173–74, 182–84
    effect on you, 59–60, 61, 73–76

encounters with, 80–82
immediate actions to take, 91–92
as parent, 61–62, 69, 78–79
reason for this label, 8–9
in relationships, 62, 76–79
suicide threats by, 67–68, 92
varieties of, 60–61
the way of, 60–73
words describing, 70
in the workplace, 62, 76, 80–81
Empathy, lack of, 22–24, 29–30, 136, 137
Entitlement, 38
Evans, Bill, 95

F

Fatal Attraction (film), 75
Fatal Flaws, 166
Fear and mistrust, irrational, 93–95, 97, 99,
    100–101, 124
Forero-Parra, Luis Alfonso, 179
Fritzl, Josef, 136

G

Gacy, John Wayne, 137, 193
Garavito Cubillos, Luis Alfredo, 178–79
Garrido, Nancy, 148
Garrido, Phillip Craig, 148
Gender bias, avoiding, 14
Gerhartsreiter, Christian Karl, 25
Gift of Fear, The, 144, 189
Giuliani, Rudolph, 132
Goodfellas (film), 23, 141
Göring, Hermann, 139
Gotti, John, 138, 148–49
Gotti, John A. "Junior," 148–49
Grandiosity, 18–19, 23
Greenawalt, Randy, 130
Guinn, Jeff, 180
Gulag Archipelago, The, 187

H

Hammarskjöld, Dag, 210
Hare, Robert, 128
Harris, Eric, 103, 185
Hartman, Brynn, 69
Hartman, Phil, 69
Hatefulness, 103
Hayward, Anthony "Tony," 22–23
Helmsley, Leona, 20

Helter Skelter, 180
Hill, Paul Jennings, 102
Hitler, Adolf, 44, 106, 113–14, 176
Hoffer, Eric, 100
Holloway, Natalee, 153
Hoyt, Tim and Waneta, 131
Hughes, Howard, 99, 113
Hypersensitivity, 63–64

I

Impulsiveness, 71–72
In the Belly of the Beast, 138
Irrational thinking, 69, 71
Isolation, 99, 110, 204

J

James, Frank, 184
James, Jesse, 184
Jeffs, Warren Steed, 181
Jobs, Steve, 201
Jones, Jim, 19, 42–43, 108, 180

K

Kaczynski, Theodore John "Ted," 97, 99, 101,
     103, 104, 106, 124, 178
Kane, Jerry, 95
Kane, Joseph, 95
Kennedy, John F., 178
Keyes, Israel, 139–40
Klebold, Dylan, 103, 185
Koresh, David, 108, 111, 181
Kuklinski, Richard Leonard, 141

L

LaBianca, Leno and Rosemary, 180
Lake, Leonard, 140, 185
Lay, Kenneth, 26, 154
Leaders, 41–44, 154–55, 181
Lincoln, Mary Todd, 81–82
Longabaugh, Harry Alonzo, 184
Looking for Mr. Goodbar (film), 72
Lucas, Henry Lee, 137, 185
Lyons, John, 130

M

MacDonald, Jeffrey Robert, 147
Madoff, Bernard, 4, 23, 131–32, 179
Madoff, Mark, 131–32

Magical thinking, 103–4
Mailer, Norman, 138
Malvo, Lee Boyd, 185
Manipulation
     avoiding, 205
     by dangerous personalities, 67–69, 132–33,
          138–39
Manson, 180
Manson, Charles, 71, 180, 184
Mass killings, 3–4
McAfee, John, 172
McGuckin, Erina, 110
McGuckin, JoAnn, 110–11
McVeigh, Timothy, 100, 102, 103, 106, 175,
     178
Mein Kampf, 106
Meloy, J. Reid, 144, 189
Menendez, Lyle and Erik, 149
Mitchell, Brian David, 148
Mladic, Ratko, 176–77
Mommie Dearest, 75
Monroe, Marilyn, 58, 73
Muhammad, John, 185

N

Narcissistic personality, 17–56
     bullying by, 18, 20–21, 30–35, 38–39
     checklist, 45–55
     combined with others, 97, 170, 176–84
     cult leaders as, 41–44
     effect on you, 29–32
     encounters with, 38–45
     immediate actions to take, 55–56
     as parent, 18, 31, 35–37
     reason for this label, 9
     in relationships, 32–37
     social predation and, 179–80
     the way of, 18–29
     words describing, 28
     in the workplace, 19, 22, 24–25, 31, 38–41
Neediness, 58, 64–67, 76
Ng, Charles, 140, 185
Nichols, Terry, 100
Nixon, Richard, 101
No Asshole Rule, The, 62
Nussbaum, Hedda, 31–32

O

Olson, Clifford Robert Jr., 139
Opinionation, 102–3
Oswald, Harvey, 177–78

P

Paranoid personality, 93–126
  checklist, 114–24
  combined with others, 97, 170, 172, 176–78,
    180–84
  effect on you, 106–8
  encounters with, 111–14
  everyday life examples of, 96–97
  immediate actions to take, 124–26
  as parent, 110–11
  as poorly understood, 95, 97
  reason for this label, 9
  in relationships, 109–11
  varieties of, 98–100
  violence of, 97, 113–14, 125
  the way of, 98–106
  words describing, 105
  in the workplace, 111–13, 125–26
Parents
  emotionally unstable personalities as,
    61–62, 69, 71, 78–79
  giving children respite, 206
  narcissistic personalities as, 18, 31, 35–37
  paranoid personalities as, 110–11
  predators as, 131, 148–51
Parker, Bonnie, 72, 184
Parker, Robert LeRoy (Butch Cassidy), 130,
  184
Pasteur, Louis, 192
Paudert, Brandon, 95
Peterson, Drew, 146–47
Peterson, Laci, 146
Peterson, Scott Lee, 146
Pol Pot, 44, 113–14, 176
Possessiveness, 38
Powell, Josh, 183
Powell, Susan, 183–84
Predators, 127–67
  checklist, 155–66
  combined with other types, 178–84
  effect on you, 141–45
  encounters with, 152–55
  exploitation as only goal of, 128–29
  help exploited by, 144–46
  immediate actions to take, 166–67
  as leaders, 154–55
  likelihood of contact with, 128, 132
  as parents, 131, 148–51
  prevalence of, 128, 130, 131
  reason for this label, 8–9
  in relationships, 145–51
  suffering spread by, 131–32, 135, 143, 145,
    148

  unnerving presence of, 127–28, 144
  varieties of, 132–34
  the way of, 132–41
  words describing, 142
  in the workplace, 143, 153–54
Professional help, 91, 124–25, 190–91, 208

Q

Quinn, Phil, 60

R

Rader, Dennis (BTK killer), 8–9, 136, 154
Ramírez, Stephany Tatiana Flores, 153
Relationships
  emotionally unstable personality in, 62,
    76–79
  narcissistic personality in, 32–37
  paranoid personality in, 109–11
  predators in, 145–51
Remorse, lack of, 136–37
Robinson, John Edward, 133–34
Rudolph, Eric, 103
Rule, Ann, 131

S

Samenow, Stanton E., 189
Sandusky, Jerry, 27, 132, 152
Savile, Jimmy, 152
Savio, Kathleen, 146–47
Sedwick, Rebecca, 21
Self-control, lack of, 140, 141
Self-defense, 188–211
  acting quickly, 199, 200, 207
  addressing financial matters, 209
  alerting your family and friends, 207
  assessing how much/how often, 197
  avoiding manipulation, 205
  cataloging behaviors, 202–3
  choosing safe times and locations, 197–98
  in complex situations, 200–202
  controlling space and distance, 195, 210
  cutting emotional strings, 196
  dealing with dangerous personalities,
    200–206
  distancing yourself, 56, 126, 166–67, 201,
    210
  from emotionally unstable personality,
    91–92
  everyday protection, 192–99
  gaining knowledge, 188–89, 192, 200

Self-defense (*cont.*)
getting professional help, 124–25, 190–91, 208
giving children respite, 206
the Great Awakening, 209
for immediate threat, 206–10
informed observation, 193–94
making yourself uninviting, 198
from narcissistic personality, 55–56
not confusing niceness with goodness, 194–95
not facing danger alone, 208
from paranoid personality, 124–26
planning your exit strategy, 208
from predators, 166–67
raising escape money, 208–9
reaching out for support, 203
remembering you're not alone, 209
resisting isolation, 204
setting boundaries, 92, 204–5
slowing things down, 196
think before talking, 207
trusting your feelings, 194
verifying trustworthiness, 198–99
Sensation seeking, 72–73
Shining, The (film), 98
Shipman, Harold, 130–31, 137
Simpson, Nicole Brown, 77, 190, 202–3
Simpson, O. J., 77, 190, 202–3
Skilling, Jeffrey Keith "Jeff," 26, 154
Smart, Elizabeth, 148
Smith, Anna Nicole, 72
Solzhenitsyn, Aleksandr I., 187
Stalin, Joseph, 44–45, 113–14, 155, 176
Statistics, reason for avoiding, 13
Steinberg, Elizabeth "Lisa," 31–32
Steinberg, Joel, 32
Steve Jobs, 201
Stevenson, Colette, 147
Stolen Life, A, 148
Stranger Beside Me, The, 131
Substance abuse, 141
Suicide threats, 67–68, 92
Sundance Kid, 184
Sutton, Robert, 62

T
Talented Mr. Ripley, The (film), 144
Tate, Sharon, 180
Taylor, Elizabeth, 58
Territo, Leonard, 64
Tinning, Marybeth, 151
Tison, Gary, 130
Toole, Ottis, 185
Trepal, George J., 130
Tsarnaev brothers, 100

V
Van der Sloot, Joran, 153
Victim, no obligation to be, 16, 211
Violence Risk and Threat Assessment, 189

W
Walker, Edwin, 177
Walker, John, 148
Walker, Michael, 148
Walsh, Adam, 185
Walsh, John, 185
Warren, Kelly Therese, 6–7
Weaver, Randy, 102, 108
Whitfield, Anthony E., 140
Williams, David Russell, 9
Williams, Nushawn, 140
Winehouse, Amy, 81
Without Conscience, 189
Workplace
handling complex situations, 200–202
narcissistic personality in, 22, 24–25, 26, 31, 38–41
paranoid personality in, 111–13, 125–26
predators in, 143, 153–54
Wound collecting, 63–64, 104, 106
Wozniak, Steven, 201

Y
Yochelson, Samuel, 189
Yudofsky, Stuart C., 166, 189